Future Librarianship in The Knowledge Society

Future Librarianship in Knowledge Society

Editors

Prof. M Bavakutty

Dr. K C Abdul Majeed

Dr. T P O Nasirudheen

Ess Ess Publications

4837/24, Ansari Road, Darya Ganj,

New Delhi-110002

Tel.: 23260807, 41563444

Fax : 011-41563334

E-mail: *info@essessreference.com*

www.essessreference.com

Ess Ess Publications
4837/24, Ansari Road,
Darya Ganj,
New Delhi-110 002.

Tel.: 23260807, 41563444
Fax: 41563334
E-mail: info@essessreference.com
www.essessreference.com

Rs.1075/-

First Published - 2008

ISBN: 81-7000-513-2 (10 Digit)
978-81-7000513-1 (13 Digit)

Published By Ess Ess Publications and printed at Salasar Imaging Systems

PRINTED IN INDIA

Preface

It is a fact that the libraries and library professionals face many challenges in the knowledge society driven by the Information Technology. It is also true that the emerging knowledge society offers many new opportunities. The Information Communication Technology has changed the ways in which the information is published, stored, organized, retrieved, accessed, communicated and utilized. The library with out walls in the form of digital repositories and portals are now accessible to users with out any barriers of space and time. It is important to discuss and comprehend the implications of these vibrant changes for the benefit of the profession. With this objective a national conference on *Future Librarianship in the Knowledge Society* was organized under the joint auspicious of Department of Library and Information Science and the CHMK Library in the University of Calicut on 28th and 29th March 2007, in connection with the farewell to Professor M. Bavakutty from the University service after forty years of splendid and very active professional career as College Librarian, Lecturer in Library Science, Deputy University Librarian, University Librarian and Professor and Head of the Department of Library and Information Science.

This volume contains 44 papers, both theoretical and practical on various facets of the theme of the conference, contributed by 78 authors, which includes practicing library professionals, Library and Information Science teachers, researchers and students. Of these 16 papers are single authored and 28 are co-authored. We sincerely hope that these papers will surely be instrumental to encourage the young library and information science professionals to understand the great responsibility they have to shoulder and the efforts they have to carry out in the coming days in the ever dynamic knowledge society.

We are thankful to the authors of the papers and to all, particularly the authorities of the University of Calicut who have helped us in our efforts of organizing the national conference in a befitting manner and to bring out this volume. We are also grateful to the library professionals, students and teachers of the Departments of Library and Information Science of University of Calicut, Annamalai University, Rajagiri College of Social Sciences, Farook College and Majalis Arts and Science College for their active participation and full involvement through out the conference.

We are particularly grateful to Sri. Sumit Sethi, the enterprising Managing Director of Ess Ess Publications, New Delhi for bringing out this work with in a short period, as in the case of our previous publications.

Prof. M. Bavakutty

Calicut University **Dr. K. C. Abdul Majeed**

10th August 2007 **Dr. T. P. O. Nasirudheen**

Contents

List of Contributing Authors

Abdul Gafoor Manningachali
Librarian, Dept. of Lib. & Infor. Science,
University of Calicut, 673635 Kerala

Dr. Abdul Majeed K C
Lecturer (Selection Grade),
Dept. of Lib. & Infor. Science,
Farook College. Calicut 673632
kcamajeedfc@yahoo.co.in

Alvi, K. S
Dept. of Lib. & Infor. Science,
Annamalai University, Chidambaram,
Tamilnadu.

Amdani, S. Y.
Lecturer, Dept. of Computer Sci. & Engg.
Babasaheb Naik College of Engineering,
Pusad, Distt. Yavatmal (M.S.)
salimamdani@yahoo.co.in

Amulraj, S
Dept. of Lib. & Infor. Science,
Annamalai University, Chidambaram, Tamilnadu.
Balamani1977@yahoo.com

Anju Govindani
Assistant Librarian, Medi-caps inst. of Tech. & Mangement,
A.B. Road, Pigdamber,
Rau, Indore (M.P.) 453331
anjugovindani@rediffmail.com

Babita Garg
Librarian, PGIMS,
Rohtak-124001(Haryana)
Babita_khushi1@yahoo.co.in

Dr. Baby, M D
Head, School of Lib. & Infor. Science,
Rajagiri College of Social Sciences,
Kalamassery, Ernakulam
shrinerose@yahoo.com

Balaji N.G
Librarian, P E S School of Engineering,
Bangalore
ngbalaji2020@rediffmail.com

Balasubramani, R
Asst. Librarian, Dayananda Sagar College of Engineering,
Bangalore – 78
lisbala@gmail.com

Dr. Bavakutty, M
Professor and Head, Dept. of Lib. & Infor. Science,
University of Calicut - 673635 Kerala
bavakuttym@yahoo.co.in

Dr. Beena, C
Asst. Librarian, Cochin University of Science & Technology,
Kochi 22. Kerala

G. Dhanasegaran
Deputy Librarian, Dr. T.P.M.Library,
Madurai Kamaraj University, Madurai-21
gdsegar@yahoo.co.in

Dhanya P
Research Scholar, Dept. of Lib. & Infor. Science,
Annamalai University
Chidambaram – 12 (T N)
nathipriyan@gmail.com

Dinesan. K
Librarian, Thalassery Campus Library (Kannur University),
Thalassery

Dipak Krushnarao, Bhalekar
Babasaheb Naik College of Engineering,
Pusad, Distt. Yavatmal (M.S.)
dkbhalekar_bnce@rediffmail.com

Elanchezhiyan, T,
Librarian, M.N. Dastur & Company,
Chennai-600 034
e_chezhiyan@yahoo.com

Gireesh A. Ganjihal
Assistant Librarian, Central Library,
Infosys Technologies, Bangalore
gireeshganjihal@gmail.com

Govinda Reddy, P.V
Librarian, V.V. Puram Evening College of Arts & Commerce,
K.R. Road, Bangalore-4
reddypvg@rediffmail.com

S. V. Gumaste,
Lecturer, Deptt. of Computer Sci.& Engg. Babasaheb Naik College of Engineering,
Pusad, Distt. Yavatmal (M.S.)
shyamraogumaste@yahoo.com

Jemsheer, N P
Library professional, CHMK Library,
University of Calicut. 673 635 Kerala

Jeyaprakash, B
Librarian, Indira Gandhi College
of Arts & Science, Puducherry-8
bjeyapragash@rediffmail.com

Johnson David
Chief Librarian, Dayananda Sagar College of Engineering,
Bangalore-78
libdavid@yahoomail.com

Krishnan, V
Dept. of Lib. & Infor. Science,
Annamalai University, Chidambaram, 12. Tamilnadu.

Kunjumohammed, V. S
Library Professional, Cochin University of Science & Technology, Kochi 22. Kerala

Maheswaran K,
Research Scholar, Dept. of Lib. & Infor. Science,
Annamalai university, Chidambaram12 Tamilanadu
Karuppiah.maheswaran@gmail.com

Manju P U
Project Assistant, DRTC, Bangalore -59
lismanju@gmail.com

Mehaboobullah, K
Research Scholar, Dept. of Lib. & Infor. Science,
University of Calicut 673635 Kerala

Milind K Labhasetwar
Librarian, Jawaharlal Darda Institute of Engg. &
Tech. MIDC, Lohara ,
Yavatmal (M S) 445001.
lmilind07@rediffmail.com

Dr. Mini Devi, B
Librarian, Dept. of Commerce,
University of Kerala,
Thiruvananthapuram 695034.
minidevi_b@yahoo.co.in

Muhammed Najeeb. V
Professional Asst. Gr I, Thalassery Campus Library,
(Kannur University), Thalassery

Nagappa V. Bakkannanavar,
Branch Head, Lib. & Infor. Centre,
Tata Consultancy Services,
Hi-tech City, Madhapur,
Hyderabad. 500 081
nagappa.b@tcs.com

Dr. Nagarajan, M
Professor, Dept. of Lib. & Infor. Science,
Annamalai University, Chidambaram-12
professormn@gmail.com

Naresh Chandara Verma
Junior Research Fellow,
Central Pulp & Paper Research Institute, Sharanpur

Dr. Nasirudheen, T.P.O,
Lecturer (Sel. Grade) and Head,
Dept. of Lib. & Infor. Science, Farook College,
Calicut 673632
thareekanakam@yahoo.co.in

Nimat R.B
Librarian, H.V.P.K.M B.P.Ed College,
Yavatmal, (MS).

Noufal. P. P
Sr. Library & Information Assistant,
P K Kelkar Library, Indian Institute of Technology,
Kanpur (UP),
noufalkodur@yahoo.co.in

Padmamma, S
Sr. lecturer, Dept. of Lib. & Infor. Science,
Kuvempu University, Shankarghatta
Shimoga District, Karnataka

Panneerselvam, P,
Librarian, B. S. Abdur Rahman Crescent
Engineering College, Chennai - 48
p_panneer@yahoo.com,

Pavalavannan, A,
Programmer, Sacs M.A.V.M.M. Engg. College,
Kidaripatty . P. O, Madurai - 625 301

Pratibha S. Kumbargoudar,
Trainee, Indian Institute of Astrophysics,
Bangalore. *pratibha.sk@gmail.com*

Praveena, K
Lecturer, Dept. of Lib. & Infor. Science,
Annamalai University, Chidamparam.12 (T N)

Raja, S
Librarian, Meenaakshi Ramasamy Arts and
Science College, Thathanur (PO),
Perambalur (Dt), Tamilnadu.
Lisraja1979@Gmail.Com

Rajasekharan, K
Librarian, Kerala Institute of Local Administration,
Mulgunnathkavu, Thrissur 680581
librariankila@hotmail.com

Ramasamy, R.U
Librarian, Sacs M.A.V.M.M. Engg College,
Kidaripatty (PO), Madurai - 625 301
Paralirur@Yahoo.co.in

Raveesh S
Infor. & Kdge. Management Trainee,
National Centre for Sci. Information,
Indian Institute of Science, Bangalore-12
sraveesh_2006@yahoo.co.in

Ravivenkat, B
Librarian, Vijaya Evening College,
R.V. Road, Bangalore-4.
bvr_69@yahoo.com

Salek Chand
Sr. Documentation Officer, NDC,
NIHFW, New Delhi 110067.
Salekchand2003@yahoo.com

Sangeetha T G
Lecturer, School of Lib. & Information Science,
Rajagiri College of Social Sciences,
Kalamassery, Ernakulam Dt.
tgsangeetha79@rediffmail.com

Santosh A. Navalur
Infor. & Kdge. Mgmt. Trainee,
National Centre for Sc. Information,
Indian Institute of Science, Bangalore- 560 012.
santoshncsi@gmail.com

Sathya A
Dept. of Lib. & Infor. Science,
Annamalai University, Chidamparam. (T N)
Balamani1977@yahoo.com

Satyanarayana, K V
Tata Consultancy Services,
54 B, Hadapsar Industrial Estate, Pune 411013
k.satyanarayana.apte@tcs.com

Seema Nair
Tata Consultancy Services, 54 B,
Hadapsar Industrial Estate, Pune 411013
seema.n.apte@tcs.com

Selvakumar R
Dept. of Lib. & Infor. Science,
Annamalai University.
Balamani1977@yahoo.com

Senthilkumar, R
Librarian, Kongunadu Arts and Sci. College,
Coimbatore (T N)
kasclibrary@yahoo.co.in

Shaini Gopinath
Library Professional, CHMK Library,
Calicut University, 673 635 Kerala

Shanmugavadivu, G
Librarian, M R Arts and Science College,
Thathanur P. O, Perambalur (Dt), Tamilnadu

Sheeba, A
Dept. of Lib. & Infor. Science,
Annamalai University, Chidambaram, Tamilnadu.

Shishir H. Mandalia,
I/C of Head, P.G. Dept. of Lib. & Infor. Science,
Bhavnagar University, Bhavnagar-364001 (Gujarat)
Shishir_Mandalia@Yahoo.Co.In

Shubhada Apte
Tata Consultancy Services, 54 B,
Hadapsar Industrial Estate, Pune 411013.
shubhada.apte@tcs.com

Sivakumaren, K.S,
Assistant University Librarian, MIT Campus Library,
Anna University, Chennai-600 044.
siva_kumaren@yahoo.co.in

Sivasekaran K
Librarian, Pavai Engg. College, Pachal, Namakkal
SivaWinsall@Yahoo.Co.In

Dr. Soman, K.N,
Assistant Librarian, CHMK Library,
University of Calicut, 673 635 Kerala

Sreejaya, P
Indian Institute of Management Kozhikode Library,
IIMK Campus, P.O., Calicut - 673570, Kerala,
sreejaya@iimk.ac.in

Sreekala P.K
Lecturer, School of Lib. & Infor. Science,
Rajagiri College of Social Sciences,
Kalamassery, Ernakulam
sreekalasudhi@yahoo.co.in

Subrata Sur
Library Assistant, Netaji Subhash Chandra
Bose Cancer Research Institute,
Kolkata. (W B)

Suja.K
Research scholar, Dept. of Lib. & Infor. Science,
University of Calicut, 673635 Kerala

Sujata Sur
Technical Assistant, Netaji Subhas Chandra
Bose Cancer Research Institute, Kolkata. (WB)

Sunitha, T
Indian Institute of Management Kozhikode Library,
IIMK Campus, P.O., Calicut 673570, Kerala
sunitha@iimk.ac.in

Suresh Kumar, N
Librarian, Fluid Control Research Institute
(Under Ministry of Heavy Industry, Govt. of India),
Palakkad - Kerala- 678623

Surulinathi, M
Research Scholar, Dept. of Lib. & Infor. Science,
Annamalai University, Chidambaram-12
surulinathi@gmail.com

Suryanarayana Sastry
Library & Information Assistant,
International Institute of Information Technology (IIIT-H),
Gachibowli, Hyderabad - 500 032
surya@iiit.ac.in

Susanta Kumar Sahoo
Assistant Librarian, ICFAI Business School,
Bhubaneswar, Orissa - 751010

Thamaraiselvi, G
Librarian, National Institute of Technology,
Tiruchirappalli - 620015 (T N)

Thenmozhi R
Dept. of Lib. & Infor. Science,
Annamalai University. Chidambaram, Tamilnadu.
Balamani1977@yahoo.com

Titiksha Goswami,
Research Scholar, Dept. of Lib. & Infor. Science,
Annamalai University, Chidambaram, Tamilanadu.
titikshaghy@gmail.com

1

Knowledge Management : A Source to enhance Libraries

K. Praveena
Dr. M. Nagarajan

ABSTRACT

The development of Knowledge management in recent years has become the key concern for librarians and libraries. This paper deals with what is Knowledge Management? Characteristics of Knowledge Management in libraries, How Knowledge Management can be applied in library so that library will become a treasure house of human knowledge, participate in knowledge innovation, and become an important link in the knowledge innovation chain. Libraries in the digital and knowledge age should be in charge of Knowledge Management in order to leverage the intellectual assets and to facilitate knowledge creation.

1. INTRODUCTION

Knowledge has become the driving force for social development, the attention of society to information and knowledge is rising and people's demand for information and knowledge are increasing step by step. This has provided a good environment for library development.

The conventional functions of a library are to collect, process, disseminate, store and utilise information to provide service for the society. In the knowledge economy era library will become a treasure house of human knowledge, participate in knowledge innovation.

Knowledge Management in libraries should be focused on effective research and development of knowledge bases, exchange and sharing of knowledge between library staffs, speeding up explicit processing of the implicit knowledge and realizing of its sharing.

2. MEANING OF KEY TERMS

Data : Data is raw, scattered, unrelated facts, numbers or symbols and each data has multiple meanings which are context dependent

Information : Information is a data that has been organised and communicated. Information relates to description, definition or perspective (What, Who, When, Where)

Knowledge : A set of organised statements of facts or ideas presenting a reasoned judgment or an experimental result which is transmitted to others through some communication medium in some systematic form.(How) Two types of knowledge have been noted one is ***explicit*** knowledge - knowledge that is documented , public, structured and externalized and the other is ***tacit*** knowledge which is personal, dynamically created and derived.

Wisdom : Wisdom embodies principle, insight or moral (Why).

Data ' information ' knowledge ' wisdom represents an emergent continuum. Everything is relative, understanding of the relation between data represent information, understanding the patterns represent knowledge and understanding the principles are the foundations of wisdom.

3. KNOWLEDGE MANAGEMENT

Knowledge management is the explicit and systematic management of vital knowledge and its associated processes of creating, gathering, organizing, diffusion, use and exploitation of information. It requires turning personal knowledge into corporate knowledge that can be widely shared throughout an organization and appropriately applied. The focus of Knowledge management is on "**doing the right thing**" instead of **doing things right**". It is how **smart minds** use **smart technologies** to leverage strategic opportunities and challenges.

3.1 Characteristics of knowledge management in libraries

The.objective of Knowledge management in libraries is to promote knowledge innovation. As base for collection, processing, storage and distribution of knowledge and information, libraries represent an indispensable link in the scientific system chain an important link in the knowledge innovation.

Libraries take part in scientific research process directly. The library work is a component of knowledge innovation.

Libraries must pay attention to diffusion and conversion of knowledge., It must act as a bridge for turning the results of knowledge innovation into realistic productive forces.

Knowledge Management is to promote relationship between libraries, between library and user. Libraries will carry out research on development and application of information resources, construction of virtual libraries, thus founding the base for knowledge innovation.

Information Technology (IT) is a tool for Knowledge management in libraries and is also indispensable in the application and exchange of knowledge. The application of IT enlarges the scope of knowledge acquisition, raises knowledge acquisition speed and reduces knowledge acquisition cost.

4. KNOWLEDGE MANAGEMENT IN LIBRARIES

The new role of libraries in the 21st century needs to be, as a learning and knowledge centre for their users as well as the intellectual commons for their respective communities. The important mission of public, academic and research library is to expand the access of knowledge for their users.

4.1. Knowledge Resources Management

Because of the exponential growth in human knowledge, libraries need to develop their resources access and sharing strategies from printed format to electronic format. Restricted by limited funding, technology, staff and space, libraries must carefully analyze the needs of the user and seek to develop co-operative acquisition plans. OPAC and other formats of knowledge should be developed and maintained. Useful websites and knowledge sources should be regularly searched and selected from the Internet and included in OPAC's.

4.2. Resources Sharing and Networking

Resource sharing and networking have been greatly expanded by the rapid development of computer, telecommunication and networking. The CORC project of OC L C (Online computer library center) should be useful for libraries to co-operatively capture digital resources of all types, describe them in a format and make them easily searchable by the user.

4.3. Information Technology Development

Knowledge management system should be built on existing computer and IT infrastructure including upgraded internet, intranet and extranet. The software programmes should facilitate the capture, analysis, organization, storage and sharing of internal and external information resources for effective knowledge exchange among users. Information management can be utilized in Knowledge management such as data warehousing, data mining text mining and content management. Knowledge Management has to transform Information retrieval systems into newer and more powerful search tools for contents on the Internet.

4.4. User Services

Knowledge management is to provide user with a variety of quality services in order to improve the communication, use and creation of knowledge. User needs should be collected through periodic user surveys. SDI can be done automatically by employing the *push technology*. Approaches in library should be user focused rather than library focused.

4.5. Human Resource Management

Library as a learning organization should allocate funds to provide continuing education and staff training to all staff members. Knowledge must be renewed and expanded to prevent it from becoming stagnant. A mentoring system should be adopted to help new comers to learn from experienced library staff. Libraries should pay attention to favorable working conditions and environment which will contribute to better staff retention.

5. CONCLUSION

As libraries enter the knowledge age of 21st century, librarians should work together with I T professionals and others to develop the appropriate Knowledge management system. Knowledge services based on high speed information networks should be out by

* Setting up virtual libraries or information centers for enterprises, governments and scientific research institutions.
* Setting up of digitalized knowledge services using the

techniques of information distribution and search with the internet as a base and web technique as the core.

* Digitizing libraries resources that is creation of databases comprising electronic journals and books in different languages and can be operated on high speed information networks.

REFERENCES

1. Davenport T H and Prusak L " *Working knowledge: How organizations manage what they know*" Harvard Business School, Boston - USA
2. Hwa-Wei Lee, "*Knowledge Management and the Role of Libraries*", Asian Division, Library of Congress, Washington, DC, USA.
3. Tang Shanhong, "*Knowledge Management in Libraries in the 21st century*", 66th IFLA council and General conference , Jerusalem, Israel 13 - 18 August.

2

Digital Libraries and Knowledge Management Trends and Developments

R. U. Ramasamy
A. Pavalavannan

ABSTRACT

Information and Knowledge Management is the driver of productivity and growth of any organization. In digital era digital libraries extend the services of traditional library to accesses materials outside the physical confines of the library. Due to electronic explosion the users find difficulties to evaluate the valuable information in electronic media. So there is need to organize the materials for the purpose of effective retrieval and manage the collection.

1. INTRODUCTION

Knowledge Management (KM) in digital era is a methodology of transferring electronics information and expertise to improve the competency and productivity of the society as a whole and individual as an entity. It is more of a challenging task of accessing valuable knowledge from various sources using it for decision making in certain environment and generating new innovative potential. Knowledge Management is practice and learning process.

2. OBJECTIVES

The objectives of Knowledge Management include the following :

- To create knowledge repositories, which store both knowledge and information, often in documentary form.
- To improve knowledge access, or to provide access to knowledge or to facilitate its transfer among individuals.
- To enhance the knowledge environment so that the environment is conducive to more effective knowledge creation, transfer and use.
- To manage knowledge as an asset and to recognize the value of knowledge to an organization.

3. CHARACTERISTICS OF KNOWLEDGE MANAGEMENT

Knowledge Management is defined by one consulting firm as a discipline that promotes an integrated approach to identifying, capturing, evaluating, retrieving and sharing all of enterprises information assets. Knowledge Management encompasses a very broad range of perspective. In particular, it deals with the complexities and nuances of human intellectual process, including tacit knowledge, learning and innovating processes, communication cultures, values and intangible assets.

Rus and Lindvall mentioned 'Knowledge Management is unique because it focuses on the individual as an expert and as the bearer of important knowledge that he or she can systematically share with an organization. Knowledge Management supports not only the know-how of a company, but also the know where, know who, know what, know when and know why'

4. KNOWLEDGE MANAGEMENT SYSTEM

It is a value added Internet with facilities to search and identify captured knowledge or identify experts who have knowledge in the area users are looking for. The Knowledge Management system also helps to establish contact with the expert and have a dialogue with them. It captures and makes available the transcripts of such discussion whether they have on chat or e-mail. The approach in building Knowledge Management system would vary in different libraries.

5. KNOWLEDGE ARCHITECTURE

Knowledge Management involves a number of parameters in which the following constitutes the key components:

People : Those who produce and those who use knowledge that will be the basis for action.

Content : The flow of data, information and knowledge that will be the success of the business.

Technology : The technical infrastructure that enables the captures, storage and delivery of content to those who need it when they need it.

6. TECHNOLOGIES FOR KNOWLEDGE MANAGEMENT

The concept of Knowledge Management would be less powerful for organizations without knowledge-oriented technologies. Technology's most valuable role in Knowledge Management is extending the reach and enhancing the speed of knowledge transfer. Knowledge engineering, digital networks, the Internet and intranets are not Knowledge Management but only enabling technologies for managing knowledge. Knowledge Management technology enables users to simultaneously access Internet sites, databases, intranets and other internal/external resources as if the information existed in a single location.

6.1. Intranet and extranet

Basically intranets/extranets are phenomenally powerful tools to streamline library services. Information disseminated on an intranet enables a high degree of coherence for the entire library because communications are consistent. By giving information seekers and information providers the ability to access time critical information, intranets improve the decision making process by empowering individuals with the knowledge necessary for faster and better informed decision making. Intranets allow the centralization of information, which makes it easier to maintain and keeps data up-to-date. The extranet further extends the Internet by allowing other libraries on sister organization to gain access to selected internal data.

7. NEED FOR KNOWLEDGE MANAGEMENT IN DIGITAL LIBRARY

Knowledge centers are slowly and steadily marching towards digital library services due to the changing needs and advent of information technology. The need is to make good choice and good decisions about information in globally competitive information saturated environment. The key for all these is knowledge management. The knowledge in libraries resides in databases, knowledge bases and text bases, web bases. The value of knowledge management relates directly to the effectiveness with which the managed knowledge enables the members of the organization to deal with today's situations and effectively envision and create their future.

8. KNOWLEDGE MANAGEMENT AND DIGITAL LIBRARIES

Digital revolution has transformed the intellectual function of traditional libraries. Digital libraries are providing the base for a set of distributed activities. It is also providing a one-stop solution for speedy delivery in a reliable fashion.

Libraries are being digitized and patrons demand is growing the concept of content management has been adapted to the library world.

9. CONCLUSION

There are several technical ways to make the link between the digital library and the Knowledge Management. As knowledge organization systems are increasingly available on the web, requirements are beginning to be defined to improve the interoperability and general use of these resources through the development of knowledge organization services on the web.

The decision of what knowledge organization system to use is central to the development of any digital library. The Knowledge Management must be applicable, either automatically or by human catalogers to the resources included in the digital library. Once the material is included in the collection, the Knowledge Management must be meaningful to its users.

REFERENCE

1. Bansal, Alka. Knowledge Management: A Review, Desidoc Bulletin of Informaiton Technology, 2000, 20(4), 3-9.
2. Ghosh, Jambekar. Networ, Digital Libraries and Knowledge Management, Desidoc Bulletin of Informaiton Technology, 2003, 23(5), 3-11.
3. Wilson, Tony. The nonsense of knowledge management. Information Research, 2002, 8(1), 1-26.

3

RFID Technology in Digital Era: A New Service

Titiksha Goswami
Dhanya P
Maheswaran K

ABSTRACT

Digital libraries are mainly aimed to overcome the time and space barriers of accessing information. However, these libraries face problems related to digitization, automation, networking and its security. Radio-Frequency Identification (RFID) technology has come to the rescue. This paper illustrates the importance of RFID technology in digital libraries in detail.

1. INTRODUCTION

The rapid growth and development of computer and communication technology has changed our society tremendously. To meet the information explosion and high demand of information the libraries are now upgraded to digital library from traditional one. Digital Library service can be regarded as a dramatic improvement of certain aspects of traditional library services. The main purpose of digitization is to overcome the twin tyrannies of time and space.

Radio-frequency identification is emerging as a good way to improve automation and security in Library Systems. For more than five years, libraries all over the world have been taking advantage of radio-frequency identification (RFID) technology. Current market research shows that RFID systems are now used in about 20 million books worldwide. The driver for today's libraries to adopt RFID is the need to increase efficiency and reduce cost. Automation and self-service can help libraries of all sizes toward achieving these aims, and RFID has the added advantage that it can also provide security for the range of different media on offer in libraries.

2. DIGITAL LIBRARY

A digital library is organization and collection of selected digital resources created to support scholarship, research, and teaching. Through the use of appropriate technological standards, a Digital Library is created to facilitate persistent access to and resource discovery of selected digital resources .Digital Library Initiatives to provide various value added services.

Gladney and Lotspiech state that Digital Library (DL) services must protect copyright holders, owners, users, and themselves against deliberate and inadvertent misuses of contents. Unobtrusive programs can provide sufficient protection, yet spare users irksome choices between distracting inconveniences and imprudent risks. Which safeguards are important depends on the kind of information resource and on the circumstances of its use. Librarians are mainly concern with authenticity; confidentiality is a basis for privacy; and security is a basis for maintaining authors' and owners' intellectual property rights. Digital Library service can deliver quality with good performance, convenience, and economy. According to Leach the security requirements are based on the nature of the requirement, aggregates and can be summarized as Security Management Practices, Identification, Authentication, Authorization, Privacy, Data Authenticity etc.

3. RFID (RADIO FREQUENCY IDENTIFICATION) TECHNOLOGY

RFID is the latest technology to be used in library theft detection systems. As of late 2005, an estimated 300 libraries were using RFID systems. Unlike EM (Electro-Mechanical) and RF (Radio Frequency) systems, which have been used in libraries for decades, RFID-based systems move beyond security to become tracking systems that combine security with more efficient tracking of materials throughout the library, including easier and faster charge and discharge, inventorying, and materials handling.

RFID is a combination of radio-frequency-based technology and microchip technology. The information contained on microchips in the tags affixed to library materials is read using radio frequency technology regardless of item orientation or alignment (i.e., the technology does not require line-of-sight or a fixed plane to read tags as do traditional theft detection systems) and distance from the item is not a critical factor except in the case of extra-wide exit gates. The corridors at the building exit(s) can be as wide as four feet because the tags can be read at a distance of up to two feet by each of two parallel exit sensors. [The devices used for circulation and inventorying are usually called "readers" while the ones used at building exits are usually called "sensors."]

The tags or targets used in RFID systems can replace both EM or RF theft detection targets and barcodes, although the system that 3M introduced in 2000 replaced only barcodes in the belief that EM is superior to RFID for security. [3M did introduce a comprehensive RFID product that replaces both EM and barcodes in 2004].

3.1. Benefits of RFID Technology

Rapid Charging/Discharging: The use of RFID reduces the amount of time required to perform circulation operations. The most significant time savings are attributable to the facts that information can be read from RFID tags much faster than from barcodes and that several items in a stack can be read at the same time.

The other time savings realized by circulation staff are modest unless the RFID tags replace both the EM security strips or RF tags of older theft detection systems and the barcodes of the automated library system—i.e., the system is a comprehensive RFID system that combines Security and the tracking. It offers very high security. Each tag is identified by a Unique Identification Number (UIN), which can be either factory or manually programmed and then password protected. The excellence of this tag is that the data on the chip that uses sophisticated algorithm techniques cannot be duplicated or manipulated. Hence making it becomes the perfect tool for Secure Access Control.

Simplified patron self-charging/discharging : For patrons using self-charging, there is a marked improvement because they do not have to carefully place materials within a designated template and they can charge several items at the same time. Patron self-discharging, which can be achieved by installing readers in book drops or with self-discharge stations, shifts work from staff to patrons.

High reliability : The readers are highly reliable. Several vendors of RFID library systems claim an almost 100 percent detection rate using RFID tags. Anecdotal evidence suggests that is the case whenever a reader is within 12 to 14 inches of the tags, but there appears to be no statistical data to support the claims.

High-speed inventorying : A unique advantage of RFID systems is their ability to scan books on the shelves without tipping them out or removing them. A hand-held inventory reader can be moved rapidly across a shelf of books to read all of the unique identification information. Using wireless technology, it is possible not only to update the inventory, but also to identify items which are out of proper order.

Automated materials handling : Another application of RFID technology is automated materials handling. This includes conveyor and sorting systems that can move library materials and sort them by category into separate bins or onto separate carts. This significantly reduces the amount of staff time required to ready materials for reshelving. Given the high cost of the equipment, this application has not been widely used. There were approximately 70 systems in use in North America as of the second quarter of 2005.

Long tag life : Finally, RFID tags last longer than barcodes because nothing comes into contact with them. Most RFID vendors claim a minimum of 100,000 transactions before a tag may need to be replaced.

3.2. Drawbacks of RFID Technology

High cost : The major drawback of RFID technology is its cost. While the readers and sensors used to read the information are comparable in cost to the components of a typical EM or RF theft detection system.

Vulnerability to compromise : It is possible to compromise an RFID system by wrapping the protected material in two to three layers of ordinary household foil to block the radio signal. Clearly, bringing household foil into a library using RFID would represent premeditated theft, just as bringing a magnet into a library using EM technology would be. It is also possible to compromise an RFID system by placing two items against one another so that one tag overlays another. That may cancel out the signals. This requires knowledge of the technology and careful alignment.

Removal of exposed tags : 3M, which recommends EM for security and RFID for tracking, argues that EM strips are concealed in the spines (30 percent of customers) or the gutters (70 percent of customers) of books and are, therefore, difficult to find and remove; while RFID tags are typically affixed to the inside back cover and are exposed for removal. The author found no evidence of removal in the libraries he visited, nor did any of the library administrators contacted by telephone report a problem. That does not mean that there won't be problems when patrons become more familiar with the role of the tags.

If a library wishes, it can insert the RFID tags in the spines of all except thin books, however, not all RFID tags are flexible enough. A library can also imprint the RFID tags with its logo and make them appear to be bookplates, or it can put a printed cover label over each tag.

Exit sensor problems : While the short-range readers used for circulation charge and discharge and inventorying appear to read the tags 100 percent of the time, the performance of the exit sensors is more problematic. They must read tags at up to twice the distance of the other readers. The author knows of no library that has done a before and after inventory to determine the loss rate when RFID is used for security. Lacking data, one can only conjecture that the performance of exist sensors is better when the antennae on the tags are larger.

Perceived Invasion of Patron Privacy : There is a perception among some that RFID is a threat to patron privacy. It is argued that the tags contain patron information and/or title information; and that the tags can be read from a distance after someone has taken the materials to home or office.

The vast majority of the tags installed in library materials contain only the item ID, usually the same number that previously has been stored on a barcode. The link between borrower and the borrowed material is maintained in the circulation module of the automated library system, and—unless a library takes the unusual step of retaining patron borrowing histories—is broken when the material is returned. When additional information is stored on the RFID tag, it is limited to information about the item, typically holding location and call number, but rarely author and/or title.

The RFID tags can only be read from a distance of two feet or less because the tags reflect a signal that comes from a reader or sensor. It is, therefore, not possible for someone to read tags from the street or an office building hallway. In order to read tags from a distance of more than two feet, it would be necessary to greatly enlarge the tags or greatly increase the power of the readers. A library has no reason to purchase larger, more costly tags. An electrical engineer at N.V. Philips in the Netherlands estimated that it would require a truck mounted reader to read the tags used by libraries from a distance of more than ten feet.

Perceptions, even when mistaken, may have real consequences. The Intellectual Freedom Committee of the American Library Association has responded to concerns about RFID raised by privacy advocates by drafting a set of principles:

- Implement and enforce an up-to-date organizational privacy policy that gives notice and full disclosure as to the use, terms of use, and any change in the terms of use for data collection via new technologies and processes, including RFID.
- Ensure that no personal information is recorded on RFID tags which, however, may contain a variety of transactional data.
- Protect data by reasonable security safeguards against interpretation by any unauthorized third part.

- Comply with relevant federal, state, and local laws as well as industry best practices and policies.
- Ensure that the four principles outlined above must be verifiable by an independent audit.

The Council of the American Library Association adopted these principles on January 19, 2005. The Intellectual Freedom Committee has continued its work and introduced a set of guidelines for RFID use for discussion at the 2006 ALA Mid-winter Meeting in San Antonio. Among them, the following are the most significant:

- Libraries should not use RFID systems to track individual library users. Libraries should remove any personally identifiable information from statistical data collected by RFID system.
- Due to the potential for eavesdropping, libraries should use hardwire connections and not wireless connections for all communications between RFID systems and the ILS involving personally identifiable information.
- Libraries should encrypt information on RFID tags.
- Libraries using "smart cards" should use an "opt-in" system that allows library users to choose between "smart cards" and barcode-enabled cards.
- Libraries should be aware that independent researchers have concluded that current RFID technology cannot preserve user privacy in the library.

The area in which RFID represents the greatest potential threat to patron privacy is the use of the "smart card" as a patron ID card. A "smart card" is an RFID card with encryption. That would make it possible to have the ID card also function as a "debit" card, with value added upon pre-payment to the library and value subtracted when a patron used a photocopier, printer, or other fee-based device, or wished to pay fines or fees. Almost none of the score of RFPs the author has examined include a mandatory requirement for 'smart cards." The few that do, ask for that as an option. All stipulate encryption to protect patron privacy. The quality of the encryption is the key to patron privacy.

Because of the attention that has been focused on privacy issues, it is important to educate library staff and patrons about the RFID technology used in libraries before implementing a program. The best way to do that is to emphasize that RFID technology is not one technology, but several. E-Z pass is RFID that is meant to be read from a distance. It would be impractical to affix tags of that size and cost to library materials. The same is true of the tags used on pallets in warehouses. Further, a library should stress that it does not store patron information on the tags in library materials, that it protects patron privacy by breaking the link between borrower and material after the material is returned, and it subscribes to the privacy guidelines in the American Library Association's Code of Ethics.

Several states are considering legislation that would pose restrictions on the use of RFID by retailers and libraries. It is, therefore, important to monitor legislative activity and to be prepared to inform legislators about the differences between retail and library applications, and how libraries protect the privacy of their patrons. Library administrators should be sure to keep their boards informed.

3.3. Components of an RFID System

A comprehensive RFID system has three components: (1) RFID tags that are electronically programmed with unique information; (2) readers or sensors to interrogate the tags; and (3) a server or docking station on which the software that interfaces with the automated library system is loaded. It is also possible to distribute the software among the readers and sensors.

3.4. Challenges

The biggest challenge for RFID technology is to provide benefits without threatening the privacy of consumers. Many solutions have been suggested but almost as many ways have been found to break them. An approach by Ohkubo, Suzuki and Kinoshita using an internal refreshment mechanism seems to protect privacy well but is not scalable. We introduce a specific time-memory trade-off that removes the scalability issue of this scheme. Additionally we prove that the system truly offers privacy and even forward privacy.

The technology can also improve circulation and inventory control, which helps to optimize the allocation of labor and financial resources. This means that libraries can relieve their professional employees of routine work and operational tasks. For scientific libraries, this frees up more time for research and other tasks.

Libraries are a fast growing application of RFID; the technology promises to relieve repetitive strain injury, speed patron self-checkout, and make possible comprehensive inventory. Unlike supply-chain RFID, library RFID requires item-level tagging, thereby raising immediate patron privacy issues. Current conventional wisdom suggests that privacy risks are negligible unless an adversary has access to library databases. The libraries and librarians globally as well as locally are facing various challenges due to the implementation of ICT, unprecedented growth in printed and electronic resources, recent trends and developments in teaching learning process. Librarians need to face various challenges for providing efficient, effective and personalized value added services and products to the stakeholders.

Some of the major challenges faced by librarians are as follows:

- Expanding Electronic Information Environment
- Development of Information Infrastructure

- Need for Web based Services
- Explosive growth of Information
- Resource Sharing and Collaboration
- Marketing of Library & Information Products
- Digital Preservation
- Security in Digital Libraries

3.5. Major Problems Faced by the Librarians

1. Lack of Trained Staff
2. Shortage of Staff
3. Removing Installed RFID Tags by Users
4. Initial Activation problem in Tags

4. CONCLUSION

Recent developments in hardware and software for RFID systems have boosted the potential of this technology in library automation and security. 'Today, the one important result for libraries is the ability to use non-proprietary systems, now that the new generation of RFID-chips with standard ISO 15693 (to be integrated into ISO 18000-3) is available. 'With this technology, libraries do not have to depend on one single supplier for tags. As libraries make a long-term investment, which mainly consists of the quantity of tags needed, this is a very important requirement.

Integration of RFID with digital libraries will ensure considerable security and facilitate the librarians and information scientists to provide more value added services to user's community for working comfortably in digital future in developed country like India too.

REFERENCES

1. http://www.eff.org/Privacy/Surveillance/RFID/20031002_sfpl_comments.php.
2. http://www.jisc.ac.uk/uploaded_documents/jtap-015.doc

3. Nicholson, S. (1995) Management of the Digital Library: New Techniques for a New Technology. Available online at http://www.bibliomining.com/nicholson/newvl.html
4. H.M. Gladney and J.B. Lotspiech, Safeguarding Digital Library Contents and Users: Assuring Convenient Security and Data Quality, D-Lib Magazine, May 1997.http://dlib.org/dlib/may97/ibm/05gladney.html
5. http://glossary.ippaper.com/default.asp?req=knowledge/article/489
6. http://www.electrocom.com.aupdfs/RFID%20vs%20Barcodes.pdf
7. Bibliotheca RFID Library Systems: http://www.bibliotheca-rfid.com/and http://www.dtechdirect.com/ (distribution partner in the UK and Ireland)
8. C.L.Borgman. Where is the Librarian in the Digital Library. Communications of the ACM, Vol.44(2001), pp66-67.

4
Knowledge Auditing in the Context of Knowledge Management

Santosh A Navalur
Raveesh S

ABSTRACT

This paper is discussing the concept of knowledge audit in the context of knowledge management in detail. It discusses the benefits of knowledge audit, its aims and objectives, major tasks involved, the outcomes etc.

1. INTRODUCTION

"The knowledge audit (K-Audit) is a systematic and scientific examination and evaluation of the explicit and tacit knowledge resources in the Organization. The K-Audit investigates and analyses the current knowledge-environment and culminates, in a diagnostic and prognostic report on the current corporate 'knowledge health'. The report provides evidence as to whether corporate knowledge value potential is being maximized. In this respect the K-Audit measures the risk and opportunities faced by the organization with respect to corporate knowledge."

2. WHAT IS A KNOWLEDGE AUDIT?

The term 'knowledge audit' is in some ways a bit of a misnomer, since the traditional concept of an audit is to check performance against a standard, as in financial auditing. A knowledge audit, however, is a more of a qualitative evaluation. It is essentially a sound investigation into an organization's knowledge 'health'. A typical audit will look at:

- What are the organization's knowledge needs?
- What knowledge assets or resources does it have and where are they?
- What gaps exist in its knowledge?
- How does knowledge flow around the organization?
- What blockages are there to that flow e.g. to what extent do its people; processes and technology currently support or hamper the effective flow of knowledge?

The knowledge audit provides an evidence-based assessment of where the organization needs to focus its knowledge management efforts. It can reveal the organization's knowledge management needs, strengths, weaknesses, opportunities, threats and risks.

3. WHAT ARE THE BENEFITS?

Among the key benefits of knowledge audit are:

- It helps the organization clearly identify what knowledge is needed to support overall organizational goals and individual and team activities.
- It gives tangible evidence of the extent to which knowledge is being effectively managed and indicates where improvements are needed.
- It provides an evidence-based account of the knowledge that exists in an organization, and how that knowledge moves around in, and is used by, that organization.

- It provides a map of what knowledge exists in the organization and where it exists, revealing both gaps and duplication.
- It reveals pockets of knowledge that are not currently being used to good advantage and therefore offer untapped potential.
- It provides a map of knowledge and communication flows and networks, revealing both examples of good practice and blockages and barriers to good practice.
- It provides an inventory of knowledge assets, allowing them to become more visible and therefore more measurable and accountable, and giving a clearer understanding of the contribution of knowledge to organizational performance.
- It provides vital information for the development of effective knowledge management programmes and initiatives that are directly relevant to the organization's specific knowledge needs and current situation.

Some examples of situations in which a knowledge audit can be beneficial include:

- you are about to embark on creating a knowledge management strategy and so need to establish exactly 'where you are now'
- people are having difficulty in finding the information and knowledge they need to make key decisions
- useful sources of information and knowledge are frequently stumbled across by accident
- there is duplication of information and knowledge gathering activities across different departments or teams, and hence duplication of costs
- questions are being raised about the value of knowledge management systems, initiatives or investments

– when findings from research and development are not making their way into practice quickly enough.

4. HOW DO I GO ABOUT IT?

There are a wide variety of approaches to conducting a knowledge audit, with varying levels of coverage and detail. As a general rule, most knowledge audits will involve some or all of the following:

4.1. Identifying Knowledge Needs

The first step in most knowledge audits involves getting clear about precisely what knowledge the organization and the people and teams within it need in order to meet their goals and objectives. A knowledge audit provides a systematic way of finding this out to some level of detail. Common approaches taken to collating this information include questionnaire-based surveys, interviews and facilitated group discussions, or a combination of these. In asking people about knowledge needs, it is important to provide a point of focus, as 'knowledge' can be seen as being quite conceptual and therefore difficult to articulate. To get around this, and to ensure that you are concentrating on vital knowledge, invite people to think about their goals and objectives, and the core processes, activities and decisions that they perform in the course of their day-to-day work. You might ask them to also consider their main problems and challenges, and how might faster access to better knowledge help them in that regard.

It is always beneficial to begin a knowledge auditing process with identifying knowledge needs. This enables you to then use your understanding of these needs to guide the rest of the auditing process, and therefore be sure that you are focusing on the knowledge that is important to the organization.

4.2. Drawing up a Knowledge Inventory

A knowledge inventory is a kind of stock-take to identify and locate knowledge assets or resources throughout the organization. It involves counting and categorizing the organization's explicit and tacit knowledge. In the case of explicit knowledge, this will include things like:

- What knowledge we have - numbers, types and categories of documents, databases, libraries, intranet websites, links and subscriptions to external resources etc?
- Where the knowledge is - locations in the organization, and in its various systems?
- Organization and access - how are knowledge resources organized, how easy is it for people to find and access them?
- Purpose, relevance and 'quality' - why do these resources exist, how relevant and appropriate are they for that purpose, are they of good 'quality' e.g. up-to-date, reliable, evidence-based etc?
- Usage - is who actually using them, how often, what for?

In the case of tacit knowledge, the inventory will focus on people and look at things like:

- Who we have - numbers and categories of people
- Where they are - locations in departments, teams and buildings
- What they do - job levels and types
- What they know -academic and professional qualifications, core knowledge and experience
- What they are learning - on the job training, learning and development.

The knowledge inventory gives you a snapshot of your knowledge assets or resources. By comparing your inventory with your earlier analysis of knowledge needs, you can begin to identify gaps in your organization's knowledge as well as areas of unnecessary duplication. This is also explored in greater detail in the next step.

4.3. Analysing Knowledge Flows

While an inventory of knowledge assets shows what knowledge resources your organization has, an analysis of knowledge flows looks at how that knowledge moves around the organization - from where it is to where it is needed. In other words, how do people find the knowledge they need, and how do they share the knowledge they have? Again, the knowledge flow analysis looks at both explicit and tacit knowledge, and at people, processes and systems:

- The relative focus in this stage is on people: their attitudes towards, habits and behaviours concerning, and skills in, knowledge sharing and use. This will usually require a combination of questionnaire-based surveys followed up with individual interviews and facilitated group discussions.
- In terms of processes, you will need to look at how people go about their daily work activities and how knowledge seeking, sharing and use are (or are not) part of those activities. In most organizations, there will be pockets of good knowledge management practice (though they may not be called knowledge management). You will also need to look at what policies and practices currently affect the flows and usage of information and knowledge, for example are there existing policies on things like information handling, records management, web publishing? Are their other wider policies and practices that, while not directly related to knowledge management, act as enablers or barriers to good knowledge practice?
- On the systems side, some assessment is needed of key

capabilities that will be used in any recommended actions or solutions. This includes the technical infrastructure: information technology systems, content management, accessibility and ease of use, and current actual levels of use. In short, to what extent do your systems effectively facilitate knowledge flows, and help to connect people with the information and other people they need.

– An analysis of knowledge flows will allow you to further identify gaps in your organization's knowledge and areas of duplication; it will also highlight examples of good practice that can be built on, as well as blockages and barriers to knowledge flows and effective use. It will show where you need to focus attention in your knowledge management initiatives in order to get knowledge moving from where it is to where it is needed.

4.5. Creating a Knowledge Map

A knowledge map is a visual representation of an organization's knowledge. There are two common approaches to knowledge mapping:

1. The first simply maps knowledge resources and assets, showing what knowledge exists in the organization and where it can be found
2. The second also includes knowledge flows, showing how that knowledge moves around the organization from where it is to where it is needed.

Clearly the second approach provides the most complete picture for the knowledge auditor. However, the first is also useful, and in some organizations is made available to all staff to help people locate the knowledge they need.

4.6. Are there Any Other Points I should be aware of?

* Be clear about your purpose. The knowledge audit is not a quick or simple process, and so the time and effort required needs to be justified by a clear purpose and a set of actions that will be taken as a result of what the audit reveals.
* When conducting a knowledge audit, bear in mind the widely-accepted statistic that around 80% of an organization's knowledge is tacit, hence beware of focusing too much time and energy on explicit knowledge and not enough on tacit knowledge.
* The ease or difficulty that you have in gathering and collating the information you need as part of the audit process is itself a good indicator of the status of your current knowledge management capabilities.
* If you decide to commission a knowledge audit from external consultants, be aware that the quality and depth of work that comes under the general banner of 'knowledge auditing' varies quite. Many vendors use the term 'knowledge audit' to describe what is in fact an information audit - which will only look at explicit knowledge. Auditing tacit knowledge is probably where the greater challenge lies, and is hence the area in which expert help is likely to be most valuable.

The first stage in adopting a knowledge strategy is performing an audit of existing data, information and knowledge contained within the organization.

This section will cover four main areas of the knowledge audit:

The aims and objectives of the audit.

- The key tasks involved.
- Process mapping.
- The audit outcomes.

There are three broad *aims of a knowledge audit*:

- Leveraging the organisation's knowledge.
- Creating new knowledge or promoting innovation.
- Increasing collaboration and hence enhancing the skill level of employees.

The objectives of a knowledge audit are:

1. Study and develop a deeper understanding of existing communities (groups that share resources, provide support and show reciprocity) content (forms and combinations of words, images and pictures) and conversations (exchanges of sentiments, observations, opinions, or ideas).
2. Identify opportunities to add value to current communities, content and conversations.
3. Develop a knowledge management strategy that delivers on the identified opportunities.

Most commonly, knowledge audits result in the following outcomes:

- Development of a knowledge repository;
- Forming and nurturing communities of practice.

However, there are many others to explore.

5. KEY TASKS

It is possible to separate a knowledge audit into seven key tasks:

1. Create a data, information and knowledge systems database : This involves creating an inter-relational database (possibly using MS Access or Oracle) with tables for:

Each section of the organization;

- Data, information and knowledge repositories
- Types of communication, such as, face-to-face, analogue and digital systems.

2. Identify areas of organizational quick gain : This can be used as a way of demonstrating to key players that you are committed to high levels of achievement in the short as well as the medium and long-term.

3. Perform process mapping : It is important to 'map' key processes as well as key players within the organization. There are a number of software tools that can be used for such mapping including MS Project and MS Visio. It is possible to take mapping a stage further by using XML image maps to illustrate processes over Intranets, Internets and extranets.

4. Organize focus groups : The composition of such groups needs to be balanced between differing levels of seniority, front/back office and differing locations. Focus groups are an important means of keeping on track. Well-balanced focus groups can be used again over time.

5. Design and pilot knowledge needs survey : The importance of a pilot project is that it sets an achievable object in the foreseeable future, say, six to twelve months. Senior managers are often very keen on pilots as, if they fail to work, resources used are limited and lessons learnt can be recorded quickly.

6. Organize feedback sessions : This is particularly important where you have a project steering group for the audit. This steering group, through its involvement with the strategy, will feel empowered and capable of enthusing and empowering others. An effective steering group should consist of:

Chair : An operational Director

Representatives : One from each Section

Quality Minutes : Rotate between members

Regular Meetings : Monthly and ad hoc

Email List : Discussion List for core, active and peripheral members

Intranet Presence : Tracking progress

Monitoring and Evaluation Procedures : Internal consultant

7. Draft strategy : This should demonstrate key findings, be well analyzed and the data should be arrayed in an accessible format.

6. PROCESS MAPPING

Process mapping is a simple exercise. It helps an organisation to know where to start making improvements that will have the biggest impact. A good definition of a process describes it as a series of connected steps or actions to achieve an outcome. A process has the following characteristics:

1. A starting and end point.
2. A purpose or aim for the outcome.
3. Rules governing the standard or quality of inputs throughout the process.
4. It is usually linked to other processes.
5. It can be simple and short, or complex and long.

Process mapping is one of the most powerful ways for multi-disciplinary teams to understand the real problems from the individual's perspective, and to identify opportunities for improvement.

A map will give you:

1. A key starting-point to any improvement project, large or small.
2. The opportunity to bring together multi-disciplinary teams from primary, secondary, and tertiary organizational levels to create a culture of ownership, responsibility and accountability
3. An overview of the complete process – helping staff to understand, often for the first time, how complicated

the systems can be.

4. An aid to help plan effectively where to test ideas for improvements that are likely to have the most impact on the project aims
5. Brilliant ideas - especially from staff who don't normally have the opportunity to contribute to service organization, but who really know how things work
6. An event that is interactive, that gets people involved and talking
7. An end product - the map - which is easy to understand and highly visual Process mapping is also easy, creative and fun.

7. OUTCOMES

The outcome of a knowledge audit tends to be marked by the production of a document. This document should be made available in both hard and soft copy. It should be accessible both as a dynamic Intranet site and interactive CD ROM.

Below is an example of the format of such a document produced as a result of a knowledge audit within a Local Authority Directorate.

Section One : The Data, Information and Knowledge Relationship Data only becomes information when it is placed in appropriate context. The Division gathers much data that is not always placed in an appropriate context and subsequently lacks quality in terms of information. Knowledge is not shared effectively and contributes to poor quality information. Systems need to be created which allow for the effective placing of a data in an appropriate context and the sharing of knowledge that adds value to that information.

Section Two : Understanding Communities & Communities of Practice

If we are to understand existing and future knowledge networks we can use the concept of community as a unit for analysing the exchange of data, information and knowledge.

A community can be defined as any group of people with a shared set of values or beliefs. Communities within the Division can be divided into:-

External : A range of subsets of Inactive Citizens x Active Citizens x Community Activists

* *Internal* : Staff x Section x Corporate x Policy x Operational
* *Management* : Senior, Middle, Junior

Communities learn from experience and in communities of practice.

A community of practice is a diverse group of people engaged in real work over a significant period of time during which they build things, solve problems, learn and invent...in short, they evolve a practice that is highly skilled and highly creative.

Section Three: Knowledge Audit

Data, Information and Knowledge are shared in three phases of activity each containing a cycle of three further activities:-

1. *Formatting* : Analogue, Digital and Intellectual
2. *Networking* : Information Exchange, Communication, and Collaboration
3. *Learning* : Action, Emotion. Knowledge

Section Four: Methodology

A methodology to compile a user-defined Knowledge Management Network (KMN) might involve the following:

— Initial Key Stakeholder Meeting : Outline of Exercise
— Best Value Performance Indicators
— An Overview of What is Available and Appropriate

– Identification of Areas of 'Quick Gain'
– Social Network Analysis
– Focus Groups of Communities of Practice
– Structured Survey of Information, Knowledge and Skills Needs
– Feedback of Draft Proposal to Key Stakeholder Group

Section Five: The Way Forward

– Draft Proposal for Discussion
– Final Draft for Implementation

Section Six: Resource Implications

– Financial
– Human
– Technological

REFERENCE

1. Bontis, N. *Assessing knowledge assets: a review of the models used to measure intellectual capital.* International Journal of Management Reviews, 2001, Volume 3 No 1, pp 41-60
2. Bouthillier France and Shearer Kathleen. Understanding knowledge management and information management: the need for an empirical perspective. Information Research, 2002, Volume 8 No 1
3. Burnett Simon, Illingworth Lorraine and Webster Linda. *Knowledge auditing and mapping: a pragmatic approach.* Knowledge and Process Management. 2004, Volume 11 Issue 1, pp 25-37
4. Liebowitz Jay, et al. *The knowledge audit.* Knowledge and Process Management. 2000, Volume 7 Issue 1, pp 3-10
5. Stevens Larry. *Knowing what your company knows: a knowledge audit is a necessary precursor to a new KM initiative.* Knowledge Management, 2000, December
6. http://www.nelh.nhs.uk/knowledge_management/km2/audit_toolkit.asp
7. http://www.communityknowledge.co.uk/KMIntro/part_e.html

5

E-journal Collection Development : Problems and Prospects

T. Sunitha

ABSTRACT

The unique advancements in information and communication technologies (ICT) and tremendous development in digital and web based technologies have led to an exponential growth of e-publishing the world over. A variety of electronic resources in an unprecedented array of publication types and in a mix of digital formats are available now for the library community to consider for their libraries. Among these e-resources, e-journals form the major publication type. E-journals extend numerous advantages to libraries and to the user community and because of these advantages, libraries are now tempted to subscribe to numerous e-Journals from a vast variety of publishers and providers. At the same time, subscription process of e-journals is a complex affair. There are many issues that libraries subscribing to e-journals must consider. It has therefore become imperative on the part of information professionals to learn the basics of digital subscriptions, digital collection development and its efficient management. This paper discusses the various issues and additional prospects relating to E-Journal collection development. It also narrates the e-journals management at IIMK and various strategies to be adopted by present day libraries in e-journal collection development and management.

1. INTRODUCTION

Fast developments in digital technologies in the recent years have given an astounding boost to electronic publishing worldwide. There has been a substantial increase in the production of electronic content, trade as well as scholarly, over the past several years. The proliferation of e-publishing across the world has brought in a revolution in scholarly publications. A variety of e-resources are penetrating into the libraries. Among these e-resources, e-journals form a major digital collection in most of our libraries and they are growing at a surpassing rate. Almost all popular journal publishers now have their electronic version in addition to their print counterparts. Most of the renowned publishers provide online access to their current as well as retrospective contents. On the other side, the user community also has been influenced by these technologies to such an extent that there has been demand from users for providing such electronic information services in the libraries. E-journals are becoming increasingly in demand both as a means of rapid desktop access to current research materials and as way to view past volumes. Generally speaking, e-journals are the electronic equivalents of their print counter parts. E-Journals often referred to interchangeably as "Electronic Serials", "Online Journals" and "Electronic Periodicals". Electronic journals have been defined in a variety of ways. Lancaster [1995] defines e-Journal as "a journal created for the electronic medium and available only in this medium". Electronic serials may be defined very broadly as any journal, magazine or newsletter which is available over the internet [E-journal Miner]. As compared to the print journals e-journals have numerous additional features. E-journals are more easily accessible and searchable than the print journals. Users can access e-journals wherever and whenever they want. E-journals can be used by more users at a time and they offer unique features like link to related items and reference liking facilities. It also supports multimedia information and less storage space is required for electronic journals. As a result of the above advantages, libraries today buy licenses for an ever-increasing number of Electronic Journals from a range of different publishers and providers, and use a diverse set of technologies for information delivery.

2. E-JOURNAL SUBSCRIPTION MODELS

Libraries get access to e-journals in a number of ways. Information professionals should have a good knowledge of various subscription models offered by the publishers. Various subscription models are practiced in India and each of them has varied features.

2.1. Direct and Second Party e-journals

Libraries can subscribe e-journals just like they subscribe to print journals. Major publishers like Elsevier, Blackwell, Wiley etc. offers e-version of the print journals. The distinction between publishers and second parties is important. In a second party electronic journal database, the entire journal is collected and users will get the look and feel of reading journal. Some examples of second party electronic journal databases include: 1. JSTOR, which offers both multidisciplinary and discipline-specific collections of e-journals provide flexibility for libraries and institutions to choose the sets of journals and collection growth paths that are most appropriate for their needs; 2. Ingenta, the most appreciated journal portal, facilitates users to read, print, and email 21,741,395 articles from 30,469 electronic journals; and 3. ProjectMUSE, which provide online access to over 300 high quality humanities, arts, and social sciences journals from 60 scholarly publishers. In India, 'J-Gate' of the Informatics

India Ltd. is an example for second party electronic journal providers. There are advantages as well as drawbacks incase of direct/second party e-journals. In the case of electronic journals, either sourced directly from the publisher or through a second party, the users have the advantage of accessing the journals direct. The disadvantage is that in the electronic journal services, mostly, search facilities are kept at a low profile.

2.2. Aggregated e-journals

Another category are aggregators. They are companies who create collections of entire journals and sell access to these collections. Aggregators use to buy the copyright of the journals in bulk and provide access to the journals through a single interface. Examples of aggregators include EBSCO Online and PROQUEST. In the aggregated services, search facilities are fairly high, with low priority for content layout, get up etc.

2.3. E-Content access to print subscription

A library may also get access to the electronic content from the publishers directly by virtue of their print subscription to a title. Most of the publishers offer free online access to the journals as part of their print subscription. The library will have to be alert and vigilant in order that these facilities are not left unnoticed or the free offer access opportunities missed out.

2.4. Consortia based Subscription

A recent trend, being observed in India, is the formation of a number of library consortia most of which are well conceived and managed. A library consortium is a collective activity of a group of libraries towards a common goal of sharing resources [Janakiraman 2002]. Consortium is a win-win situation for all its stakeholders, users, publishers, and libraries - all alike. Users are the ultimate end beneficiaries of such initiatives. For publishers, the consortium offers reduced attrition, improved income stability, incremental revenue, and greater visibility of their products. For the participating libraries, the consortia offer several benefits which include access to otherwise un-subscribed materials, scope for electronic archives, availability and monitoring of usage statistics, getting deep discounts through joint pricing negotiations - hence lower unit cost of information, reduced storage costs, developing common resources databases, effective document delivery systems, a single interface and access point, enhanced search facilities, better scope for developing a union catalogue among participating libraries etc.

2.5. Open Access Archives / Open Access Journals

Recent trend in scholarly communication is open archives/open access publishing. Open-access (OA) literature is digital, online, free of charge, and free of most copyright and licensing restrictions [earlham]. It is all about democratizing the scientific intellectual capital, which often draws its energy from publicly or privately funded research. It is not against proprietary or peer reviewed scholarly journals. According to Stevan Harnad, the world renowned proponent of Open Access, it is just self-archiving the articles the author has published in (peer-reviewed) non-OA journals. Hence it neither bypasses nor replaces peer-review. It has nothing to do with changing peer review. Self-archiving is a way of supplementing non-OA journal access with an OA version for those would-be users whose institutions cannot afford the non-OA journal. First and most important preprint server and archive is physics preprint archive. [arXiv). This archive contains over 3,60,000 e-prints in Physics, Mathematics, Computer Science and Quantitative Biology. Directory of open access journals (DOAJ) [doaj] is a service that provides access to quality controlled Open Access Journals. The Directory aims to be comprehensive and cover all open access scientific and scholarly journals that use an appropriate quality control system, and it will not be limited to particular languages or subject areas. The aim of the Directory is to increase the visibility and ease of use of open access scientific and scholarly journals thereby promoting their increased usage and impact covers 2586 journals and 127317 articles.

3. COLLECTION DEVELOPMENT ISSUES

Collection development of e-journals is a tricky job, as there is a great deal of difference between the traditional print information resources being handled by libraries and the new genre of electronic and digital information being sourced and accessed. In the traditional paradigm, the journals bought and subscribed to by the libraries were naturally owned by them, allowing them to make the best use of the resources within the 'fair use' clause or principle. Whereas in the electronic publishing scenario all the traditional belief, approach and understanding about the digital documents that the library purchases / subscribes to, have a world of difference. Libraries get only a license to use the electronic information while purchasing, and even this license is issued only for a prescribed period of time. Librarians at the same time, have the professional responsibility to assure uninterrupted as well as perpetual access to the information subscribed to by the library. Issues of copyright, intellectual property and fair use are very much important to libraries [Orsdel 2002]. Considering the prevailing socio-cultural-economic situations, the libraries need to follow a pragmatic hybrid approach to collection development activities [Sreekumar & Sunitha].

Hence the collection development and management is far more complex process for electronic journals than for print journals. In the changed scenario it is observed that the librarian is becoming more and more involved in negotiating complex licensing agreements, addressing issues of copyright, organizing methods of access to information through networked resources and aggressively engaged in liaising with the academic community in the purchase of information products [Ashcroft 2000]. There are many issues that libraries subscribing to e-journals must consider: budget provisions, IT infrastructure, user awareness/preferences, access issues, copyright/IPR issues, preservation/archival considerations, swinging pricing models, license etc. Serious attention should be paid to find the solution to these issues. Major dilemmas in e-journals collection development are illustrated in the figure 1.

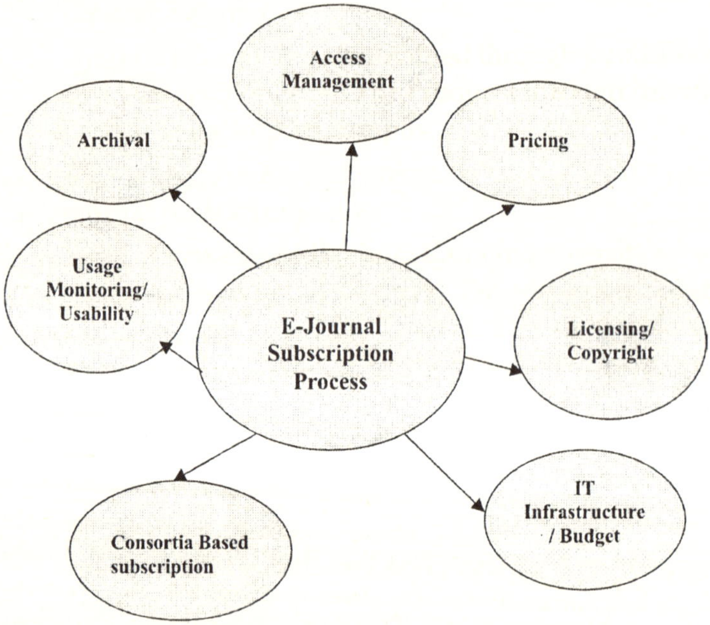

Fig.1. Issues in E-Journal Collection Development

3.1. Access related Issues

There are a host of issues and problems that keep haunting the libraries while arranging subscriptions to electronic journals as well as providing long term and perpetual access to the vast amount of digital scholarly content spread across the world. Access to E-Journals could be arranged from the respective publishers against UserID/ Password or through IP authentication. For a wider audience, IP based access is mostly preferred, as the users need not have to bother about the UserID and Password every time. A useful alternative is to provide the UserID/Password in the library's portal / website so that users can pick them up during usage, and over a period of time, they also by-heart them.

Among the third party journals access services, 'Athens' is an Access Management system for controlling secure access to E-Journals and other web based services. It offers number of features like secured single sign-on access to multiple web-based services; devolved administration facilities at organisation level; remote access user accounts; encrypted bulk user account upload services; highly scalable services - supports millions of user accounts; replicated, load balanced and fully resilient architecture.

Libraries need to take care of the 'site license' aspects of content access, as some publishers lay stringent rules on this, making the life of the Librarian miserable. Before jumping into such services, the Librarian should ensure necessary Internet bandwidth also, failing which complaints will pile up, resulting in a growing aversion against the electronic services in general. Another important aspect is the local administration of access management by the users. Users are to be properly oriented towards effective and efficient use of the Net as well as the journal sites. Unnecessary and unscrupulous hits, revisits and downloads can result in frequent choking of the Net connectivity, posing unwanted problems to the entire user community on campus.

3.2. Copyright, IPR/Licensing issues

Issues of copyright, intellectual property and fair use

are important to libraries, yet they are struggling to make sense of all these issues in the new Digital Age. There are a number of issues that the library should be highly careful while entering into digital subscriptions. Catches can come in multiple forms with the vague yet meticulously manipulated term "licensing". The e-journal subscription and access model allows licensing of the content for a stipulated period of time which has several restrictions and binding on licensee. Proper measures and back-up agreements for access to the retrospective content are to be assured from the publishers/vendors.

3.3. Pricing Issues

There are no universally acceptable pricing and licensing models for e-journals. Pricing strategies vary widely from publisher to publisher. Pricing should be market based and not formulaic. There exist a number of pricing models for electronic journals such as the online only, online and print, print and online, flip-pricing, pay-per-hit, pay-per-view, pay-per-download, pay-per-print, deeply discounted pricing etc. Some of the other popular models include the "Base price plus consortium premium", the FTE (Full Time Equivalence) based pricing", "core subscription plus pay-per-view", "usage based pricing", "licensee membership fees" etc. Based on the nature of the subscription / licensing arrangements and the availability of funds a number of models can coexist in a practical library setting at the moment. Here what is more important is that the price offered by the publishers should be economically viable for the library.

3.4. IT Infrastructure and Budget Provision

Moving towards e-journals requires libraries to develop IT infrastructure at their end. But most of the libraries in India do not make the effective use of information technology for e-journals collection development as they are either weak in their IT infrastructure or that the right methodologies are not known to the library professionals. Non-availability of sufficient funds as well as lack of encouragement and support from management is another factor contributing to this scenario. Librarians should convince the authorities to obtain special funds for the acquisition of e-collection as well as developing infrastructure for providing access to the e-collection to the users.

3.5. Usage Monitoring and Usability issues

This area requires much attention. Libraries are investing huge amount of money in e- resources. So they should ensure that these resources are effectively and efficiently being utilized. Users are to be trained properly towards effective utilization of e-resources.

3.6. Consortia based subscription issues

By forming consortia, groups of libraries are often able to negotiate access to additional e-journal titles, without increasing cost. The main aim of a consortium is to achieve what the members of the group cannot achieve. By employing this strategy, the libraries have been able to increase the number of journal available on campus, without increasing cost. Issues like pricing, copyright/IPR issues, licensing, access models, archival access etc are to be considered while signing the consortia agreement.

3.7. Archival Issues

Internet and the e-Journals have created new paradigms for archiving journals resulting in controversial debates and throwing in new technological complexities. The very process of delivery is being reversed in the e-journal system. While the print journals were delivered to the libraries by publishers or the subscription agents, the libraries may have to now electronically visit the publishers to collect the journals. This alone adds a new set of cost and infrastructure dimension to the libraries. Currently, not all publishers allow archiving rights for e-journals to libraries. Each publisher is evolving his own commercial policy and is exercising customized technical features and controls for delivering e-journals to libraries for archiving. All these issues require thoughtful debate and understanding to formulate effective archiving strategy by the library community.

4. CONCLUSION

In the present digital environment, there has been a substantial increase in the production of e-journals across the world. E-journals have become the major digital resources in our libraries and they bring in numerous benefits to the end users. On the other hand, e-journal subscription is a complex and complicated process. Naturally there will be a host of issues and problems that keep haunting libraries involved in e-journals collection building activities. Role of information professionals have become more crucial in major decision making activities like selection of best subscription models, licensing, pricing decisions, access control and management. So, information professionals should be equipped with necessary skill sets and working knowledge on e-journal management. What is more important here is the development of a collection development policy and strategy for e-journals. At IIMK, we have been using various strategies and techniques for e-journal collection development and management. These models can be adopted and practiced by any libraries in the country. From our experience over the past seven years, we can confidently say that development of strong e-journal base is possible for any libraries with meticulous and continuous efforts.

REFERENCES

1. Lancaster F.W. 1995 The evolution of electronic publishing *Library Trends*, 43(4) : 518-527.

2. E-Journal Miner. <http://ejournal.coalliance.org/faqs.cfm> accessed on May 25, 2006
3. J-Stor. < www.jstor.org> accessed on February 23, 2007
4. Ingenta < www.ingenta.com> accessed on February 23, 2007
5. Project Muse < http://muse.jhu.edu/> accessed on February 23, 2007
6. J-Gate < www.j-gate.informindia.co.in> accessed on February 23, 2007
7. Janakiraman, S. 2002 Thoughts on Library Consortium. In *Proceedings of the Round Table on Sharing of E-Journals through Consortia in Indian Libraries,* Indian Institute of Astrophysics, Bangalore, India. [Proceedings of the Round Table on Sharing of E-Journals through Consortia in Indian Libraries, Bangalore. 28-29 November 2002].
8. Peter Suber <http://www.earlham.edu/~peters/fos/overview.htm>
9. Physics Preprint Archive < www.arXiv.org>
10. **Directory of Open Access Journals** <http://www.doaj.org>
11. Sreekumar, M.G and Sunitha,T. 2006. Community Acceptance of e-journals as a Robust Print Surrogate and Scholarship Supplement: The IIMK Experience . In *Proceedings of the International Conference on Digital Libraries (ICDL 2006).* New Delhi. TERI. Pp.531-541.
12. [Proceedings of the International Conference on Digital Libraries (ICDL 2004). New Delhi, India. 24-27 February 2004. Organized by TERI, India
13. **Orsdel, Lee Van; Born, Kathleen. 2002. Doing the Digital Flip. *Library Journal,* 127 (7): 51-55.**
14. Ashcroft, L. 2000. Win-win-win: Can the evaluation and promotion of electronic journals bring benefits to library suppliers, information professionals and users? *Library Management,* 21(9) : 466 - 471.

6

Upcoming Trends in Library Acquisitions with Special Reference to E-books

Sreejaya P

ABSTRACT

Rapid advancements in information communication technologies have led to the emergence of electronic publishing, especially scholarly electronic publishing, which deliver the content in electronic/digital format. E-journals and e-books have become predominant types / formats in the e-publishing era. E-books are rapidly becoming a viable alternative over the traditional medium and will continue to stay in one form or another. E-books are more efficient than paper-based books from the various perspectives such as storage, transfer, delivery, and accessibility. However, in spite of the advantages, the acceptance of e-book technology in India is slow due to several obstacles which include lack of reliable suppliers / vendors. This paper discusses the various types of e-books, the issues involved in the collection development of e-books, the factors associated with the selection process like availability of content, quality of content, access / subscription issues, pricing models and distribution. It also highlights the important market players in the e-book industry. This article also shares the experience of the Indian Institute of

Management Kozhikode with regard to the collection development, services and management of e-books.

1. INTRODUCTION

Libraries are undergoing a paradigm shift on one side by the complexities of information in an array of different types and formats and on the other side the increasing broad user demand. Application of information and communication technologies in information management has made a drastic change in library services. The advent of electronic publication has led to the emergence of electronic resources. Libraries today buy, subscribe to, license and accumulate information in an unprecedented array of content categories or publication types and in a rapidly proliferating mix of formats such as digital and print. Today libraries are faced with the challenges of integrating the traditional and emerging formats and balancing the resource allocation between the traditional and upcoming technologies and building new information management processes and procedures. Now the content no longer penetrates into our research and academic libraries through the print media alone. The recorded knowledge reaches libraries by way of established scholarly publication types. In the changing information environment, drastic shifts have taken place in the format and media of publication. The variety of publication types include books (published as such or issued as accompaniment), journals, portals, vortals, reports, cases, databases, CBTs, WBTs etc. This proliferation of different file formats, standards and platforms in which documents are published unprecedentedly increase the challenges associated with the selection, acquisition, storage and information delivery. Irrespective of these challenges and issues confronted with, the digital formats have become the predominant format. All these prevalent changes in the scholarly communication reveal that the collection development mission of libraries can not avoid their impact.

As libraries cope with the pace and magnitude of these changes collection development is one of the areas which need high attention. There is a great deal of difference in the modus operandi in the digital collection building as against the traditional collection building. In the traditional paradigm the books and journals bought and subscribed to by the libraries are naturally owned by them so as to allow the libraries to make best use of them, whereas in the electronic publishing scenario, the libraries get only a 'license' or 'permission' to use the electronic information, that also for a particular period of time.

2. COLLECTION DEVELOPMENT IN THE ELECTRONIC ERA

Collection development is a natural and common place activity of libraries across the world and being followed for several centuries. It is the process of planning a stock acquisition programme not simply to cater for immediate needs, but to build a coherent and reliable collection over a number of years, to meet the objectives of the service (Harrold Librarian Glossary).

As libraries rapidly move into a new paradigm, the collection development processes are also to be properly planned and tuned, incorporating such procedural changes with explicit collection development policies, user needs and analysis, selection and acquisition in order to satisfy the real and potential needs of the Organization.

Electronic material are either produced exclusively electronic (born digital), or simultaneously in print and electronic, while some are exact reproduction of the same text (made electronic or digitized). Proper care has to be taken when electronic products are being purchased, the librarian should be careful about the hurdles and also aware about the tricks of the publishers / vendors. The acquisition librarian should make sure that he/she avoids buying something already in stock in another format, while entering into licensing agreement for e-resources. A well formulated collection development policy acts as a guide to libraries in overcoming the issues and processes involved in e-subscriptions. The main difference between the traditional collection development policy and electronic resources collection development policy is that the former is based on ownership of material and later is based access from the vendors. Selection and acquisition of e-resources imply an array of complex factors which need to be carefully considered and they include content, cost, ease of use, availability, technical support, infrastructure needed, updating, archiving, licensing etc. The current information environment calls for the skilled librarians who act as an intermediary between the ever challenging domain and ever demanding user community. S/he should be able to explore the various electronic resources available and be able to make the intelligent selection decisions as deem fit for each occasion. Financial resources and IT infrastructure are other important factors which are to be considered in e-resources collection development. As reflected in the title, this paper focuses on the features with regard to e-books and the issues involved in collection development of e-books.

3. E-BOOKS

E-books have been around for a quite while now and although different stake holders have various expectations of how they could fit in to both academic and everyday life. An e-book is an electronic representation of a book, usually a parallel publication of a print copy, but occasionally born digital. It can be defined as a digital monograph that is searchable, able to be enhanced with cross-references, and linked to other sources and multimedia. The market for e-books is still new but at the same time it is in a rapid change.

Depending on the nature and type of the digital format,

access / delivery mode, subscription / licensing pattern, e-books could be categorised into the following:

3.1. Downloadable e-books

Downloadable e-books are of three types, viz., i). Downloading to a PC - where the books could be downloaded from the internet e-book services to the PC, and no separate reading devices are needed; ii). Downloading to a handheld devices such as palm pilots and PDAs which provide another means of accessing e-books. These handheld machines allow users to read e-books as long as they have a specific piece of software installed (eg. Microsoft reader); iii) Downloading to e-book specific devise - wherein the contents are downloaded to a dedicated hardware device with high quality screen. They are light and portable and they provide good storage.

3.2. Print on demand (POD) e-books

This form of e-books provide great deal of freedom and flexibility to users by allowing them to purchase books in parts (say a chapter) as against the whole copy. It also facilitates users to get print copies of the e-books.

3.3. Web accessible e-books

The Web interface allows the user to read the text, it also opens up the possibilities of linking to other resources, cross-text searching etc. Here Publisher's or providers web site may be accessed on a fee or purchase the e-books to receive indefinite access, ebrary, Netlibrary, Books 24X7 etc. are the examples.

3.4. Features of e-books

E-books are evolving as a viable part of library collections. E-books offer libraries the potential to make considerable savings. Most importantly they can be accessed 24 hours a day which is not possible by a library in the traditional way. Also it could be used in a network, and shared unlimitedly within an organization. They do have advantages over print titles for libraries as well as users. They do not occupy shelf space. In addition, e-books cannot be damaged, lost or stolen, they may free staff from routine tasks such as shelving and issuing and returning books. However, apart from the advantages of e-books, there are also some disadvantages. Shortcomings of current e-book technology and its derivatives include the inconsistent costs, absolute dependency on a variety of gadgets, inappropriate pace with the current user expectations about how books are handled, quality of reading experiences, ensured accessibility etc. E-books create a state of bewilderment and pose a number intimidating issues to libraries in complex technicalities and management, as a developing model.

Since their introduction in the late 1990s, e-books have evolved from simple digital reproductions of their print counterparts to content that can be purchased and used in a much more flexible manner. While the models are still evolving for content, licensing, and purchase, the new generation of e-book serves both the librarian and the user better than ever before. Vendors are making it easier for librarians to integrate e-books into their regular selection and acquisition workflow. But it is necessary to allow multiple methods for the user to find the information they seek. The options include searching, navigation, e-book features, usage statistics, integration, MARC records etc.

3.5. Guidelines for selection of e-books

The guidelines involved in the selection process of the e-books are to find out duplication of electronic and print monograph, ensure that which both format is preferred and books for which electronic format is preferred. There are number of factors libraries need to consider while opting for a specific e-book service. Flexibility is an important factor, which help to choose a collection and model that meets your library's needs and budget. Accessibility is another factor and it is to be ensured that simultaneous access for all authenticated users are made available. The issues related to extensibility and inter-operability are also to be well taken care of. One feature among the inter-operability is ensuring of seamless integration with catalogues and portals. Utility is another factor which help user to get maximum benefit from the service.

4. COLLECTION DEVELOPMENT ISSUES

The biggest problem collection developers face are locating the e-books of choice, lack of consistent information about their availability, established trade channels as available for their print counterparts etc. This has become a major constraint in the acquisition of the e-books. Looking at the market, one can see that a mixture of old and new material are being produced electronically by the publishers. One has to be therefore careful about balancing the print and the e-book collection. Publishers should ensure quality of e-books, but there are still questions to consider in the realm of distribution and licensing them. Most of the publishers' website and catalogues provide information whether titles are available electronically.

In India e-books are currently in a relatively early stage of development, as in most libraries the collections are in hybrid stages, as a mix of print and electronic material. In this transitional stage of development we are facing lot of problems in the collection development of e-books.

The companies associated with the selling of e-content negotiate with publishers to digitize their titles and sell them with on a license. Consortium deals are also made for e-book collections or selections. Secure technology protects the publisher's copyright. Due to publisher's concerns about rights, e-book vendors are normally able to offer only limited usage rights for printing, downloading and copying. Access is another issue which includes user awareness and the ability to accommodate simultaneous users.

4.1. Purchase / pricing models

This is one area which needs utmost attention both from the publishers' side as well as the library front. E-books can be purchased from online bookstores (amazon.com, Barnes & Noble), aggregators (NetLibrary, ebrary, EBL), reference books directly from publishers (Elsevier, Oxford, Gale), monograph vendors' online ordering system (YBP, Blackwell), or through consortium options. The methods by which libraries can select e-books are in two types, choose to access the titles on a time bound licensing or choose to acquire access on a permanent basis. But libraries need to consider the different means by which their users will utilize their e-books and what combination of models will best meet their needs. Publishers and aggregators offer libraries several different pricing options for e-books. E-books can be acquired as single copies or in collections. Pricing can be based on the number of potential users in the organization, or the resources can be acquired through restricted simultaneous user licenses. Pricing may also be based on annual subscriptions or the books may be purchased separately.

Perpetual access for e-books by which individual books can be purchased separately for long term use helps us to gain permanent access for one time payment, but it can be costly. One-time purchases of e-books are well suited to resources that have a long-term use value and do not need to be continually updated. The advantages of consortium acquisitions show up particularly well in one-time purchases of e-books. One-time purchases give the consortium negotiating power over price.

Annual subscription is another model. This model help us to get to access to the collections of e-books. With annual subscriptions, libraries may acquire user rights to collections of e-books considerably more cheaply than the purchase price of an equivalent collection of printed books. In some cases, the addition of new e-books to the collection is included in the annual subscription_price.

Pricing based on number of users is another upcoming model which is based on full-time equivalent (FTE) figure, the prices of the collections are calculated on the basis of the number of potential users in the organisation. The price may also be defined on the basis of FTE figures for separate subject areas.

Pricing of e-books may also be based on a restricted number of simultaneous users. The library can choose how many customers are able to use the collection at the same time. The greater the number of simultaneous users, higher the subscription price. Restricting the number of simultaneous users is undesirable from the library's point of view, as it may prevent potential users from gaining access to the resources.

4.2. E-book players in the market

There are many vendors active in e-book market, the major aggregators who are involved in selling e-books are listed below;

Netlibrary (www.netlibrary.com) : NetLibrary is a division of OCLC Online Computer Library Center, Inc. (www.oclc.org). They provide versatile e-content for libraries and publishers today. More than 100,000 titles have been digitized now. Additionally, NetLibrary offers e-books, audio books, databases and even some e-journals online. It supports the most content from more than 400 leading publishers. The books are available searchable full text and in some cases can be printed/annotated. The publisher of the content determines the e-book price, but the majority of the e-book titles are the same price as the hard copy book. An access fee is charged to libraries and institutions to cover the costs of maintaining a digital library, such as use of search capabilities and related Web-based features. The access fee can be paid as a one-time charge for ongoing access to the e-book title, or can be paid on an annual basis.

Ebrary (www.ebrary.com) : Ebrary is a leading e-Content services and technology provider that has been serving the library, publishing, and corporate markets since 1999. This e-book service provides More than 60,000 full-text, digital books and other authoritative content from over 200 leading publishers. The ebrary platform is PDF based. The Dynamic Content Platform of ebrary includes the ebrary Reader, which optimizes page-by-page delivery of PDF documents, and InfoTools , which seamlessly links search queries to multiple online databases and information on the Web. It is a multi user access model.

Books24X7 (www.books24x7.com) : Books24x7, a SkillSoft Company, is a leading provider of web-based digital technical and business reference content, containing thousands of digitized "best-in-class" reference books, research reports, documentation and articles. Books24x7's hosted web-based platform enables users to search, browse, read and collaborate with vast professional "Referenceware" libraries assembled through its relationships with the world's top IT and business publishers. This includes, in the technical publishing arena, imprints like Microsoft Press, Osborne/McGraw Hill, Artech House and many others. In the business field, prominent publishing partners include AMACOM, ASTD Press, Berrett-Koehler, Harvard Business School Publishing, John Wiley, MIT Press, Oxford University Press and others. Prominent customers that have adopted Books24x7 solutions include: Bank of America, Lockheed-Martin and many more.

Questia (www.questia.com) : Questia claims to be the first online library that provides 24/7 access to the world's largest online collection of books and journal articles in the humanities and social sciences, plus magazine and newspaper articles. Its service offers Over 67,000 complete books, available cover to cover from over 250 publishers as well as 155,000 journal articles. Individual subscription fee is $99.95/Year. Users must read the works on the screen and can not print more than one page at a time, a restriction that helps prevent piracy.

Safari online (http//www.safaribooksonline.com): Safari Books Online a joint venture of Oreilly and Addison Wesley is a searchable e-reference library containing the broadest range of technical and business content available from O'Reilly Media, Pearson, Adobe, Sun Microsystems Press, IBM, Microsoft and many more. Safari provides immediate access to fully searchable technical content from leading publishers for problem solving, learning and skill enhancement. Safari offers two plans: Safari Library and Safari Bookshelf. Safari Library offers complete unlimited access to all content. Safari Bookshelf limits how much book content can be viewed at one time.

4.3. Major Publishers

Almost all reputed publishers have their e-book presence in the market. E-books are being published by a wide range of publishers. Established publishers are already making available e-book versions of some of their new mainstream publications.

Simon & Schuster

Simon & Schuster, Inc. is a global leader in the field of general interest publishing, providing consumers worldwide with a diverse range of quality books and multimedia products across a wide. Their e-book saysshop.com is an e-book store with more than 3000 titles.

Springer (www.springer.com)

The Springer e-book Collection spans the world of science, technology and medicine, publishing 15000 e-books. The collection offers high resolution illustrations, exceptional search capabilities and bookmarks, making research as fast and easy as possible. Accessible via PDF and HTML formats.

Pricing option includes institutional and individual access. Book Collection is a cost-effective, patron-pleasing choice for academic and corporate libraries.

Science Direct (www.sciencedirect.com)

Science Direct is a part of Elsevier (www.elsevier.com) and they offer one of the world's most advanced web delivery systems for scientific, technical and medical information. .Apart from their e journal content, more than hundreds of e book series, reference works and handbooks are available via science direct.

Apart from the above mentioned publishers, there are major publishers like John Wiley, Blackwell and Taylor and Francis, Baker & Taylor etc are also deal with the e-book selling.

5. FREE E-BOOKS

Many of the greatest books in the world are available on the net, free of charge. A few Sources of free and public domain e-books are listed below:

Project Gutenberg (www.gutenberg.org) **–** This e-book service offers18000 classics and books in the public domain as free.

On Line Books Page (www.digital.library.upenn.edu/books) - Thousands of texts are listed in this site.

Literature.org (www.literature.org) - A number of novels written by famous authors in easy-to-read HTML format are available in this site

Classic Book Library (www.classicbook.info) - Free online classics are available in this library.

Many books.Net (www.manybooks.net) - This is a well-organized site supporting multiple formats for both public domain and more recent, freely available titles.

6. CONCLUSION

The fundamentals and the basic philosophies of / about libraries are undergoing revolutionary changes with the advent of technologies. There is a paradigm shift in libraries - the perceptions, processes, procedures, practices and the usages are changed drastically. Collection development has become a process of building diverse combination of print and electronic resources. E-books are now arguably becoming a significant collection and a type of publication on its own. Libraries, especially those attached to the research and higher learning institutions, are therefore to be prepared in sourcing them as well as serving them for the benefit of their user community. There is of course an element of uncertainty and confusion among most of the publishers with regard to the selling, subscription and management of e-books, but that could not be an excuse for librarians to prevent the provision of e-books in libraries. As time pass by and as technologies and processes evolve, there will be more and more clarity in the provision of e-books as has happened in the case of its other surrogates such as e-journals.

REFERENCES

1. Chapman, Liz. Managing acquisitions in library and information London: Facet publishing, 2004. p.18-21
2. Lee, Stuart D and Boyle, Frances. Building an electronic resource collection: A practical guide.2nd ed. London: facet Publishing, 2004. p.48-51
3. Siriginidi Subba Rao (2005) Electronic books: Their integration into library and information centers. Electronic Library, Volume 23 Number 1,pp. 116-140
4. Kebede Gessesse (2000). Collection development and management in the twenty-first century with special reference to academic libraries: An over view. Library Management Volume 21, Number 7, pp. 365-372.
5. Paula Mikkonen (2006).Analyzing e-book pricing options and models based on FinELib e-book strategy. World library and

information congress: 72nd IFLA General Conference and Council, 20-24 August 2006,Seoul,Korea, http://www.ifla.org/IV/ifla72/index.htm

6. Ebrary: www.ebrary.com
7. Questia: www.questia.com
8. Netlibrary: www.netlibrary.com
9. Books 24X7: www.books24x7.com)
10. Safari online :http//www.safaribooksonline.com

7

Knowledge Management and Present Libraries

Padmamma, S

ABSTRACT

This paper mainly focuses on the concept of Knowledge Management, and the role of the Library professionals in managing the knowledge. The paper states the value of knowledge for an organization and also highlights the importance of librarians and information creation, capture, acquisition and sharing is described. Paper also touched the topics like the barriers and the role of the librarians.

1. INTRODUCTION

From the last few years the KM has become one of the latest hot topics in the library science field. Knowledge management is not a new term. Over the past few years it has become a generic term used by business organizations and government organizations and more in library field. There has been a phenomenal growth in interest and activity, as seen in many new publications, conferences, IT products, and job advertisements.

Knowledge is a product of human experience and reflection. The accumulated information in a particular area is known as 'knowledge'. San Segundo Mannuel (2001) observed "the pillars of the new society of knowledge are settling on the basis of productivity and utility and this has turned knowledge into nothing more than productive information". Singh and Singh (2004) expressed KM as "is a discipline that promotes an integrated approach to identifying, managing and sharing of an organizations information assets regardless of how or where they are located. It is strategic in nature and involves the careful interaction of people "Simply speaking knowledge management is concerned with managing both recorded (i.e., explicit) and tacit knowledge"

Santosus, Megan and Surmacz, Jon (2005) summarizes "unfortunately, there is no universal definition of KM just as there is no agreement as to what constitute knowledge in the first place. For this reason, it is best to think of KM in the broadest context.

2. KNOWLEDGE MANAGEMENT

KM is the management of knowledge resources and embodied knowledge. Knowledge is the totality of all existing information that is known. Every piece of information that is recorded in logical and systematic manner creates knowledge. According to Webster's New World Dictionary, "Knowledge is organized information available to problem solving".

Knowledge can be defined as the management of creating, sustaining, applying, and renewing knowledge resources of an organization including its relationship with customers and suppliers.

Knowledge can be divided into two types. Tacit knowledge and another one is explicit knowledge. Tacit knowledge is the "know how" acquired by persons. But one of the goals of the knowledge management is to make tacit knowledge more available. Explicit knowledge is systematically documented records in any kind of format, which guides the users to gain the knowledge and to expand the knowledge base further. These both knowledge is important in the library and information community. Knowledge management is very essential and vital process in order to achieve the goal and aspirations of organization. The Libraries have applied knowledge management principles to provide effective library services.

3. KNOWLEDGE MANAGEMENT PROCESS

- Knowledge creation
- Knowledge acquisition/capture
- Knowledge organization
- Knowledge sharing
- Knowledge renewal

4. USE OF KNOWLEDGE MANAGEMENT IN LIBRARIES

At present libraries are defined as a house of knowledge. The libraries actively engaging in their service dissemination with need based services. Today's libraries are completely plays as a mediator between knowledge containers and knowledge seeking. Librarian as a facilitator of knowledge which containing by outside and acquiring, organizing, and explicating the same.

The library personnel must have a clear view of the "know how" of information sources, management, retrieval and dissemination as well as global access to information with the tacit knowledge and this knowledge helps the end users to gain explicit knowledge. They must be guided to the gateway of knowledge. The objective of knowledge management in libraries is to promote knowledge innovation, relationship in and between libraries and between library and user.

Libraries are universally recognized a important social institutions for diffusion of knowledge and information as process of that brought and will continue to bring profound changes to library world in terms of both technology and involvement of people. So that today they used technology in their libraries for fost service. Hence, they are setting their knowledge management along with technology.

Knowledge management tools are technologies broadly defined, which enhance and enable knowledge generation, codification (know how) and transfer (Ruggles, 1997). The main roles of information technology in knowledge management are to accelerate the speed of knowledge transfer and creation. Knowledge management tools intend to help the processes of collecting and organizing the knowledge of groups of individuals in order to make this knowledge available in a shared base (Carvalho & Ferrira, 2001). Libraries use a combination of strategies and tools towards knowledge creation, knowledge adaptation, knowledge distribution and knowledge review. The working style of librarians has been replaced and enhanced by the advent of new information technologies and the power of knowledge is now substantially recognized as an organization asset.

According to Kim (1999) knowledge management is not about managing or organizing books or journals, searching the inherent for clients or arranging for the circulation of materials. However each of these activities can in some way be part of knowledge management spectrum and processes. Knowledge management is about enhancing the use of organizational knowledge through sound practices of knowledge management and organizational learning. Thus, knowledge management is a "combination of information management communication and human resources" how to manage knowledge will become an important subject facing libraries in near future. Knowledge management in libraries should be focused on effective research and development of knowledge, creation of knowledge base, exchange and sharing of knowledge between library staffs (including its users), training of library staff, speeding up explicit processing of the implicit knowledge and realizing of its sharing (shanhong, 2000).

5. ROLE OF LIBRARIANS IN KNOWLEDGE MANAGEMENT

The role of knowledge management in library and library services is not a new one. From the centuries they can have a KM and using them properly for information dissemination. But at present knowledge management along with Information Technologies and their usage, not only in administration point of view and also user point of view, to set and give the direction to the users to use the sources with satisfactory. Reardom (1998) has stated that "There is a need for significant changes in thinking, attitudes, education and training before we can confidently face the knowledge management future that waits in many important areas of the information and library professions".

The Librarians should have following type of knowledge:

- Knowledge about library's information source or assets, products and services;
- Knowledge about where these sources stored are and what is its use
- Knowledge about users including teaching staff and researcher and who is using these information sources
- What are the current usage of these sources and how to increase its uses?
- Knowledge about the library's own competencies and capabilities
- Knowledge about the emerging library trends and technologies

6. BARRIERS OF KNOWLEDGE MANAGEMENT IN LIBRARIES

- The library profession may not have proper knowledge about resources sharing.
- Generally, the Junior Staff cannot share their knowledge and ideas when they feel there is no benefit of this in terms of salary increases.
- Lack of communication skills.
- Fearing in asking questions and gives ideas.
- Between the staff there is no cooperation.
- Every library cannot participate in terms of modern technology and its management.
- Lack of staff training.

7. CONCLUSION

Every library should develop their own knowledge management systems. An efficient knowledge management system is one that will enable libraries to store information sources manually or electronically and facilitate the process of retrieving, sharing, tracking, revising and distributing these information sources efficiently with their users. Knowledge management and the sharing of knowledge can help libraries with the improvement of the quality of their services as well as the creation and maintenance of a learning culture (Mphidi and Snyman, 2004). Libraries should adopt some practice of KM from successful companies and reward library staff for seeking, sharing and creating knowledge.

REFERENCE

1. Liebowitz, J.Building Organizatinal Intelligence: A knowledge Management Primer, CRC Press, Boca Raton, FI, 200.
2. Koskinen, Kaj U. Knowledge management to improve project communication and implementation. Project management Journal, 2004, vol.135 (2), 13-19.
3. Jantz, R. Knowledge Management in Academic Libraries: Special

Tools and Processes to Support Information Professionals. Reference Service Review, 2001, 29 (1), 33-39.

4. Lytros, Militiadis D. Pouloudi, Athanasia and Poulymenakou, Angeliki. Knowledge Management Convergence-Expanding Learning Frontiers. Journal of Knowledge Management, 2002, vol.16 (1), p40-51.
5. Duffy, Jan. The Tools and Technologies Needed for Knowledge Management. Information Management Journal, 2001, v35 (1), p 64.
6. Mphidi, Hamilton and Snyman, Retha. The Utilization of an Intranet as Knowledge Management Tool in Academic Libraries. The Electronic Library, 2004, 22 (5), 393-400.
7. Ruggles, Rudy. Working paper. Knowledge Tools: Using Technology to Manage Knowledge Better. (available at www.cs.totonto.edu/-mkolp/lis2103/kmtools.pdf)
8. Mphidi, Hamilton and Snyman, Retha. The Utilization of an Internet as Knowledge Management Tool in Academic Libraries. The Electronic Library, 2004, 22 (5), 393-400.
9. Award, Elias M and Ghaziri, Hassan M. Knowledge Management. -Delhi: Pearson Education, 2004. P.1-456.
10. Teng, Sharon and Hawamdeh, Suliman. Knowledge Management in Public Libraries. Aslib proceedings, 2002, 54 (2), 188-197.

8

Future Librarianship in Knowledge Society

B. Ravivenkat
P V Govinda Reddy.

ABSTRACT

Libraries and information centres are the places where knowledge sources are collected, processed, organized, retrieved and disseminated according to the requirements of the users. There are changes in all spheres of libraries and information centers due to the developments in the area of printing, publishing, computer and communication technologies etc. There is a paradigm shift in libraries, especially in the area of collection, tools, services, staff, and users. This paper is an attempt to disclose the paradigm shift of libraries and information centres.

1. INTRODUCTION

Librarianship is the art of organizing knowledge sources in various forms . It is imperative that knowledge sources need to be organized in order to put them to proper use. It is rather easy to generate knowledge as mankind has the required talent and technique to think and evolve. But to visualize the use of that knowledge and disseminate it to the right people at the right time in right personal way requires an extra skill, which is an art by itself. This art can be best described as Librarianship.

2. KNOWLEDGE ORGANISATION

Libraries are no doubt storehouses of documents. But merely putting the documents in a place and go on piling up documents to fill up the shelf space does not mean anything to the librarian or the user of that library. Organisation methods are essential to practise the fundamental principles of Library Science. As the literature is exploding more and more documents are produced to capture knowledge. A demand for organization of the documents has been agitating the minds of knowledge organizers and information handling personnel. Evaluation of various forms and types of documents also added difficulties to the organization of knowledge. Librarianship has been devising ways and means of organizing the collection in a library . In a broad sense the following house keeping functions have been identified to organize the collection in most of the libraries in the world.

- Acquistion process including book selection and collection development
- Techinical Processing(Classification, Cataloguing, Indexing and Abstracting)
- Circulation transactions
- Reference Services(Ready Reference and Long Range)
- Information Processing Retrieval

The above functions are manual intensive and require professional or trained manpower to perform. Professional Courses have been evolved to impart education and training in Librarianship. These courses have been introduced in academic institutions at the undergraduate, graduate and post graduate levels by giving equal status on par with other science subjects including humanities and social sciences.

Suitable syllabi has been formulated and continuously updated with the rapid changes in users' requirements and demands for up to date information.

3. PARADIGM SHIFT

The convergence of communication and information technologies demolished the concept of distance and made the world a global village. In the last two decades many transformations have taken place in the area of Information Technology such as the Information Superhighways, Hotlines, Transborder Networks, Internet, World Wide Web, Electronic Library and Virtual Library which seem to have indelible impact on all walks of life. The world community has become a telecommunity, with the possibilities of access to information to anyone, anywhere, anytime. The developed countries which are already living in information age moving fast into knowledge based societies whereas the developing countries or third world economies are slowly transforming themselves into information age. The Information Technology is causing a radical change in all activities of all Library and Information Centres.

The indicators in the Paradigm Shift are Collection, Tool, Services, Staff, Education, User.

3.1. Collection

The Print Media dominated in the 20th Century. At the end of the century there are films CDs and other micrographics on a low scale in the libraries. Mostly the electronic materials began to appear in the last two decades of the 20th century in the special libraries. Contrary to this the future is on the collection of digital materials like CD-ROMS ,DVD, FMD, and computer databases. But there will be both and former will be confined to humanistic literature like poetry, drama, fiction and children libraries. The multimedia collection of the library and information centers will pose problems of acquisiton, organization, retrieval and dissemination of information which were not experienced in the yesteryears.

3.2. Library Tools

The traditional tools such as typerwriters, card duplicators, catalogue cabinets, photocopiers, microfilm cameras, microfilm and microfiche readers etc. has paved way for Compact racks, Laser Printers, Computers, Automatic Xerox Machines, Digital Database,E-Readers,OPAC, Airconditioned and fully equipped reading rooms. There is every possibility that robots and gizmos will attend ciruculation work, maintenance and reference work in future. Cyber libraries will reduce their professional staff and their places will be occupied by the machines.

3.3. Library Services

Services to the users are the forte of libraries and information centers. They also changed in form and focus. In the beginning the services provided were on the basis of on demand or responsive services (Lending, information Services, Reference Services, Bibliographic Services, User Education, Photocopying Services). Later in the transition period which is also called as Active Services period consisted CAS, SDI, Indexing, Translation, Abstracting, Documentation. In the 21st century the services is of Acute and Specific they are Literature Search, Subject DC, DVD Information Analysis, Technical Reports. Scanning , Internet, Automatic Xeroxing, Library Publication, Portal Dot.com , Downloading Structured and Unstructured information. The need and use of information by the users will increase in the future. The information services will be mostly directed towards repackaging and analysis of information. Virtual libraries will come into existence and the LIS professionals should be able to get information which is available in distant libraries and serve the users on online. The librarians should be conversant with the different formats of information and their databases to download such information for their clientle.

3.4. Staff

The LIS professional are trained to collect, organize, retrieve and disseminate information to satisfy the intellectual needs of readers and scholars. The needs of the readers largely depend on the environment and situation they live in many such as economic, political, social and cultural constantly churn the readers and their needs. The LIS professionals have to keep these factors of the users in mind. Further developments in the information work such as the information explosion, information technology, intellectual property rights, information networks, world wide web, cybernetics, artificial intelligence, information handling robots and user behaviour have their pressure on the professionals at different levels.

The Special Library Association has developed a list of competencies for librarians that, with little or no modification, would apply to a librarian in any setting-academic, public, or special library. These competencies include:

- Knowledge of evaluation and filter information resources.
- Specialized subject knowledge.
- Provision of convenient, accessible, and cost-effective information services.
- Provision of excellent instruction for using the information resources and support for users.
- Provision of market value-added information services and products.
- Expertise in using information technology to acquire, organize and disseminate information.
- Efficiency in communicating the importance of information services with senior management.

- Developing of specialized information products.
- Evaluates the outcomes of information use.
- Continually improves the information services.
- Commited to service excellence.
- Becoming an effective staff member.
- Seeks out challenges and opportunities.
- Looks for partnerships and alliances
- Creates an environment of respect and trust.
- Has effective communication skills.
- Works well with colleagues and users.

The LIS Professionals have to sharpen their communication and Information analysis skills. They will transform into knowledge worker, Information Technicians, Information engineers, Information entrepreneurs, Navigators and computer specialists.

4. TECHNOLOGY IN LIBRARIES

The increasing role of technology in has a significant impact on the changing role of librarians. New technologies are dramatically increasing the accessibility of information and librarians are adapting to the evolving needs of users that emerge from the adoption of these new technologies. The most significant example of how technology has changed the role of librarians in the last 50 years has been the move from traditional card catalogs to online public access catalog (OPAC). The same could be said of other technology developments, from electronic databases including internet, to logistical functions such as barcodes, RFID, Many librarians provide virtual reference services(via web based chat, instant messaging, text messaging, and e-mail), development of information architectures for improving access and search functionality.

5. CONCLUSION

The human action and the information flow shall be the two most dominant inputs to sound development strategy. For this, the right information to right user needs to be the hands of the right people at the right time. The success does not rely on individual's knowledge, but the knowledge of the organization. Information revolution and knowledge society are the two most important buzzwords of the 21st century. But world is yet to devise a clear concept and/ or definition of information, and for that purpose the relation between information and knowledge is not so differ. The situation is so alarming that there emerges a view that nobody knows what the information is!

REFERENCE

1. Mathai K J & Soni S K , Digital Library and Archivers, Indian Journal of Techinical Education Vol.25,1, Jan -Mar 2002.
2. Arora R C & Sharma V K , Resource Sharing and Networking for Human Resource Development , Indian Journal of Technical Education , June 2002.
3. Sridhar V. Libraries in the global village , front line 2002.
4. Talwar V G. et.al , Proceeding of 2nd ASSIST seminar , Bangalore 2003.
5. http://www.webindia123.com/career/options/library/intro.htm
6. http://en.wikipedia.org/wiki/librarian. Professional_organizations_and_activities
7. http://www.eduref.org/cgi-bin/res.cgi/Librarianship
8. http://eprints.rclis.org/archive/00003073/

9

Knowledge Management in Libraries

Dr. M. Nagarajan
V. Krishnan
K.S. Alvi
A. Sheeba

ABSTRACT

Definition, characteristics and objectives of knowledge management are provided. In the knowledge society the library will become a treasure house of human knowledge. It participates in knowledge innovation, and becomse an important link in the knowledge innovation chain. The library will inevitably face the new challenges of knowledge management.

1. INTRODUCTION

Early in the industrial era, organizations improved their efficiency, effectiveness and hence their competitive edge, by automating manual labor and reducing redundancy. Now in the age of Knowledge workers, many organizations have gone through massive restructuring to eliminate redundant workers and jobs. Sometimes these efforts lead to the ideas of business process engineering. Downsizing resulted in major loses, sometimes irreplaceable, of core knowledge assets as employees walked out the door with their knowledge. The effects of such knowledge dissipation are stunned innovation, teamwork and productivity.

2. DEFINITION

Knowledge management is a discipline that promotes an integrated approach to identifying, managing and sharing all of an enterprise's information assets. These information assets may include database, documents, policies and procedures as well as previously unarticulated expertise and experience resident in individuals. Knowledge management issues include developing, implementing and maintaining the appropriate technical and organisational infrastructure to enable knowledge sharing.

2.1. What is Knowledge Management?

Knowledge management is fundamentally the management of corporate knowledge and intellectual assets that can improve a range of organizational performance characteristics and add value by enabling an enterprise to act more intelligently.

Knowledge Management is a process that helps organizations identify, select, organize, disseminate and transfer important information and expertise that are a part of the organizational memory that typically resides within an organization in an unstructured manner. This enables effective and efficient problem solving, dynamic learning, strategic planning and decision-making. Knowledge management focuses on identifying knowledge, explicating it in a way so that it can be shared in a formal manner, and thus reusing it.

Knowledge management enables the communication of knowledge from one person to another so that the other person can use it. The domains in which knowledge concepts are leveraged in organization through knowledge initiatives are:

- Sharing knowledge and best practices
- Instilling responsibility for sharing knowledge
- Capturing and reusing best practices
- Embedding knowledge in products, services and processes
- Producing knowledge as a product
- Driving knowledge generation for innovation
- Mapping networks of experts
- Building and mining customer knowledge bases
- Understanding and measuring the value of knowledge
- Leveraging intellectual assets.

Knowledge management is the art of performing knowledge actions such as organizing, blocking, filtering, storing gathering, sharing, disseminating and using knowledge objects such as data, information, experiences, evaluations, insights, wisdom and initiatives. In general terms it is the performance of knowledge actions on knowledge objects.

3. CHARACTERISTICS OF KNOWLEDGE MANAGEMENT IN LIBRARIES

The role of knowledge management in libraries will become more and more important along with the development of knowledge economy. It is a new management mode, boasts the following superiority and characteristics incomparable with conventional management:

Human Resource Management is the Core of Knowledge Management in Libraries

The most important resource in the knowledge economy system is the talents who grasp knowledge. The talent competition has become the focus of market competition in the knowledge economy era. In the knowledge economy era, the libraries will attach importance to vocational training and lifelong education of library staffs to raise their scientific knowledge level and ability of acquiring and innovating knowledge. They also will and fully respect the human value, guide and bring into play wisdom potentialities of library staffs, take developing knowledge resources in the brains of library staffs as an important way for rising work efficiency. An all-round improvement of library staff's quality and positioning of the human value will become important objectives of knowledge management in libraries.

The Objective of Knowledge Management in Libraries is to Promote Knowledge Innovation

Knowledge innovation is the core of the knowledge economy society. As bases for collection, processing, storage and distribution of knowledge and information, libraries represent an indispensable link in the scientific system chain, an important link in the knowledge innovation. Secondly, libraries take part in scientific research process directly. The library work is a component of knowledge innovation. Thirdly, libraries must pay attention to diffusion and conversion of knowledge. They act as bridges for turning the results of knowledge innovation into realistic productive forces. Knowledge management in libraries is to promote relationship in and between libraries, between library and user, to strengthen knowledge internetworking and to quicken knowledge flow. In the knowledge economy era, libraries will carry out researches on development and application of information resources, construction of virtual libraries, protection of intellectual property rights in the electronic era etc., thus founding the base for knowledge innovation.

Knowledge acquisition is the starting point of knowledge management in libraries. The application of information technologies enlarges the scope of knowledge acquisition, raises knowledge acquisition speed and reduces knowledge acquisition cost. It is impossible to accomplish such important tasks by using man's brains only in the modern society in which the knowledge changes with each passing day. It will be possible to link closely knowledge sources and knowledge workers by computer networks, thus constructing knowledge networks in libraries based on realization of single-point informatization.

The knowledge acquired must be accumulated and converged into knowledge warehouses of libraries. The priority of information technologies in the field of knowledge storage not only finds expression in quantity, but also in retrieval, sorting and security of the knowledge. Information technology is also indispensable in the application and exchange of knowledge and other fields. It functions as a source and tool for knowledge innovation.

4. Contents of Knowledge Management in Libraries

As a completely new method of management, knowledge management in libraries leaves much to be desired in its theoretical system. In my opinion, knowledge management in libraries should include such respects as follows:

4.1. Knowledge Innovation Management

Knowledge innovation management in libraries refers to the management of the production, diffusion and transfer of knowledge as well as of the network systems constructed by related institutions and organizations. It includes three aspects, namely, theoretical innovation management of knowledge, technical innovation management and organizational innovation management.

Theoretical innovation management is to enrich and enlarge the theoretical and practical research fields of library science and information science through pursuing the latest development trends in library science the world over.

Technical innovation management is to manage the network systems constructed by institutions and organizations that relate to the full course of technical innovation. In their evolution from conventional libraries to electronic libraries, or digital libraries, Libraries should make technical breakthroughs and progress and build up technical facilities to support knowledge management. Organizational innovation management is to create a set of effective organizational management systems adaptable to the requirements in the electronic library era to support and strengthen knowledge management activities, by optimizing the functional departments and operation procedures of libraries.

In these systems, it firstly requires that leaders who take charge of knowledge management activities should undertake to formulate the management plans and coordinate all knowledge management related activities. Secondly, it requires establishment of special leading groups of knowledge flow for accomplishing all tasks relating to knowledge management activities. Electronic resources committees are established composed of various types of specialists to take charge of evaluating, procuring and creating the electronic resources on the one hand, and coordinating activities of business departments and spurring them on to close cooperation in such fields as procurement and organization of the electronic information resources as well as providing services on the other hand.

4.2. Knowledge Dissemination Management

Knowledge dissemination is of equal importance as compared to knowledge innovation. Knowledge creators do not have much time and energy to look for knowledge users. Though there are a multitude of knowledge users, it is very difficult to acquire knowledge that already exists in the minds of knowledge creators as restricted by various objective and subjective conditions. Therefore, libraries may play the part of knowledge tosser, use diverse media and channels to disseminate various new knowledge. The Internet, with its mass information and extensive contents, will provide people with the main approach to searching knowledge and acquiring information. But now there emerge absurd, salacious, false and uncivil information resulting from seeking for commercial profits and political objectives on the Net. Therefore, it is necessary to strengthen knowledge dissemination management in libraries as follows:

1. Uninterruptedly strengthening the creation of libraries' own document resources and deepening the development of document information resources;
2. Continuously raising the quality of libraries' staffs and strengthening continuous engineering education of working staffs;
3. Giving full play to the special role of the expert system in knowledge dissemination;
4. Making a comprehensive utilization of all media to ensure security of operation of networks, and prevent online criminal activities and online dissemination of inappropriate information.

4.3. Knowledge Application Management

The libraries should also attach importance to provision of services for people to acquire knowledge and achieve maximum functions and efficiency of knowledge information. Therefore, knowledge services based on high-speed information networks should be carried out by:

1. Setting up virtual libraries or information centers for enterprises, governments, public organizations and scientific research institutions. It is difficult for an enterprise or a social organization to put sufficient manpower, material and financial resources on information gathering, organizing and developing. It is also impossible and unnecessary to spend a large

amount of funds on information resources for their own use. Libraries can create virtual libraries or information centers for these organs separately according to their respective information requirements by using abundant information resources on the high-speed information networks.

2. Setting up digitized knowledge services, which is actually a development trend of libraries. This presupposes: creating step by step the users-oriented information service systems such as information dissemination, information search and special supply of information; quickening the creation of digitized libraries; studying the methods, means and techniques of information distribution and search with the Internet as the base and WEB technique as the core.
3. Digitizing libraries' resources. The electronic libraries or digitized libraries are the technical modes and development trends of libraries in the knowledge economy era. The knowledge services of libraries in the future will start with creation of databases comprising electronic journals and books in different languages that have discipline features and can operate on high-speed information networks. Great efforts should be made to transform all existing large non-electronic information resources into electronic information and integrate them into electronic libraries.

4.4. Human Resources Management

Human resources management takes it as its basic starting point to train high quality specialized talents and to revitalize the library undertaking. In practice, we should pay full attention to diversity and variation of library staffs' requirements, strengthened management of different library staffs by applying contingency management approach. That is, to some people, rigid management method is applied, rigorous supervision and control imposed, and quantity and quality requirements of work according to regulations and procedures are made clear. And, to the rest of people, more flexible management method is applied to let them participate in decision-making and consultation and undertake more jobs so as to bring their management abilities into full play and realize organizational and personal objectives. Doing well in continuous engineering education of specialized staffs, which should not only focus on the theory of library science and related disciplines, but also cover the latest technical knowledge. And strengthening professional ethics education.

5. CONCLUSIONS

Economic environment and information environment is changing quickly today. Knowledge management has become a powerful tool for promoting innovation and realizing reengineering the various walks of life. It occupies very outstanding position in the creation of the knowledge innovation systems of a country. How for the library circles to meet the challenge of knowledge economy and to build the knowledge management systems of libraries is a subject that demands our urgent study and solution.

REFERENCE

1. Tang Shanhong, Knowledge Management in Libraries in the 21st Century, Library management 1999.
2. Wang Yunhua. Knowledge Economy and the Development of the Library, Library Work & Research. 1999(6), 17-19
3. Cao Yi. The Reorientation of Libraries in the Knowledge Economy Era, Library Work & Research, 1999(3), 24-26
4. Wang Delu. The Collection and Processing of Knowledge. February 4,199. http://www.bsti.ac.cn/bsti_kmchina/gei/048_001.htm
5. Allee, V. (1997). "12 Principles Of Knowledge Management". Training And Development, Vol . 51, No. 11.
6. Barth, S. (2000). "Knowledge As A Function Of X. ", Knowledge Management

7. Clarke, P. (1998). "Implementing A Knowledge Strategy For Your Firm". Research Technology Management.
8. Dyer, G. (2000). "Knowledge Management Crosses The Chasm". Knowledge Management.
9. Davenport, T.H., Delong D.W., & Beers, M.C. (1998). "Successful Knowledge Management Projects". Sloan Management Review, Vol. 39, No. 2.

10

Knowledge Management Emerging Perspectives

P. Panneerselvam

ABSTRACT

The major objectives of this paper are to give an overview of Knowledge Management (KM) with definition, KM types, characteristics, benefits, importance and major criticism.

1. KNOWLEDGE MANAGEMENT

The term knowledge management was first introduced in a 1986 keynote address to a European management conference (American Productivity and Quality Center 1996).

The most common type of definition describes knowledge management as a set of processes directed at "creating-capturing-storing-sharing-applying-reusing" knowledge.

This type of definition is criticized for making knowledge management appear to involve somewhat mechanistic and sequential process steps and for focusing attention on explicit knowledge artifacts as opposed to tacit knowledge. Knowledge engineering reflects this view of knowledge management. A definition with similar problems sees knowledge management as "delivering the right knowledge to the right persons at the right time."

2. TYPES OF KNOWLEDGE

Knowledge can be broadly categorized in to two

– Tacit Knowledge
– Explicit Knowledge

Tacit knowledge consists often of habits and culture that we do not recognize in ourselves. In other words "We know more than we can tell." In the field of knowledge management the concept of tacit knowledge refers to a knowledge which is only known by an individual and that is difficult to communicate to the rest of an organization. The process of transforming tacit knowledge into explicit knowledge is known as codification or articulation.

Explicit knowledge is knowledge that has been or can be articulated, codified, and stored in certain media. It can be readily transmitted to others. The most common forms of explicit knowledge are manuals, documents and procedures. Knowledge also can be audio-visual. Works of art and product design can be seen as other forms of explicit knowledge where human skills, motives and knowledge are externalized. Knowledge that is easy to communicate is called explicit knowledge.

3. CHARACTERISTICS OF KNOWLEDGE MANAGEMENT

Knowledge vs. Information : The challenge of Knowledge Management is to determine what information within an organization qualifies as" valuable". All information is not knowledge, and all knowledge is not valuable. The key is to find the worthwhile knowledge within a vast sea of information.

Knowledge Management is about people : It is directly linked to what people know, and how what they know can support business and organizational objectives. It draws on human competency, intuition, ideas, and motivations. It is not a technology-based concept. Although technology can support a Knowledge Management effort, it shouldn't begin there.

Knowledge Management is orderly and goal-directed: It is inextricably tied to the strategic objectives of the organization. It uses only the information that is the most meaningful, practical, and purposeful.

Knowledge Management is ever changing : There is no such thing as an immutable law in Knowledge Management. Knowledge is constantly tested, updated, revised, and sometimes even "obsoleted" when it is no longer practicable. It is a fluid, ongoing process.

Knowledge Management is value-added : It draws upon pooled expertise, relationships, and alliances. Organizations can further the two-way exchange of ideas by bringing in experts from the field to advise or educate managers on recent trends and developments. Forums, councils, and boards can be instrumental in creating common ground and organizational cohesiveness.

Knowledge Management is visionary : This vision is expressed in strategic business terms rather than technical terms, and in a manner that generates enthusiasm, buy-in, and motivates managers to work together toward reaching common goals.

Knowledge Management is complementary : It can be integrated with other organizational learning initiatives such as Total Quality Management (TQM). It is important for knowledge managers to show interim successes along with progress made on more protracted efforts such as multiyear systems developments infrastructure, or enterprise architecture projects.

3. TYPES OF KNOWLEDGE MANAGEMENT

1. Data,
2. Information,
3. Knowledge and
4. Wisdom.

The following chart indicates how knowledge can be transferred as Wisdom.

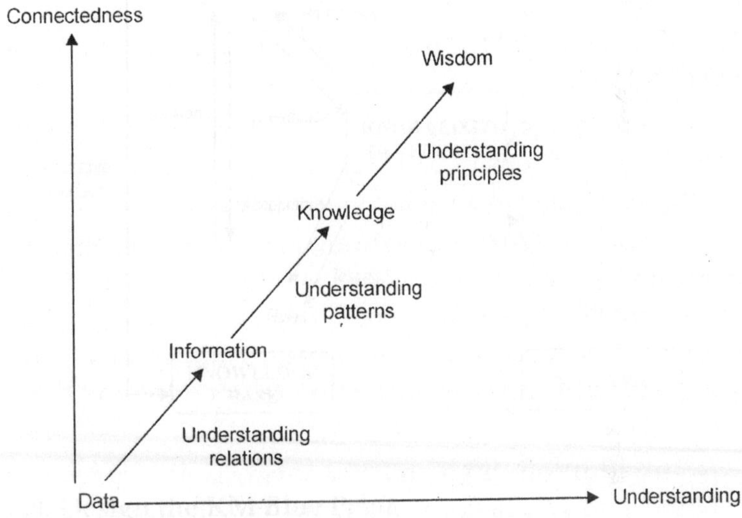

Data : is represented as an item or event out of context with no relation to other things. *Information* is represented by relationships between data, and possibly other information. The relationships may represent information, yet the relationships do not actually constitute information until they are understood. Also, the relationships, which represent data, have a tendency to be limited in context, mostly about the past or present, with little if any implication for the future. *Knowledge* is represented by patterns between data, information, and possible other knowledge. These patterns may represent knowledge, yet the patterns do not actually constitute knowledge until they are understood.

Also, the patterns, which represent knowledge, have a high level of predictability associated with them such that the pattern suggests its past, its present, and its future. *Wisdom* is the patterns, which represent knowledge, are what they are because of foundational principles, which for a time I called eternal truths but people beat me up so much I stopped. When one understands these foundational principles they then understand why the knowledge is what it is.

4. KNOWLEDGE MANAGEMENT: HUMAN POTENTIAL

Knowledge management is so important to public sector organizations in part because of the prospective loss of employees due to an aging workforce.

A recent GAO report indicated that a substantial portion of the federal workforce would become eligible to retire or will retire over the next five to 10 years, and that workforce planning is critical to ensure that agencies have sufficient and appropriate staff to account for these retirements.

In addition, high staff turnover, lack of adequate training, and a tendency to maintain the status quo, further impact and impede the success of knowledge retention and growth.

Oftentimes, when people leave an organization, they take a wealth of knowledge about their jobs with them.

Knowledge management attempts to secure and replenish the learning experiences, as well as the work products, of the individuals who comprise an organization.

5. BENEFITS OF KNOWLEDGE MANAGEMENT

Whether to minimize loss and risk, improve organizational efficiency, or embrace innovation, knowledge management efforts and initiatives add great value to an organization.

Some of the benefits of KM include:

- Facilitates better, more informed decisions;
- Contributes to the intellectual capital of an organization;
- Encourages the free flow of ideas, which leads to insight and innovation;
- Eliminates redundant processes, streamlines operations, and enhances employee retention rates;
- Improves customer service and efficiency; and
- Leads to greater productivity

6. IMPORTANCE OF KNOWLEDGE MANAGEMENT

Knowledge management is the hottest subject of the day. The question is: what is this activity called knowledge management, and why is it so important to each and every one of us? The following writings, articles, and links offer some emerging perspectives in response to these questions. As you read on, you can determine whether it all makes any sense or not.

7. MAJOR CRITICISMS OF KNOWLEDGE MANAGEMENT

1. It has traditionally conjured up too close an association with information management and information technology (IT).
2. It implies that knowledge can be managed.
3. It tends to be so broad and vague as to have little meaning.
4. It tends to focus on the nuts and bolts of knowledge creation, capture, sharing, use and reuse, rather than providing a true vision and strategy that conveys how knowledge-based enterprises will function and succeed in the new knowledge-based economy.

5. In addition, more specific criticisms have been leveled at particular views of knowledge management.

8. CONCLUSION

Economic environment and information environment is changing quickly today. Knowledge management has become a powerful tool for promoting innovation and realizing reengineering the various walks of life. It occupies very outstanding position in the creation of the knowledge innovation systems of a country. How far the library circles to meet the challenge of knowledge economy and to build the knowledge management systems of libraries is a subject that demands our urgent study and solution.

REFERENCE

1. Wang Yunhua. *Knowledge Economy and the Development of the Library,* Library Work & Research. 1999
2. Cao Yi. The *Reorientation of Libraries in the Knowledge Economy Era,* Library Work & Research, 1999
3. Cristension H Peter, *Knowledge Management: perspective & pitfalls,* copenhean school press, 2003.
4. Liebowitz. Jay Knowledge Management: learning from knowledge engineering, CRC press, 2001.
5. Wang Delu. The Collection and Processing of Knowledge. February 4,199. http://www.bsti.ac.cn/bsti_kmchina/gei /048_001.htm

11

Changing Role of Library Professionals in Cyber Era

Balasubramani R
Manju P U
Surulinathi M

ABSTRACT

Information Technology is making drastic changes in all fields, including library and information science. Libraries are changing due to the increased use of information technology in the works and services. Since the libraries are largely using computers and related technologies, there should be a corresponding change in the information technology skills and knowledge of library and information professionals. This paper is an attempt to illustrate the changing role of library and information professionals in the age of information technology.

1. INTRODUCTION

The information technology is bringing revolutionary changes across all sectors of society and library is not an exception to it. However, the fast changing technologies are posing a great threat to the library professionals. There is a growing impression among the LIS professionals that they will be replaced by the computer professionals due to the major changes taking place in the sphere of technology.

LIS professionals need to equip themselves to work in the network environment. Concepts of databank, data warehouse are coming up, so the library should move in the direction of becoming a knowledge center and the LIS professionals are required to equip themselves to be able to work in the network environment and be capable enough to provide web-based services as well.

Their primary responsibility is to collect, organize, store and disseminate information to the large community of users. Today information has been considered as a strategic or economic resource, a marketable commodity and a social wealth. Considering the important of information, the employees of libraries and information centers need to update their knowledge and skills. This is a creative process in which education and training become strong foundations.

2. CHANGING ROLE OF LIBRARY PROFESSIONALS

Today the word 'Library ' itself is replacing by the term 'Information Centre' and the term librarian is replacing by different terms, i.e. UNESCO guidelines identified these professional categories as follows:

- Information Educator
- Information Manager
- Information Scientist
- Information Researcher
- Information Analyst

Blaise Cronin rightly called the library professional as 'the electronic librarian'. In his model he suggested library work at three level, top level called 'strategist' concerned with long range planning, trend analysis etc. 'Network Managers' in the middle level concerned with system design and its implementation, networking, user and staff training etc. and in operative level concerned with database searching, cataloguing, indexing, information analysis, reformatting, repackaging etc.

Human resource development in the field of library and information science can be done by various methods, which could under:

3. TRAINING AND SUPPORT OF STAFF AND USERS

Every professional required training. IT has brought in many changes in LIS education and professional. To keep up with the technological development and learn to accept these changes and pressure they belong above, the library professionals needs continuous training and development of IT skills. It is essential at this time of upsetting changes to ensure that such training is not enabling them to improve their job performance, but also providing them with supportive help as they acquire new and essential skills.

Many electronics journals are being published in variety of different interfaces; searching and retrieval skills are becoming necessary, professionals who are well versed with the latest developments should be appointed in the library and existing staff should be trained well so that the user will get proper assistance to find out the relevant information. The academic libraries should have professionals who are familiar with bibliographic software packages, www and related technologies. The information needs of people is under going a rapid change, so library professionals should keep abreast of changes to provide better services.

4. CONTINUING EDUCATION PROGRAMMES

Continuing Education Programmes (CEP) provide opportunities to the professionals to develop managerial skills, problem-solving skills, etc. The present day profession demand new skills, methods and approaches. Information providers, information specialists, information intermediaries and end-users have become increasingly significant. The radical changes make it imperative for a good system of continuing education. Education and training of professionals, and converting them into information professionals need changes at three levels, viz

- Library and information science education Curriculum
- Continuing education programmes and
- Specialized Training.

Computer-based learning such as multimedia technologies, artificial intelligences expert system, networking hypermedia, etc. will change the working environment of information professionals as well as pattern of education and learning. In the modern times, the library and information science personnel have to acquire and cultivate knowledge and skills for communicating the sought information to a variety of users in efficient and effective manners.

Apart form the above the following factors will also be considered as the HRD in LIS:

- The present curriculum of library and information science needs to be revised to include new technologies.
- Upgrading skills of employees/ library staff to ensure quality services to its readers.
- Professional library staff should be accorded full academic and management status. This need to be linked to a proper plan of professional's human resource development, to ensure that librarians are able to cope with the new technologies.
- HRD programme for the training of in-service personnel should be organized on a regular basis.
- LIS professional associations and groups should organize national and international seminars/ conferences for updating / sharing knowledge.
- A developmental plan and policy at the national level is essential for a planned growth of LIS professionals.

5. IT SKILL FOR DIGITAL LIBRARIAN

There are plenty of skills that librarians will need to master to enable them to deal with the requirement of digital libraries. They break down into three main area of expertise.

5.1. Technical Skills

The technical skills required are probably better understood and defined in the literature than the managerial skills.

Imaging technologies : the means of capturing images from physical objects.

OCR : the means of converting imaged text into machine-readable text.

Scripting languages : the means of adding metadata or structuring digital content (PHP, PERL and ASP etc.,)

Cataloguing and metadata : identifying the resources for future access.

Indexing and database technology : building search system or supporting finding aids.

User interfaces design : the creative function enhancing user interactions with data. (Subject Gateway, Portal etc.,)

Programming : basic understanding of programming techniques and some languages. (C, C++, and VB)

Web-technology : being well versed in every aspect of the primary delivery medium of digital libraries. (www, browser etc.,)

Open Source Software : Knowledge about Dspace, Greenstone and E-prints etc.,

These technical skills are not all required for every job and no individual should expect to be highly skilled and experienced in all of them. What is essential is that there is at least a familiarity with all these skills and what they encompass.

On the basis of these considerations, Borgman (1986, 1996) proposes a model for knowledge and skills the users and/or librarians will need. It includes:

- Conceptual knowledge;
- Semantic and syntactic knowledge; and
- Technical skills.

Conceptual knowledge denotes the user's model or understanding of the type of digital library with which they are dealing. The conceptual knowledge of the search process is used for translating an information need into a plan for executing the search. The success of searching in digital libraries depends heavily on the user's ability to construct a mental model of the given information space. In contrast with the conceptual knowledge, which is used to plan and refine searches, semantic and syntactic knowledge is more concerned with details and with individual systems or applications. Semantic knowledge means knowledge of the operations available to execute a search plan. Shneiderman (1992) defines syntactic knowledge as the user's understanding of the commands or actions in a specific system. The expert user possesses the following semantic and syntactic knowledge:

- Understanding of the general characteristics common to most information systems;
- Understanding of the features characteristic for specific kinds of information systems; and
- Ability to become familiar with the features of a new system, and then to adapt the search strategy to these features.

By "technical skills" it is meant those basic computer skills, which are prerequisite for developing conceptual, syntactic, and semantic knowledge, within the context of a digital library. These skills include knowing how to use computer devices and being familiar with the digital conventions, e.g. screen display. It is important to be aware that the levels of these skills in the population are very diverse, and also that different applications and systems require very diverse levels of these skills. Borgman (2003, p. 109) states, "as digital libraries are designed for more general audiences, a broader range of skill levels will need to be accommodated in many applications".

5.2. Library activities

The library professionals should actively participate in various library activities:

- Involvement in teaching and education.
- Information management and information access.
- Building collections and making them accessible.
- Managing in general.
- Creating electronic libraries.
- Co-operation and resource sharing.
- Support for research and reference.
- Social activities

5.3. Skills of librarian

- Communication/training skills.
- IT skills.
- Managerial.
- Commitment.
- Subject knowledge/profiling.

6. PROBLEMS WITH NEW TECHNOLOGIES / ELECTRONIC MEDIA

- Managing electronic information.
- Dealing with pace of change.
- Legal.
- Finance.

– People (human factor).
– Competitiveness.

7. CONCLUSION

The importance of library and information science manpower in India has also risen considerably. Since the modern library movement, the importance of the contribution of library personnel has been gaining strength all over the world. Maintaining currency in the information professionals has become increasingly difficult in the light of fast paced societal and technological changes. Professionals in this field have started realizing the type of education and training they believe is needed to practice. Developments in educational technology and the changing pattern of education and learning indicate senior's challenges for the library and information community to upgrade their information technology skills.

An organization can achieve its goal, if sufficient opportunities are provided to its employees to enrich their potential by proper policies and programmes in the area of their interest. Professional competencies are further identified by knowledge in the area of information, resources, technology, management and research. The ability to use these areas of knowledge for providing library and information services can be enhanced by the organizations HRD polices.

REFERENCE

1. Borgman, C L (1986), "Why are online catalogs hard to use? Lessons learned from information retrieval studies", Journal of the American Society for Information Science, Vol. 37 No. 6, pp. 387-400.
2. Borgman, C L (1996), "Why are online catalogs still hard to use?" Journal of the American Society for Information Science, Vol. 47 No. 7, pp. 493-503.
3. Shniderman, B (1992), Designing the User Interface: Strategies for

Effective Human-Computer Interaction, 2nd ed., Addison-Wesley, Reading, MA.

4. Borgman, C L (2003), "Designing digital libraries for usability", in Bishop, A.P., Van House, N.A. and Buttenfield, B.P. (Eds), Digital Library Use: Social Practice and Evaluation, MIT Press, Cambridge, pp. 85-118.

12

The Role of Digital Libraries in Future Librarianship

R. Senthilkumar
N.G. Balaji
P.U. Manju

ABSTRACT

Digital libraries are providing access to information resources such as books and journals and other kinds of information resources available in digital form. The traditional libraries are developing digital resources and use digital resources online to meet the increased information requirements of users. The present day librarians require additional knowledge in computers, digital library development and management, networking etc. this paper is an attempt to describe the digital resources and the networks in detail.

1. INTRODUCTION

Digital Libraries encodes those books, journals and other resources into digital format in which large numbers of geographically distributed users can access the contents of large and diverse repositories of electronic. A digital library is expected to provide access to the digital information collections.

A digital library may be considered to be any of these

- machine-readable data files;
- components of the emerging National Information Infrastructure;
- various online databases and CD-ROM information products;
- computer information storage devices on which information resides;
- computerized networked library systems.

2. CULTURAL CHANGE VS TECHNOLOGICAL CHANGE

The advent of digital technologies has helped reinvent the profession, not render it out of date. However, there is another way of looking at the nature of the digital library, which is in fact more challenging to the values of the profession than the argument that technical advances supersede human skills. This view challenges us to think of the contemporary information revolution in cultural terms rather than technological terms. If we think back to the previous information revolution, when printed text displaced the manuscript, then the economics of "thc information industry" did see a great deal of labour market displacement.

However, had the "Financial Times" run a Renaissance edition, it would have said that employment levels in the information industry remained high, with opportunities in moveable type printing mopping up structural unemployment in the labour market for manuscript clerks. So in a sense, one form of human impact of a revolutionary, but purely technical change, was rather limited. By contrast, the higher level impact of changed information technology on Medieval- Renaissance culture was seismic. Megabytes of profound textual analysis have charted the way in which wider access to the printed Bible in more readily available translations meant that the faithful individual could decide their theology for themselves, in a direct personal dialogue with God which was firmly Biblical in its authority.

This is not the place to provide a brief chronicle of the rise of print, Protestantism and the birth of capitalism. But a simplistic rehearsal of the commonplaces of Medieval-Renaissance history does give a hint of how to view contemporary digital library change. That is, not as a change in mechanical and technological processes, but as a fundamental change in social beliefs, viewed in terms of both cultural theory and cultural practices.

3. CHANGE MANAGEMENT

It is a truism to state that technological change makes new things possible and old things no longer possible. The more difficult challenge is to make value judgments about the nature of these changes, saying whether what is lost was better than what replaces it, and vice versa. A devout Roman Catholic theocrat living during the Counter Reformation will probably have viewed new information technology as a failure in religious-human terms, while grudgingly acknowledging its success in narrowly technical terms. The most important judgment remains human and cultural. If one believes that a technological improvement has led to the splintering of the true church and the wider prevalence of sin, then one must believe that that new technology has failed in every important sense. The next step in this argument is thus to challenge the rather complacent and self congratulatory view of the digital librarian who sees their successful creation of a new digital library in the image of the old print library, as a triumph of change management. By contrast, in many ways such "facsimile" digital libraries are merely reincarnations of old media, repressing the intrinsic nature of new digital media in order to make change manageable. In this vision of IT change, digital librarians are like effective Counter Reformation Jesuits, with Cranmer's Prayer Book unprinted and unpublished, and Henry Tudor still happily undivorced. But we have to ask, for how much longer is such a status quo preservable?

4. NEED FOR A DIGITAL LIBRARIAN IN THE MANAGEMENT OF DIS

Necessity is the mother of invention. The emerging global digital libraries or worldwide digital information centers generate the need for creating a new job-title "digital librarian" to manage their digital knowledge resources. The huge digital libraries are emerging as knowledge warehouses. Digital librarians are required to:

- manage the digital libraries;
- organize digital knowledge and information; (content Management)
- disseminate digital information from the computer-held digital information;
- provide digital reference services and electronic information services;
- handle the tasks of massive digitization,
- digital storage process, and digital preservation; (Institutional Repository)
- provide universal access and retrieval of digital knowledge, ultimately access to all; (Knowledge Portal or Subject Gateway)
- catalogue and classify digital documents and digital knowledge (taxonomy).

5. NEW TYPES OF DIGITAL RESOURCE

The advent of techniques to support 'paperless publishing' (Ref 22) has meant that many new types of information artefact has become available for users of library systems. In some cases these are merely emulations of conventional paper-based publications. In other cases, however, these artefacts are quite sophisticated publications that have no corresponding counterpart in the domain of paper-based publishing. This section of the paper briefly discusses three basic electronic resources that are now playing an important part in the development of digital library systems: electronic books, electronic journals and network-based facilities and services.

5.1. Electronic Books

The potential of electronic books as a mechanism for the dissemination of information and knowledge has been discussed by numerous authors An electronic book is essentially a computer-based information storage/ dissemination artefact that embeds a 'book metaphor'. That is, the appearance of such an object on a computer screen is visually very similar to a conventional paper-based book. In many ways, most of the properties and behaviour of an electronic book are similar to those of their paper-based counterparts. However, because of the special characteristics of electronic media, the properties and behaviour of electronic books can be extended in numerous ways over and above those of conventional books

Undoubtedly, within the context of a digital library system, three of the most useful properties of electronic books are: (1) the ease with which such books can be simultaneously shared between multiple users; (2) the ability to search through an individual book or a complete collection of books in order to locate particular items of sought-after information; and (3) the possibility of embedding hyperlinks at particular points in a book which can be used to link to related items of information in other parts of that book, in other books or in other digital libraries that might be located anywhere in the world. This latter facility is very important from the point of view of allowing students to create personalised web structures that reflect the information that is needed to solve the particular problems that they are working on.

5.2. Electronic Journals

Electronic journals represent another very important resource for use in digital libraries. For a variety of different reasons, both publishers and academics have undertaken a considerable amount of research into: the feasibility of their production; their potential cost-effectiveness; techniques for their creation; and mechanisms for their dissemination

As is the case with electronic books, electronic journals could easily be implemented as emulations of their paper-based counter-parts. Although this does happen, most of the more sophisticated journals are designed in ways that take advantage of the many new publishing opportunities that electronic media can offer. For example, an electronic journal might contain 3-D images, animations, video clips and/or sound effects. In addition, it might also make available important data sets containing experimental data so that users of particular scientific papers can check the calculations that have been performed or analyse the data using different statistical techniques.

Typical examples of the wide range of electronic journals that are now becoming available from publishers are reflected in the online materials that are available at the following World Wide Web sites:

http://www.elsevier.nl/locate/mathcompcog

http://www.iee.org.uk/publish/journals/journals.html

http://www.springer.de/server/svjps.html

Some publishers of electronic journals provide an 'alerting' facility based upon the use of electronic mail. Elsevier, for example, runs a 'ContentsDirect' service, which provides copies of the contents pages of selected journals. These are embedded (in ASCII text format) within email messages that are sent to subscribers to the service. Users can quickly scan through these in order to identify items of interest.

Naturally, research and development in electronic journals is currently an active growth area - both with respect to the creation of new titles and the provision of new types of facility and service. Obviously, the possibilities offered by the ability to automatically embed electronic journals into digital library systems offer tremendous potential as a stepping-stone for the creation of suitable library facilities for the development of virtual university systems.

5.3. Network Facilities and Services

The efficient delivery of electronic journals to individual library sites (from a remote distribution centre) depends upon those libraries having an appropriate connection to a suitable global computer network such as the Internet. Naturally, such a connection can also be used to facilitate remote access to other libraries' Web pages and digital services, publisher's Web sites, listervers, news-groups and online bookstores such as *Amazon* (*http://www.amazon.com*). These are just some specific examples of the new types of service and facility that communications networks are bringing into library systems. Of course, in general terms, the Internet and World Wide Web can now be used to bring, hitherto, unparalleled access to a wide variety of information services and sources from anywhere in the world 'at the touch of a button'.

As well as providing access to the Internet and World Wide Web, another important development (both for conventional libraries and digital library systems) is the availability of private, local, in-house networks that are based on the use of Internet-like protocols. These are often referred to as 'intranets'. As is discussed later, intranet facilities are an important building block for digital library systems that are used as a basis for electronic course delivery within virtual university systems.

Within library systems, intranets can form the basis of

a wide range of services and facilities for local users. For example, they can be used to provide 'bulletin board' services, online help facilities and instruction on how to use various library resources (such as searching online catalogues, submitting inter-library loan requests or completing book requisition forms). It is also possible to make available an electronic mail facility so that users can communicate electronically with library staff. Intranets can also be used to provide new types of online tool for users.

6. CONCLUSION

The rapid development of information technology and the constant emergence of new kinds of information services, Digital Libraries are facing more and more challenges and issues. This new environment puts more and more requirements upon librarians. It is imperative to improve the quality of library staff and to train more qualified librarians in digital environment. The future librarians should not only have profound knowledge of the management of libraries but also be skilled in the operation of advanced information technologies.

REFERENCE

1. http://www.ifla.org/IV/ifla62/62-qinh.htm
2. Liu, Deyou. (1995) "Advancing on a New Step with the Advantage of the Evaluation of Chinese Libraries". Chinese Library Journal, (2): 3-9,25.
3. Barker, P.G., (1994). Electronic Libraries - Visions of the Future, *The Electronic Library*, 12(4), 221-230.
4. Raitt, D., (1997). *Libraries for the New Millennium - Implications for Managers*, Library Association Publishing, London.

13

The Challenging Role of Librarianship in The Knowledge Society

G. Thamaraiselvi

ABSTRACT

As the information Technologies are changing day-to-day and growing at a tremendous speed, the knowledge society is becoming more complex, competitive and dependent on technological changes, information explosion, and globalization of Networks. This transition of the society from an economy based to knowledge based information society has been shaking the very foundations of traditional Librarianship. The information revolution and the pervasive thinking that everything is available on the Web have created new challenges to these traditional professional ethics. The enormous increase in Internet-based communication serves to shift attention to the virtual, rather than the physical, library. In the context of a knowledge society, many teenagers or university students are now keyboard literate, but have no skills in conducting a sensible search or using such techniques as Boolean logic. Librarians have been trained in a variety of research techniques and know how to play a very active role in providing coaching, training and support in developing both the formal skills base and the informal values round information and knowledge sharing and storing which are critical to organizations in the 21st century. The changing role implies a different skill set in which Communication is the main skill needed very much within a working group of knowledge management system. Librarians of this Digital era are in the position to change their role as arbitrary information scientists/gatekeepers and to meet the challenges of the Internet, World Wide Web, and On-line access in the knowledge society.

1. INTRODUCTION

As the information Technologies are changing day-to-day and growing at a tremendous speed, the knowledge society is becoming more complex, competitive and dependent on technological changes, information explosion, and globalization of Networks. This transition of the society from an economy based to knowledge based information society has been shaking the very foundations of traditional Librarianship. The information revolution and the pervasive thinking that everything is available on the Web have created new challenges to these traditional professional ethics. Acquiring and providing access to electronic knowledge resources require librarians to change their role from traditional librarian to Information Scientist by learning and applying new skills to understand the evolving technologies to manage and provide quality on-line information service to the knowledge society. The primary objective of libraries is to organize and provide access to information. This objective will never change, although the format and the methods that are used can change dramatically, providing new opportunities and challenges. A librarian who is aware of computer technology, communications technology, and information technology can face the challenges of the new millennium.

As information and knowledge has become an important productive factor for the modern economic system, the society will inevitably require intensified management of information and knowledge. How to manage knowledge will become an important subject facing libraries in the near future. Knowledge management in libraries should be focused on effective research and development of knowledge, creation of knowledge bases, exchange and sharing of knowledge between library staffs including its users, training of library staff, speeding up explicit processing of the implicit knowledge and realizing of its sharing.

2. THE CHANGING ENVIRONMENT OF THE KNOWLEDGE SOCIETY

From information society to knowledge society of more immediate impact than the globalization and co modification of mass media is the introduction from the late 1980s on of computers and later the Internet and mobile media. In the 1980s, 'the information society' becomes a synonym of societal development. In such a society, the levers of development are information processing, i.e. efficient and reliable generation, transfer and retrieval of data, whose appropriation is often closely tied to formal sites of labour or education.

The competences necessary to advance such a society is information literacy. In its simplest form, the concept denotes the individual's ability to access, retrieve and process data of relevance to concrete problem-solving and decision-making, while in its more advanced versions, information literacy is contextualized and related to actual learning sites and wider societal and personal criteria of relevance and reflection. Still, the concept of information literacy is closely tied to the technologies of computing and Internet access, and knowledge is defined in terms of reflexive and responsible use of information.

The definitions of libraries and of librarians change accordingly. The enormous increase in Internet-based communication serves to shift attention to the virtual, rather than the physical, library. Digital reference services, free access to large-scale data banks and secure retrieval become vital areas of professional development, and there is certainly more to come in this decisive domain of innovation.

The librarian's traditional role as 'cultural custodian' or, in the 1980s as 'cultural guide', is downplayed in favour of the librarian's function as effective information disseminator assisting in the user's development of information literacy. Focus is on developing user-friendly information searches that gradually become more and more attuned to actual problems and activities rather than stand-alone tools.

The role of information specialists is to facilitate the interactions between the potential information user community and the body of recorded information. The traditional information access and management roles played by the information professions are expanding, particularly in the design and development of new information products and services and of tools to support information seeking and selection, the analysis and synthesis of information content on behalf of users, and information of user instruction.

The major change that has had an impact on the way librarians work is the modern computer, and hence the technical push with the growth in the amount and production of technical and other documentation. Computers have been able to help in the processing, storage, and management of information and their application is increasing even more dramatically at present.

One of the major events that has had a significant effect on the way librarians function and perform was the evolution of telecommunications and computer networking, which evolved from dedicated fixed connections to circuit switching, and then more recently to packet switching. Circuit switching has actually been around for quite some time. In 1990, the concept of the national research and education network evolved, which links all the government agencies, government installations and research labs, and academic and educational institutions at present and we are now in the Global Information Network system.

The power of the Global Information technologies of increasingly more sophisticated and powerful computers at very reasonable prices, and the evolution of networks to include both wired and wireless networks, as remote mobile communications increases, offers opportunities that have never before been available. Some of the ideas and thoughts that librarians had in the 1960s and 1970s and even in the early 1980s that were not feasible for implementation in the technology of the day now become much more realistic in terms of today's technologies. The opportunities are there for us to take advantage of the technology.

3. CHANGING THE ROLE OF LIBRARIANSHIP

One primary role of librarians is to provide leadership and expertise in the design, development, and ethical management of knowledge-based information systems in order to meet the information needs and obligations of the patron or institution. Electronic information provides librarians with challenges that are not necessarily new; however, as the nature of the librarians' roles changes, so do the challenges to long-standing professional codes of ethics. Marshall Keys writes that in the future, as now, "we can expect the virtual library to be the organization that identifies, selects, negotiates for, and provides access to an incredible range of information resources on our behalf ".

Keys writes that the evolution toward a digital library creates a change in the "locus of control". "The library's collection is moving outside the library itself. Digital collections can be stored off-site, and the individual library will have far less control than today over the actual availability of information to the end user". Electronic information creates challenges for the library community at its very foundation, moving it away from the traditional paper-and-print format to an ethereal world of circuits and connectivity. The library is no longer defined simply as a building or a physical repository that houses information. The analysis, synthesis, and packaging processes are going to increase dramatically. This has been the situation for a considerable period of time and these activities are going to continue to increase as the amount of information and the number of resources grows.

In the context of a knowledge society, many teenagers or university students are now keyboard literate, but have no skills in conducting a sensible search or using such techniques as Boolean logic. The fast-changing information environment is also increasing the emphasis on the need for lifelong learning, a move away from the classroom and towards learning resource centers for non-teacher based learning. Librarians have been trained in a variety of research techniques and know how to question a wide range of sources to find answers. They also have the training in how to order, summarize and catalogue documents so that well organized repositories can be made available. Because of their training in these areas, librarians can play a very active role in providing coaching, training and support in developing both the formal skills base and the informal values round information and knowledge sharing and storing which are critical to organizations in the 21st century.

4. THE FUTURE CHALLENGES AND THE CHANGING ROLE OF LIBRARIANS

The modern trend is for the role of the librarian to move from that of a passive Intermediary responsible for guiding patrons to appropriate information resources to-ward that of a much more proactive professional whose role includes analyzing and repackaging information. Librarians have faced this challenge head on by becoming masters of the Web. Librarians create powerful Web sites such as the National Library of Medicine's PubMed database. Librarians see the Web as an easier way to share what they know with others. They gather electronic information and create electronic pathfinders and front-end search tools to help users. Librarians create online tutorials and instructional Web pages to help patron's per-form the best searchers. They gather links to web-sites on specific topics and lead patrons to these evaluated sites as a starting point.

According to Mary Ellen Bates, another role change technology brings is that the "library and information center managers are often asked to negotiate these electronic subscriptions. This requires a new set of skills and even an entirely new relationship with publishers".

The increasing cost of both print and electronic journals causes many libraries to cut subscriptions and to purchase data for a particular audience. It is the job of the librarian to choose what is to be cancelled and to decide who will suffer least from the lack of access to particular information. In the decision to cancel subscriptions, the librarian considers, among other things, the needs of the community the library serves and whether the information is also available within the organization. Price and timeliness in retrieving the information are also considered. When negotiating access with a publisher, the librarian must agree to certain restrictions on photocopying or distribution of electronic materials. Despite copyright notices and efforts to educate employees about intellectual property rights, electronic publications can be easily forwarded to people outside the licensed user group. The library is responsible for maintaining the awareness of all employees about copyright issues. Some key active roles for librarians in the knowledge society are information editors, investigators, locators, gatekeepers, drivers, collectors, curators, producers, originators, guides, classifiers, advisers, educators, catalysts, facilitators, partners, standard bearers, researchers, navigators, storytellers etc. One of the challenges in developing the influence of librarians in these roles is that many of the people who used to visit libraries to find resources and information can now gain access to these things from a distance. This provides less opportunity for face-to-face encounter which can lead to the development of a strong bond between librarians and their clients.

5. THE CHANGING ROLE OF LIBRARIANSHIP IN THE CONTEXT OF DIGITAL / VIRTUAL LIBRARIES

Virtual Library can be simply defined as the Internet based Digital Library or a Library without walls. Timothy Green, Director of Business Research, defines Virtual Library as "a set of services that gives customers the knowledge they need to make the highest quality business decisions in the least amount of time"

The virtual or digital library will have many familiar library features, but there will be a change in the way in which the library acquires and provides access to collections and in the composition and roles of the library staff. Moving toward a digital or virtual library challenges not only the accessibility of the information but also the entire philosophy of what constitutes a document. Many librarians had heard that by the year 2000 all new resources would be digital. Although we have not quite reached that point, today most libraries are struggling to maintain a "transitional library" collecting and organizing both print and electronic resources. Walt Crawford says that "ongoing complexity and unpredictable currents of change will mark the future of libraries". Even the terminology describing information is changing.

Once we described information in a printed,

permanent format as a "document"; now, information is described as a "resource". Once, a user can be looked at one book or journal at a time. Now, electronic information can be stored and accessed by millions of users simultaneously from personal computers (PCs) with modems or through direct Internet connections from home, work, or practically anywhere. Patrons no longer have to physically visit the library to retrieve information. This ability to access full-text resources electronically from within the institution or from any PC provides the user with convenient and immediate access to information. Expanded use of interlibrary loan and document delivery also offers the potential to provide access to all materials, rather than only to materials owned locally.

6. SPECIAL SKILLS NEEDED FOR LIBRARIANSHIP IN THE KNOWLEDGE SOCIETY

The changing role implies a different skill set. The emphasis will shift from technical skills in the library to communication, facilitation, training and management skills. Although technology presents the librarian with ethical challenges, the librarian is ready for the role of information professional in the connected world. Communication is the main skill needed very much within a working group of knowledge management system. The communication channel must be kept open always in order to react promptly to problems due both to people and modern technology. Communication among members can be developed in many ways like, frequent meetings, shared documentation, pair programming etc.

Information professionals have to acquire skills that can be contributed to success in their new roles. Duberman describes four skills that information professionals already possess:

1. they "know about changes, the problems, and the opportunities the new technologies and new content can provide;

2. [they are] used to learning new things;
3. [they have] negotiation skills; and
4. [they possess a] deep knowledge of information systems and databases that really enables them to turn questions inside out and look beyond the obvious".

Libraries have frequently been early adopters of new technology, and librarians continue to be at the forefront in learning and teaching new technologies. Librarians see the Internet and electronic information as tools that are used to provide information. Crawford writes that the librarian must "recognize that technology offers tools that those tools interact in complex ways, and that tools aren't ends in themselves". Librarians are accountable for the information they provide. If they are not now doing so, they should take every precaution to avoid the distribution of misinformation. The provision of false or misleading information through carelessness breaches the trust the patron puts in the librarian's ethical duty to supply the highest level of service to library patrons, no matter the format of that information. In the end, librarians know that *"a good library is defined by the principles of librarianship, the mission of the specific library, and the persons and services that make that mission a reality"*.

7. CONCLUSION

The remarkable growth of Internet has made significant revolution in all the areas of science and technology. Rather than using it as a tool for searching and retrieving information, Internet has become the king of all media, by which we can access virtual information and can build a virtual library to provide timely, quality service to the users. As more and more end-users acquire desktop access to information in an intuitive, seamless search environment, the word 'librarian' itself will become a misnomer. Librarians of this Digital era are in the position to change their role as arbitrary information scientists/

gatekeepers and to meet the challenges of the Internet, World Wide Web, and On-line access in the knowledge society. So they must enrich their knowledge with special skills of the latest IT developments, to browse, access and retrieve a particular information across the Global Networks and to organize and manage the information by building digital libraries and by which they can provide quality e-information service to the knowledge society.

REFERENCE

1. Malwad (N M) et al. , "Digital Libraries: Dynamic storehouse of digitized Information". 1996. New Age International.
2. DLIB MAGAZINE - January 2003 to January 2006 / http://www.dlib.org
3. http://www.vlib.org
4. http://www.sap.com
5. http://www.nla.gov.au/padi
6. Kirk Hastings and Roy Tennant: How to Build a Digital Librarian: Digital Library Research & Development, "D-Lib Magazine", November 1996.ISSN 1082-9873.

14

The Emerging Role of Librarians as Knowledge Managers in the Digital Age

K. Rajasekharan

ABSTRACT

Libraries, the depositories of diverse forms of knowledge, will continue to be the keepers of knowledge. Modern libraries should keep the users at the centre-stage and promote use of knowledge resources. Information and Communication Technologies play a great role in this task. Librarians, the keepers of information sources, should function as managers of knowledge and not of books. Therefore, they should enhance their skills in the Information & Communication Technologies. Digital library technology is the frontier developing area, which the librarians cannot afford to ignore. Remote access to documents and easy delivery of information even to multiple users are the advantages it offers. But the librarians cannot dispense with the traditional library practices too. In order to become successful knowledge mangers, librarians should apply the book selection strategies and skills along with their understanding of the universe of knowledge, they learned from library schools, in the new scenarios of abundant information sources of diverse kinds. In a chaotic and fluid state of information technologies, the role of librarians, as information managers, are emerging as more crucial than ever before. Librarians, in this context, should enhance their knowledge on information technologies, horn their skills in selection of knowledge materials and reinforce their vision about the use of information/knowledge in the society so as to emerge themselves as successful knowledge mangers.

1. KNOWLEDGE MANAGEMENT

We have been moving ahead in a knowledge society dominated with a knowledge-oriented paradigm of development. In our society, the Knowledge Management, a subject so close to libraries and librarianship, has been gaining prominence particularly among management experts and computer professionals.

Knowledge management is a set of processes that govern the generation, collection, distribution and use of variant forms of knowledge and is about enhancing the overall gathering and use of it for human advancement. Some consider it as a refined label for information management, but is much more than that. The management of knowledge requires technical, organizational and interpersonal skills and everyone involved in the process, as managers in varying degrees, should have basic competence in handling information and using information technology.

2. LIBRARIES ARE KNOWLEDGE CENTERS

Libraries have been the repositories of an intangible asset, the divergent forms of knowledge. The asset has been termed diversely as facts, figures, data, information, knowledge or wisdom, depending on the level in its processing. Our libraries that existed ever since the human history and the libraries that we can see around us have been the keepers of that human intellectual asset - the knowledge in diverse formats. Probably the libraries in the future will continue to be the major repositories of knowledge in a more diversified manner.

Libraries in the past were mainly focusing on the then onerous task of preservation of the fewer knowledge materials available at that time whereas the libraries of the present day are giving thrust on promoting the use of abundantly available knowledge among more number of users for bettering the living conditions of humanity. Present day libraries seek newer ways to place the key users at the centre stage and to open up new mechanisms to enhance the access and retrieval from the emerging flood of information as the thrust activities. Libraries are now finding it difficult to carry out the twin duties of providing worlds literature -not only in print form, but also in other forms- for today's readers and preserving it for future generations.

With the advent of computer, and its alliance with the telecommunication technologies, our society - the environment where we work - had been transforming itself into an information society where every human endeavour is built upon the building blocks of information. In such a situation, the role of the library as a keeper, manager and provider of information has become divergent and probably more crucial than in the past where the body of knowledge was so limited. Internet, the amazing contribution of our times as a repository of digital knowledge, has revolutionised the way in which we publish, disseminate and use information. The resource abundance in print and digital forms poses challenges in the library scenario. Knowledge is essential to succeed in any endeavor particularly in an information society that deals with abundant information materials in diverse formats.

3. DIGITAL LIBRARIES AND MANAGEMENT OF KNOWLEDGE

In the emerging knowledge society, the digital library technologies that use computers and web applications are emerging out as an important area of development in library services. *Digital library* is an organized collection of digital documents, in any format, such as text, image, audio or video that would permit easy access and retrieval of information by users and selection, organization and maintenance by professional librarians. Digital library replaces the idea of a library as a mere repository of knowledge with the concept of it as a provider of information services to users. Digital libraries offer easier remote access, powerful search/browse facility, and electronic delivery of information to distant and multiple recipients without ease. As many would think, they do not replace the physical libraries that have been built with brick and mortar containing printed documents and having a quite place for comfortable reading. The concept of a digital library does not aim at de-constructing the existing libraries and putting their contents in tiny electronic computers. Converting a conventional library into digital form is the most ambitious and expensive one. Before embarking on it, consider whether you need that expensive digitization. The digital libraries are transforming the ways of dealing with information, managing the source materials and promoting portability of information. They are of interest to both users and librarians as easily manageable knowledge resources of our times.

Digital libraries are libraries devoid of walls having obvious practical advantages over physical ones and both of them can work in unison. In order to stay relevant, we need to redefine the forms and roles of our digital libraries carefully. Even though the digital libraries do not have walls, they should have clearly delineated boundaries in limiting their collection in this age of exponential growth of information, that adds around 3 lakhs books to our knowledge base every year. Digital libraries should have a purpose with clearly stated objectives and a set of principles that will guide the library managers to determine what should be included and what else should be excluded. We should not refrain from the imminent need to digitize absolutely essential documents, make them accessible over network and archive them for posterity. But we should not channelise our resources on digitalizing any inessential document. There should be a perfect balance in our choice of digitalization.

Libraries that keep and issue one copy each of the title of books, normally cater their services to a small constituency of people whereas the digital libraries can store and disseminate information resources to multitudes of users simultaneously reaching remotely anywhere at any time at the users will. Digital libraries can be made far more accessible to a virtually unlimited audience than the physical libraries. But remember that we cannot ignore the comforts our magnificent physical libraries provide, we cannot neglect the inviting atmosphere of the quite large reading halls our libraries have and we cannot dispense with the message that an edifice of library spread across the society, on the importance of knowledge. As well we can never ignore the digital libraries that would pay rich dividends nor we can build digital libraries without taking the difficult course of learning many new things.

4. NEED TO DEVELOP CAPABILITY AS KNOWLEDGE MANAGERS

If we have a propensity to think that our libraries are resource houses of knowledge, stored for current use and preserved for future generations, we should keep in mind that the librarians who manage them are not managers of physical documents, but managers of knowledge. With this in mind, we should look back and around us to see how far we treat our selves as managers of knowledge who selected, stored and handled the knowledge sources on which we have been exercising considerable control. We should have exercised a great role in the selection, organisation and serving of knowledge materials not only in books or other physical formats, but also in the abstract form data, information and knowledge, as such. We should have exercised our intelligence, learning and prudence in selection of the right information materials for the right kind of users based on the lessons that we learned from our library science schools where we learned book selection as a specialised subject. No one else in the members of the faculty who have been recommending books for the library has had any chance to get education on that subject. So we should have emerged as selectors of the most suitable books that tally with the needs of the users by learning more and more about the diverse areas of knowledge content contained in the documents that we handle. As well, we are the rare group of people who learned something about every other subject - the universe of knowledge - as part of our curriculum unlike others who learned only a few subjects and hence are ignorant of many other academic subjects. So we must have utilized that advantage in our complex task of knowledge management positively.

5. REFINE THE KNOWLEDGE MANAGEMENT SKILLS

We, as librarians, should go above our routine concerns in lending books, preparing bibliographies, creating catalogues, distributing new additions lists etc. We should not have unnecessarily concentrated on hotly debating on the need to have a coma in the place of a fullstop in a catalogue entry and should not have treated the books and other information materials as mere lifeless physical objects. We should have treated information materials as embodiment of knowledge and end products of thinking process by great minds lived around us. Then the libraries should have been the temples of learning and we should have been the well-revered priests in the academic world. We should treat out libraries as a sacred place if we treat the documents as embodiment of thoughts of the intellectual giants.

We should bear in mind that all the roles played by a traditional librarian in the era of print, have direct parallels in the electronic age. The user-educational role - educating the users in knowing, learning and handling knowledge - is a growing one which librarians are uniquely qualified to handle. Perhaps the oldest and the most traditional role of the library, stretching back to their very origin, is the protection of human kind's cultural record from damage or loss. The digital technologies offer stable ways to preserve the knowledge for future use not only in one place but in multiple locations without much ease. Now the digital technologies help the libraries to move much ahead in putting that knowledge to work, transforming themselves as centers for dissemination of pieces of knowledge to a wider group of academic clients.

The role of library and information professionals in reference work has been on the increase, rather than the reverse, as electronic information sources accessible to library are growing exponentially. It was probably never possible that users could use all the resources of a library unaided, but many have a propensity to think that they can. The growing variety in bibliographic databases, numerical databanks, electronic journals, and Internet resources, that exist today make it difficult for many users to exploit the optimal use of them all. The software needed to search those electronic sources, the command languages and the facilities available for getting the output or transfer of retrieved information to other files for further processing etc are so complex that professional help of trained people is normally needed to use them effectively. Learning the nuances of information tracking and helping the users in identifying the right knowledge materials by exposing them to strategic searching are important tasks librarians have to play in this cyber age.

The most intellectually rigorous part of the work of a

librarian is the information service where the users ask the librarian for pieces of information needed by them. The task of providing right information requires broad based knowledge on the specific subjects and on the types of sources of information on the subjects. This requires, the librarians to have a sound knowledge on information resources that exist in the library and elsewhere with a broad understanding on the internal structure of those information sources and information repositories existing around the world. Otherwise we cannot emerge ourselves as knowledge providers or knowledge facilitators.

Digital libraries need digital librarians. Organizing a digital collection has very little in common with organizing a print collection. The digital library technology is advancing at a rapid pace that what is learned today will soon be outdated. Therefore, the digital librarians should possess innate personal qualities rather than specific technical expertise that can be learned. Digital librarians should thrive on change. They should read constantly, but selectively and experiment endlessly. They need to love learning, mainly self learning, and be inclined to take risks. And they must have a keen sense of both the potentials and pitfalls of technology.

In addition to personal qualities, Digital Librarians need to have technical expertise on:-

- imaging technologies
- scanning and optical character recognition (OCR)
- markup languages, including HTML, SGML, and XML
- cataloging and metadata
- indexing and database technology
- user interface design
- Web technology, and
- project management.

In short, the librarians should focus on developing the skills required to identify, find, retrieve, evaluate, use and communicate information from a variety of sources by making use of his innate personal qualities and technological expertise.

6. DIGITAL AGE OFFERS MORE CRUCIAL ROLE

There are a growing number of people who believe quite firmly that once the transition from print to electronic documents has been made, there will be no role for libraries or librarians in the knowledge generation and use chain where electronic documents can be delivered directly from the publisher to the user's desktop. Such a scenario is certainly possible, but it is unlikely to happen. Many believed that the traditional functions of a librarian have become redundant in an era when increasing amounts of information are available directly to users via the Internet. The Internet right now is completely chaotic and therefore the users had to waste much time in searching fruitlessly for precise information that they need from among the abundant digital materials it will bring. The skills of a librarian are in fact so relevant in the electronic age on a broad spectrum of areas including helping the Internet users in obtaining the needed information without hassles. The librarian has obligation to advise the Internet users on the best resources to access, how to access those resources, and how to formulate their queries for search and retrieval of relevant items. We should as well remember that a source material that is available in Internet might disappear at any moment. Permanence is an impossible quality that one can expect from Internet. This implies that keep them aware of the need to download and keep away the Internet information material, if they are so particular about having the document. Despite the popularity of the Internet and supposed user-friendliness of the World Wide Web, users need far more guidance in using electronic resources than in using a library of print materials. The libraries should organise orientation or exposure training on Internet use in which the librarians, and not the computer professionals, should take lead roles as facilitators. This implies that the librarians need to learn a lot about information technologies to serve as competent librarians in digital era.

7. LIBRARIANS CAN BE CHANGE AGENTS IN MANY WAYS

Librarians, as knowledge managers and providers can play a lead role in many knowledge-oriented activities that would trigger great changes in the society. Librarians, through many services, can encourage people to increase their competitive ability in the globalised market, enhance their accumulation of experience indirectly from documents, help them in bringing out better products and services through enhanced access to information, allow them to improve their life-skills, provide the decision makers with all sorts of information needed for taking well-informed decisions etc. We can, through better information services, push the frontiers of academic disciplines, help preserve traditional culture through archiving documents, support human development by popularizing development information and can do so many similar things if we emerge ourselves as real knowledge managers with a purpose. For this we should continue to engage in capturing all kinds of knowledge within our reach, organize or manage them effectively and disseminate the information contained in them through excellent services by utilising the exciting information technologies including Internet available at our disposal.

We, as information managers, should concentrate more than ever before on continuous improvement of our competencies in successfully fulfilling our new roles. We should exercise constant care and control over the management of information resources through a range of activities such as identifying, selecting, evaluating, securing and providing access to information pertinent to the users. We should take care in all aspects of information services, from the concept stage through the design, development and delivery of services, based on print and digital documents so as to have effective and efficient services. We should as well choose, modify and develop tools, and technologies of the digital era that would enhance the effectiveness of dissemination of information to all. To become good knowledge managers, librarians will have to refine and redefine their skills, in wide ranging activities like classification, indexing, abstracting, filtering of information, networking of experts, need assessment of users, web page development, database development, teaching and training, compiling status papers, writing for publications etc. Information professionals should have personal competencies in presenting ideas clearly, negotiating confidently and dealing with persuasively with the organization in which they are a part. They should be able to plan, prioritize and focus on new initiatives and think creatively and innovatively as silent revolutionaries who transformed the world. If we need to be instrumental in making changes in the society, we should emerge ourselves as knowledge facilitators.

8. CONCLUSION

We need librarians who learnt in the past, engage in learning the rapid advancements of the present day world and look at the distant future with a vision of a knowledge society and not those who look back to the glory of the past, worry about the unstable present and ignore the unpredictable future. Our learning in the past, engagements in the present digital world and the vision about the future based on both should bring in new traces of knowledge-enhanced skills and appropriate attitudes for dealing with the complexities of the emerging knowledge oriented world. It will help groom ourselves as knowledge managers. Unless we groom ourselves as knowledge managers, we may not have meaningful existence in the future.

So we should build our library as a knowledge house from where knowledge flows out through various means and not as a storehouse of printed documents. Librarians should emerge as knowledge managers rather than mere book keepers. For that we should learn the specific subjects our library handle with the enthusiasm of a professor and keep in touch with the information technologies like that of an enthusiastic computer man. We must continue to keep thinking on newer ways of information gathering and dissemination in the emerging scenario. All this is possible only if we improve the skill-sets including leadership abilities needed constantly for a knowledge manager.

Library schools do have a dominant role to play in that process and the seminars like this should throw up those concepts for detailed deliberations and putting the outcome into practice.

REFERENCE

1. David Stern (1999): *Digital Libraries- Philosophies, Technical Design Consideration, and Example Scenarios.* Haworth Press.
2. William Y Arms (2000): *Digital Libraries.* MIT Press.
3. Michael Lesk (1997): *Practical Digital Libraries.* Morgan Kaufmann.
4. Allen Kent *Ed* (2002): *Encyclopedia of Library and Information Science.* CRC Press.
5. Ian Witten & David Bainbridge (2002): *How to Build a Digital Library.* Morgan Kaufmann.

15

Professional Skill and Computer Educational Requirements for Future Librarians

Milind K. Labhasetwar
R.B. Nimat

ABSTRACT

The libraries of the 21st century have to be conceived not merely as the store house of knowledge but an effective mechanism to facilitate dissemination of knowledge, promoting information and knowledge sharing, while, at the same time supporting the growth of intellectual property. In the context of the impact of information technology on the libraries it is worthwhile to ponder over the challenges to be met by the library professionals. In this paper we mentioned that the up gradation of skill and professional education required for the handle and manage the information systems of 21st century.

1. INTRODUCTION

The libraries of the 21st century have to be conceived not merely as the store house of knowledge but an effective mechanism to facilitate dissemination of knowledge, promoting information and knowledge sharing, while, at the same time supporting the growth of intellectual property. In the context of the impact of information technology on the libraries it is worthwhile to ponder over the challenges to be met by the library professionals. There is a requirement of additional skills to the library and information professionals to meet the future requirements of the libraries.

2. SKILL REQUIREMENT IN FUTURE FOR BETTER PROFESSIONAL SERVICES

Following skills will require for the successful Library professional in the future.

1. **Adaptability** - Information professionals must be able to cope with constant change
2. **Creativity** - Resolving many challenges will require ingenuity and lateral thinking
3. **Willingness to take risks** - Characteristic normally associated with librarians
4. **Self-starters** - Much of the responsibility for self-improvement will fall to the individual
5. Project management skills
6. **Change management skills** - Essential in today's environment
7. **Interpersonal and communication skills** - Librarians are the 'human face' of technology for many people and, as we progress to be managers, we need good people skills to help both staff and users adjust to the changes facing them
8. **Sense of humor** - Last but not least, this is an essential component of any job

3. ESSENTIAL REQUIREMENT FOR BETTER SERVICES

* Management of Information Organizations - administration skills

* Information Resources and Services – advanced reference skills
* Introduction to Information Technology - Computer programming/data analysis (Details are given below)
* Intro to Bibliographic Control – advanced cataloguing skills
* Online Information Retrieval - introduction to electronic databases
* Research Methods - research methodology, types of research
* Information and its Social Contexts - Economic/political/social impact of society's emphasis on information

Somehow, library schools need to structure their curricula so that the seeds of these attitudes and skills can be sown. Continuing education, with a strong emphasis on mentoring, is also essential. The possible career paths open to library graduates have widened dramatically in recent years and will continue to do so. If the information professionals of the future are equipped with these characteristics and skills, they will be capable of meeting the numerous exciting challenges ahead.

4. SKILLS REQUIRED FOR BETTER LIBRARIANSHIP

- Archives Management
- Records Management
- Supervisory Management
- Information Retrieval
- Technical processing
- Research Skills
- Information Provision
- Information Analysis

- Basic Information Systems
- Communication for Management
- Reference service
- Interpersonal communication
- Provision of Information Services
- Information search and retrieval

5. CONTINUING EDUCATION

The terms 'life-long learning' and 'knowledge nation' are in our daily conversation. This orientation towards a continual upgrading of skills, especially technological skills, is a requirement of most working professionals and is certainly true in our discipline. No information professional graduating today assumes that they have done all that is required to last them until they retire. Many graduates will combine their library degree with another higher degree such as business administration or IT. Frequent and diverse on-the-job training is becoming an essential component of working life and the importance of devoting resources to this is now recognized by senior library managers. Involvement in professional associations is another method through which information professionals can remain current. In addition to conferences and formal training opportunities, the opportunity to network and learn from others is a vital component in our rapidly changing professional world .Recently distance education provider institutes available for carrier advancement programme the institutes provide the degree, postgraduate as well as doctorate level degree courses in library and information science

A key role for librarians will still be filtering or sifting information. The 'information overload' that most people feel bad in our favour. One of the eminent personality's keynote address, talked about two categories of end-users - the 'do it for me' group and the 'let me do it myself' group.

In my opinion, librarians have something to contribute to both those groups.

6. COMMUNICATION SKILL

Excellent communication and interpersonal skills have always been important but are increasingly essential as librarians are called upon to explain the complexity of electronic resources to their clients. Information literacy, with its increasing emphasis on developing self-sufficiency in the end-user, will solidify the role of librarian as educator. In all environments, we hear about developing 'partnerships' which requires good listening, communication, diplomacy and negotiation skills.

7. REQUIRED COMPUTER RELATED KNOWLEDGE OF LIBRARIANS IN FUTURE

1. Computer system Components : Micro Computer systems, Mini Computer Systems, mainframe Computer Systems, Networked computer systems

2. Computer Software : System Software, operating Systems, database Management Systems language Transfer Programmes

3. Application Software : Application Software for users, database Management Packages, Graphic Packages

4. Digital Technology Media Processing : Internet/ WWW for publishing support through integrated with HTML, Suit Design Network Filter Enhancement, Searches against Keywords.

5. Manage wise Systems : Asset Management, Server Management, desktop Management, Network Analysis, Virus Protection, macromedia Director Systems

6. Interface : Navigation, Browsing, Filtering, Searching, Multimedia Systems, Document Analysis, Classification

7. Surrogation and Storage : Indexing, Abstracting, Content Conversion, database, E Commerce, Electronic Publishing, E Journals, E Book, Online Archive, Image Processing.

8. Management Processing : Archiving, Digital Preservation, Security of Data, Sustainable Interaction, World Wide Web, Network Systems Virtual Library.

9. Digital Information Systems : Basic Structure, Importance, Technology, System Concepts, Feedback and Control, System Characteristics, Components, Human Resources, Hardware Resources, Software Resources, Information Systems Activity, Types.

8. SKILL DEVELOPMENT TOWARDS TOTAL QUALITY MANAGEMENT

Libraries are ideal places to implement TQM. They are service organizations dedicated to their customers, the patrons. By develop the skill professionals must create a strategic plan, and following it with a commitment to continuous quality improvement, librarian can transform and improve their organizations. Riggs (1992) summarizes the notable principles of TQM: (1) manage by fact: make library decisions after careful analysis of data gathered with tools such as check sheets, histograms, and Pareto charts; (2) eliminate rework: library work is often labor intensive—simplify it and make sure it is done properly the first time; (3) respect people and ideas: staff are the library's most valuable resources, and they should be encouraged to point out problems without fear of management; and (4) empower people: trust library staff to act responsibly and give them the appropriate authority to make decisions that can improve the quality of work they do.

9. DEVELOP MARKETING SKILL

Training in personal selling remains a pronounced gap

between retailers and librarians. "Hey how's it going? May I help you find what you are looking for? Let me know if you need any assistance while you are in the store. While we are better trained in our profession than many retail salespeople are, librarians shy away from thinking of contact with the public as "selling." Yet personal selling is the most powerful promotion tool, and it's underutilized by most librarians. By and large, retail stores rely on quickly hired and trained minimum-wage employees to operate daily functions. While this direct contact can backfire if the person is not knowledgeable about the product, it is also a golden opportunity to respond directly to customer questions and unique needs. If we would retrain our staff members to proactively "sell" library services through making eye contact, communicating new services and materials, and handling complaints in a professional manner, libraries could take the lead in this most powerful form of promotion.

10. INFORMATION LITERACY SKILL

In the information age every one needs to become competent and confident information users. Information literacy can contribute to develop the information skill needed to handle the Information Technology use by the end user. Information literacy empowers the ability to access, evaluate, and use information effectively. Users need to master the skills of finding ,handling , evaluating and using it because it is scattered in print , electronic, and digital forms and format .Suggested step for develop the skill is follows:

- Development of thinking skill such as problem solving reasoning and critical evaluation.
- Information gathering and reflection which in turn promotes deep learning
- Promote to users for develop acquisition of effective information skill through conceptual awareness of nature of information and its diversity.

– Encourage information skills development trough self directed learning.

11. KNOWLEDGE MANAGEMENT SKILL

Human Resource Management Is the Core of Knowledge Management in Libraries.

The most important resource in the knowledge economy system is the talents who grasp knowledge. The talent competition has become the focus of market competition in the knowledge economy era. In the knowledge economy era, the libraries will attach importance to vocational training and lifelong education of library staffs to raise their scientific knowledge level and ability of acquiring and innovating knowledge. They also will and fully respect the human value, guide and bring into play wisdom potentialities of library staffs, take developing knowledge resources in the brains of library staffs as an important way for rising work efficiency. An all-round improvement of library staff's quality and positioning of the human value will become important objectives of knowledge management in libraries.

The objective of Knowledge Management in Libraries is to promote Knowledge Innovation. Knowledge innovation is the core of the knowledge economy society. As bases for collection, processing, storage and distribution of knowledge and information, libraries represent an indispensable link in the scientific system chain, an important link in the knowledge innovation. Secondly, libraries take part in scientific research process directly. The library work is a component of knowledge innovation. Thirdly, libraries must pay attention to diffusion and conversion of knowledge. They act as bridges for turning the results of knowledge innovation into realistic productive forces. Knowledge management in libraries is to promote relationship in and between libraries, between library and user, to strengthen knowledge internetworking and to quicken knowledge flow. In the knowledge economy era, libraries will carry out researches on development and application of information resources, construction of virtual libraries, protection of intellectual property rights in the electronic era etc., thus founding the base for knowledge innovation·

Information Technology Is a Tool for Knowledge Management in Libraries. The knowledge acquired must be accumulated and converged into knowledge warehouses of libraries. The priority of information technologies in the field of knowledge storage not only finds expression in quantity, but also in retrieval, sorting and security of the knowledge. Information technology is also indispensable in the application and exchange of knowledge and other fields. It functions as a source and tool for knowledge innovation.

12. CONCLUSION

In the 21st century libraries should also attach importance to provision of services for people to acquire knowledge and achieve maximum functions and efficiency of knowledge information. Therefore, knowledge services based on high-speed information networks should be carried out by:

1. Setting up virtual libraries or information centers for enterprises, governments, public organizations and scientific research institutions
2. Setting up digitized knowledge services which is actually a development trend of libraries in the 21st century
3. Digitizing libraries' resources. The electronic libraries or digitized libraries are the technical modes and development trends of libraries in the knowledge economy era
4. Human Resources Management-Human resources management takes it as its basic starting point to train

high quality specialized talents and to revitalize the library undertaking. In practice, we should pay full attention to diversity and variation of library staffs' requirements, strengthened management of different library staffs by applying contingency management approach

The library professionals and those working and managing modern information systems are therefore required to posses the knowledge and skills to handle the challenges of 21st century. They are required to constantly update their own knowledge and skill base so as to work in today's rapidly changing information and knowledge systems.

REFERENCE

1. http://www.anu.edu.au/~culture
2. Delany, Paul, and George P. Landow. 1991. *Hypermedia and literary studies, Technical communications*. Cambridge, Mass.: MIT Press; London,
3. George P. 1994. *Hyper text theory*. Baltimore ; London: Johns Hopkins University Press
4. http://etext.lib.virginia.edu/TEI.html
5. Malwad,N M et al., "Digital Libraries: Dynamic storehouse of digitized Information. 1996. New Age International.

16

Knowledge Management An Emerging Concept

Shishir H. Mandalia

ABSTRACT

Describes that both knowledge and information have been essential ingredients to change our society for future vision and shows the different approaches of knowledge activities. Knowledge management in libraries should be focused on effective research and development of knowledge, creation of knowledge bases, exchange and sharing of knowledge Mention the modules and processes of knowledge management and also discuss the knowledge management techniques in libraries.

1. INTRODUCTION

In the present age of information technology both information and knowledge have become essential ingredients due to multidimensional use and application in the society. They have also been playing an important role to change and improve the current society for future vision. Organizing information for its gainful use in social development interventions against the environment of information explosion all over the world has become a highly contentious issue that poses a great challenge for today's librarians and information professionals.

Knowledge economy is a knowledge-based economy. In the knowledge economy era, the management refers to effectively identify, acquire, develop, resolve, use, store and share knowledge, to create an approach to transforming and sharing of tacit and explicit knowledge, and to raise the emergency and innovation capability by utilizing the wisdom of the team. Since knowledge has become the driving force for social development, the attention of the society to information and knowledge is rising and people's demands for information and knowledge are increasing step by step. This has provided a good environment for library development. Moreover, as information and knowledge has become an important productive factor for the modern economic system, the society will inevitably require intensified management of information and knowledge. How to manage knowledge will become an important subject facing libraries in the near future.

Knowledge management in libraries should be focused on effective research and development of knowledge, creation of knowledge bases, exchange and sharing of knowledge between library staffs (including its users), training of library staff, speeding up explicit processing of the implicit knowledge and realizing of its sharing.

2. WHAT AND WHY KNOWLEDGE MANAGEMENT?

Knowledge management is about enhancing the use of organizational knowledge through sound practices of information management and organizational learning. It is the process of transforming information and intellectual assets into enduring value.

In the words of Marquardt (1998) the economy has shifted from brawn to 'brain' and knowledge is becoming more and more of every nation's GNP. So knowledge management is necessary for survival.

3. OBJECTIVE OF KNOWLEDGE MANAGEMENT

The Objective of Knowledge Management in Libraries is to Promote Knowledge Innovation. Knowledge innovation is the core of the knowledge economy society. As bases for collection, processing, storage and distribution of knowledge and information, libraries represent an indispensable link in the scientific system chain, an important link in the knowledge innovation. Secondly, libraries take part in scientific research process directly. The library work is a component of knowledge innovation. Thirdly, libraries must pay attention to diffusion and conversion of knowledge. They act as bridges for turning the results of knowledge innovation into realistic productive forces. Knowledge management in libraries is to promote relationship in and between libraries, between library and user, to strengthen knowledge internetworking and to quicken knowledge flow. In the knowledge economy era, libraries will carry out researches on development and application of information resources, construction of virtual libraries, protection of intellectual property rights in the electronic era etc., thus founding the base for knowledge innovation.

More, Knowledge management is concerned with the exploitation and development of the knowledge assets of an organization with a view to furthering the organizations objective. The knowledge to be managed includes both explicit, documentary knowledge and tacit or subjective knowledge, which resides in the minds of employees, knowledge management embraces all of the processes associated with the identification, sharing and creation of information successful knowledge management required. System for the management of knowledge repositories, and to cultivate and facilitate the sharing of knowledge and organization learning. Knowledge management projects focus on more of the following objective:

- To create knowledge repositories, which store both

knowledge and information, often in documentary form. A common feature is "added value" through categorization and pruning.

- To improve knowledge access, or to provide access to knowledge or to facilitate its transfer among individuals: here the emphasis is on connectivity, access and transfer, and technologies such as video conferencing systems, document scanning and telecommunication networks are central to this objective.
- To enhance the knowledge environment so that the environment is conductive to more effective knowledge creation, transfer and use. This involves talking organizational norms and value as they relate to knowledge.
- To manage knowledge as an asset, and to recognize the value of knowledge to an organization .Assets, such as technologies that are sold under license or have potential value, customer databases and detailed parts catalogues are typical of companies intangible assets to which a value can be assign.

4. CHARACTERISTICS OF KNOWLEDGE MANAGEMENT

The role of knowledge management in libraries will become more and more important along with the development of knowledge economy. It is a new management mode, boasts the following superiority and characteristics incomparable with conventional management:

4.1. Human Resource

The most important resource in the knowledge economy system is the talents who grasp knowledge. The talent competition has become the focus of market competition in the knowledge economy era. In the knowledge economy era, the libraries will attach importance to vocational training and lifelong education of library staffs to raise their scientific knowledge level and ability of acquiring and innovating knowledge. They also will and fully respect the human value, guide and bring into play wisdom potentialities of library staffs, take developing knowledge resources in the brains of library staffs as an important way for rising work efficiency. An all-round improvement of library staff's quality and positioning of the human value will become important objectives of knowledge management in libraries.

4.2. Information Technology

Information Technology is a Tool for Knowledge Management in Libraries

4.3. Knowledge acquisition

Knowledge acquisition is the starting point of knowledge management in libraries. The application of information technologies enlarges the scope of knowledge acquisition, raises knowledge acquisition speed and reduces knowledge acquisition cost. It is impossible to accomplish such important tasks by using man's brains only in the modern society in which the knowledge changes with each passing day. It will be possible to link closely knowledge sources and knowledge workers by computer networks, thus constructing knowledge networks in libraries based on realization of single-point information.

4.4. Knowledge acquired

Knowledge acquired must be accumulated and converged into knowledge warehouses of libraries. The priority of information technologies in the field of knowledge storage not only finds expression in quantity, but also in retrieval, sorting and security of the knowledge. Information technology is also indispensable in the application and exchange of knowledge and other fields. It functions as a source and tool for knowledge innovation.

4.5. Modules of Knowledge Management

Knowledge management system is primarily base on eight vital modules such as

1. Information: the most important bezel, acts as an instant access to update and customize information.
2. Expertise: Expertise lancets in seal time experts in an organization to members who earn assistance even the tacit knowledge can made explicit.
3. Collaboration: Collaboration plays an important role to facilitate on-line brain storming sessions and reserves information.
4. Team: Team ensures efficient and systematic management among share skills.
5. Learning: Learning abridges skill gap with the help of on-line sessions.
6. Intelligence: Intelligence deals mainly with the explicit knowledge raise.
7. knowledge transfer: knowledge transfer in a structured electronic form according to William saffody relates to,
   (i) Machine readable data files
   (ii) Various on-line databases and CD-ROM information products
   (iii) Computer storage devices in which information resides in the shape of optical disks, juck boxes or magnetic tape, autoloaders and
   (iv) Computerized network systems.
8. Knowledge Mapping: knowledge mapping identifies the body of knowledge within the organization which is primarily concerned with mute knowledge base and

makes a repository of all skills and expertise in the organization.

4.6. Scope of Knowledge Management

The current state of knowledge management field is that it encompasses four overlapping areas:

1. Managing organization
2. Organizational Learning
3. Intellectual capital
4. Knowledge economics

The aim of knowledge management is for library to become more competitive through the capacities of their staff and clients to be more flexible and innovative.

4.7. Contents of Knowledge Management

As a completely new method of management, knowledge management in libraries leaves much to be desired in its theoretical system. In my opinion, knowledge management in libraries should include such respects as follows:

(a) Knowledge Innovation Management

Knowledge innovation management in libraries refers to the management of the production, diffusion and transfer of knowledge as well as of the network systems constructed by related institutions and organizations. It includes three aspects, namely, theoretical innovation management of knowledge, technical innovation management and organizational innovation management.

(b) Knowledge Dissemination Management

Knowledge dissemination is of equal importance as compared to knowledge innovation. Knowledge creators do not have much time and energy to look for knowledge users. Though there are a multitude of knowledge users, it is very difficult to acquire knowledge that already exists in the minds of knowledge creators as restricted by various objective and subjective conditions. Therefore, libraries may play the part of knowledge tosses, use diverse media and channels to disseminate various new knowledge. In the 21st century, the Internet, with its mass information and extensive contents, will provide people with the main approach to searching knowledge and acquiring information. But now there emerge absurd, salacious, false and uncivil information resulting from seeking for commercial profits and political objectives on the Net. Therefore, it is necessary to strengthen knowledge dissemination management in libraries as follows:

- Uninterruptedly strengthening the creation of libraries' own document resources and deepening the development of document information resources;
- Continuously raising the quality of libraries' staffs and strengthening continuous engineering education of working staffs;
- Giving full play to the special role of the expert system in knowledge dissemination;
- Making a comprehensive utilization of all media to ensure security of operation of networks, and prevent online criminal activities and online dissemination of inappropriate information.

(c) Knowledge Application Management

In the 21st century libraries should also attach importance to provision of services for people to acquire knowledge and achieve maximum functions and efficiency of knowledge information. Therefore, knowledge services based on high-speed information networks should be carried out by:

- Setting up virtual libraries or information centers for enterprises, governments, public organizations and scientific research institutions. It is difficult for an enterprise or a social organization to put sufficient manpower, material and financial resources on information gathering, organizing and developing. It is also impossible and unnecessary to spend a large amount of funds on information resources for their own use. Libraries can create virtual libraries or information centers for these organs separately according to their respective information requirements by using abundant information resources on the high-speed information networks.

- Setting up digitized knowledge services which is actually a development trend of libraries in the 21st century. This presupposes: creating step by step the users-oriented information service systems such as information dissemination, information search and special supply of information; quickening the creation of digitized libraries; studying the methods, means and techniques of information distribution and search with the Internet as the base and WEB technique as the core.
- Digitizing libraries' resources. The electronic libraries or digitized libraries are the technical modes and development trends of libraries in the knowledge economy era. The knowledge services of libraries in the future will start with creation of databases comprising electronic journals and books in different languages that have discipline features and can operate on high-speed information networks. Great efforts should be made to transform all existing large non-electronic information resources into electronic information and integrate them into electronic libraries.

(d) Human Resources Management

Human resources management takes it as its basic starting point to train high quality specialized talents and to revitalize the library undertaking. In practice, we should pay full attention to diversity and variation of library staffs' requirements, strengthened management of different library staffs by applying contingency management approach. That is, to some people, rigid management method is applied, rigorous supervision and control imposed, and quantity and quality requirements of work according to regulations and procedures are made clear. And, to the rest of people, more flexible management method is applied to let them participate in decision-making and consultation and undertake more jobs so as to bring their management abilities into full play and realize organizational and personal objectives. Doing well in continuous engineering education of specialized staffs, which should not only focus on the theory of library science and related disciplines, but also cover the latest technical knowledge. And strengthening professional ethics education.

5. CONCLUSION

Knowledge management understands of dimensions of knowledge work. Knowledge management has become a powerful tool for promoting innovation and realizing and recognizing the various walks of life. Knowledge management in libraries should be help on effective research and development of knowledge, creation of knowledge bases, exchange and sharing of knowledge between library and users.

REFERENCE

1. Tang Shanhong, Knowledge Management in Libraries in the 21st Century,66th IFLA Council and General Conference, Jerusalem, Israel, 13-18 August-2000.
2. L.S.R.V.Ramesh, A.V. S. S. Naga Raju & B. Isthari, Implementation of knowledge management in library : A powerful tool for future survival, Indian Journal of Information, Library & Society,Vol.18,N 3-4,July-December,2005.
3. Kumar, P.S.G. Information and Communication, New Delhi: B.R. Publishing Corporation, p. 419

17

Issues and Challenges in Knowledge Management

S. Raja
G. Shanmugavadivu

ABSTRACT

Knowledge Management and Information Resource Management involve similar processes such as acquisition, creation, and renewal, archival, dissemination. Present Colloquium is about the various issues and challenges in Knowledge management of Information Resources. This study proposes to analyze the management of the most important resource that is knowledge.

1. INTRODUCTION

Over the past several years, a number of authors have proposed a variety of approaches for the various issues and challenges in knowledge management of Information Resources. Knowledge management is not a single discipline. Rather, it an integration of numerous endeavors and fields of study. The traditional knowledge model emphasizes convergence and compliance to achieve pre-specified organizational goals. This study proposes to analysis the management of the most important resource that is Knowledge.

Knowledge is created through an individual process of changing cognitive structure and enables people to act. Knowledge is intrinsically linked to people.

2. WHAT IS KNOWLEDGE?

- "Knowledge is the small part of ignorance that we arrange and classify." – Ambrose Bierce (1842 - 1914)
- What we know – purified by reality
- Knowledge continuum:

  Data ----Information ----Knowledge (Tacit & Explicit)

2.1. Kinds of Knowledge

Organizations have numerous kinds of knowledge resources. The Intellectual and Knowledge based assets fall into one of two categories:

- **Explicit** : formal; systematized; recorded for posterity; "book knowledge;" "white papers;" policy manuals; general documents
- **Tacit** : personal "know-how;" "tricks of the trade;" seasoned intuition; resident in individuals; typically developed from experience

3. KNOWLEDGE MANAGEMENT

Not the "managing of knowledge", but the establishing of a relevant framework to support and promote the application of available knowledge in value creating process can also be described as the management of the organizational knowledge base

Information Resource Management is all about recognizing the value of Information resource. Here main problem lies in handling / managing the various information resources, specially the resources which provide tacit knowledge. Tacit knowledge is that knowledge which can't be communicated in words, i.e., the Knowledge that is retained in the mind of human.

Knowledge Management (KM) has structural and functional basis in the Information management or Information Resource Management. The main difference is the high degree of dynamic activity involved in the Knowledge Management. According to Aslib the scope and definitions and activities under the denotation of Information Resource Management is totally encompassed by Knowledge Management, which is the latest context in the information arena and a nature extension of the ideas of Information Resource Management. Both the Knowledge Management and Information Resource Management involve similar processes such as acquisition, creation, and renewal, archival, dissemination.

3.1. What is Knowledge Management?

- "A discipline that promotes an integrated approach to identifying, capturing, evaluating, retrieving and sharing enterprise information assets." (Gartner Group)
- "KM is the process through which an enterprise uses its collective intelligence to accomplish its strategic objectives." (Ramon Barquin, Barquin International, Inc.)
- A "people enabler" not a technological solution
- Steps of KM process:
  - Creation
  - Capture
  - Application
  - K measurement

3.2. Components of Knowledge Management

- People management
- Process management
- Information Management

3.3. Implementation of Knowledge Management

- High-level commitment to change.
- Human Resource of organization.
- To and fro communication in the hierarchical structure of management.
- Understanding among the staff.
- Keeping track of the process of workflow in the organization.

3.4. Process of Knowledge Management

Knowledge Acquisition : finding existing knowledge, understanding requirements, searching among multiple sources.

Knowledge Creation : research activities, creative processes in advertising, writing books or articles, making movies, and so on.

Packaging : publishing, editing, design work.

Applying or using existing knowledge : auditing, medical diagnosis;

Reuse of knowledge for new purpose : leveraging knowledge product development processes, software development.

4. LIBRARIANS AS KNOWLEDGE MANAGERS

Tools of Knowledge Management consists 70% of services and 30% of Technologies. Librarians provide these 70% services. This indicates the role of Librarians as Knowledge Manager. Where their functions are: -

- Providing services to the user community
- Sharing of information and understanding of user needs.
- Analyzing documents, classifying and sorting them for easy retrieval.

– Building the index etc.

5. CHALLENGES OF KNOWLEDGE MANAGEMENT

Intellectual Capital : managing of tacit knowledge is not easy. Because, we don't know what is in human mind. It is not possible to document tacit knowledge.

Culture : Because of narrow mindedness or insecurity majority of people don't want to share their knowledge; some people don't want to interfere they want to stay neutral and they are away from knowledge sharing.

Obsolescence : There are types of information, which gets obsolete as soon as it is generated for, ex: Stock market information. Because of these types of ever changing information it is difficult to give this information quickly to capable user.

Overloading : Knowledge gets accumulated. If obsolete information is not removed it leads overload. And it is difficult to identify which is useful from this information.

Technology : Due to rapid changes in technology it is difficult to communicate the knowledge to the user because, technology helps Knowledge Management to a large extent. Technology is tool for Knowledge Management.

Structure : Structure of Knowledge management should show overall economy. Whether to follow centralized or decentralized system.

6. ISSUES INVOLVED

Knowledge maps : This involves building an actual map of special databases, which points towards the resource./required data.

Acquisition : Acquisition along with external sources should also be extended to internal sources of knowledge. The librarian works with the knowledge team to survey the various in house documents to identify and digitize, like standards, reports, and reports of technical discussions.

Categorizing : The knowledge which is located inside or outside has to be represented in a way which is suitable for access or transfer on the basis of controlled vocabulary in a hierarchy.

Narratives : Extracting and diffusing the success stories and technical anecdotes from resource persons.

- Managing databases
- Capturing tacit knowledge

7. QUALITY KM SITE FUNCTIONAL CAPABILITIES

- Quick, easy, immediate, ubiquitous access
- Single sign-on access to all linked sites
- Email account
- Links to sources of explicit K (where it's maintained!)
- "Chat rooms"
- "Threaded discussions"
- Customization - presentation & content delivery based on criteria set by user
- Personalization - tailor the presentation of content to individuals or classes of customers based on profile info
- Alerting - matches incoming streams of new information against users' profiles & "pushes" it to them by user-selected means
- Search & Retrieval with Filtering
  * Can find out who else has been searching on a topic
  * Can direct search agent to push new info to desktop, cell phone, or hand-held computer
- Virtual work space or "e-room" where docs are easily exchanged
- Web conferencing

- Virtual communities of practice (e.g., Contract Specialists, Price & Cost Analysts, Procurement Analysts)
- Shared presentations
- Networks of subject matter experts

8. CONCLUSION

Knowledge Management is not managing or organizing books or journals, searching the Internet for clients or arranging the circulation of materials. Knowledge Management is about enhancing the use of organizational knowledge through sound practices of Knowledge Management and Organizational learning. Thus Knowledge Management is a combination of Information Management, Communication and Human Resources.

REFERENCE

1. Bawden, David - The shifting terminologies of Information - Aslib proceedings, Vol. 53, No.3, More on the ways in which tacit knowledge can be addressed by knowledge management efforts can be found in *The Siamese Twins: Documents and Knowledge* (Newman, 1997). March 2001- pp. 93 - 98.
2. Binwal, J.C - Knowledge Management -IASLIC Bulletin 46 (2), 2001, p. 65 - 78.
3. Devika.P.Madalli-ed: Information Resource Management- DRTC Work shop 13-15 March 2002- DRTC- Bangalore, 2002.
4. Haravu, L.J. - Lectures on Knowledge Management: Paradigm, Challenges and Opportunities - Sarada Ranganathan Endowment for Library Science- Bangalore, 2002.
5. Kim, Seonghee- The Role of Knowledge Professionals for Knowledge Management: Libraries in the Information Society - Ed by- V.Ershova, Tatiana and E.Hohlov, Yuri-IFLA Publications 102- KG.Saur.
6. Michael Polanyi, *The Tacit Dimension* (New York, Doubleday, 1966), p. 4.
7. M. David Merrill 'Knowledge Objects' *CBT Solutions* Mar/Apr 1998.

8. Richard Close and James Li, 'White Paper: The promise of e-Learning and the practice of knowledge System Design' (Irvine, California: Leading way Corporation, 2000) p.5.

9. "Knowledge management Application in Libraries and Information Centers - Pramod Kumar Singh - DRTC Project-2, 1999-2001.

18

Measuring the Quality of Libraries : Role of SERVQUAL

Dr. Abdul Majeed K.C
Dr. M. Bavakutty

ABSTRACT

The face of libraries is changing day-by-day. Traditional libraries are gradually switching over to computerized libraries, digital libraries or online libraries. There is a corresponding concern over the quality of the library products and services also. More over, the funders, library authorities, users and the library and information professionals demand service quality in every respect. Here comes the relevance of SERVQUAL, a tool for measuring service quality of products, services and service organizations. This paper discusses the SERVQUAL tool in detail and mentions the other tools such as LibQUAL, WebQUAL, DigQUAL etc developed. LibQUAL is the modified SERVQUAL tool suited to measure the service quality of library and information centers. Similarly the WebQUAL can be modified to suit to measure the service quality of library websites. DigQUAL is yet to be developed for measuring the service quality of digital libraries.

1. INTRODUCTION

Libraries and information centers are service organizations charged with the responsibility of providing different information services based on collection of suitable resources. It contains tangible assets namely library building, furniture, equipment, information resources and staff, and intangible information services. The tangible assets and intangible services of libraries are changing greatly due to the developments and changes in the area of Science and Technology, especially in Information Communication Technology and Computer Technology. Application of information and computer technology gives new faces to libraries. There are libraries functioning in traditional, computerized, digital and online environments. It gives rise to new terminologies such as traditional libraries, computerized libraries, digital libraries, online libraries or virtual libraries etc. Traditional libraries are gradually switching over to computerized, digital or online libraries. Future libraries are expected to be computerized, digital or online that may face many threats such as the Internet, private lending libraries, commercial and non-commercial information products and services, escalating price of information sources, budget cut, competition from other libraries and information centers, etc. Existence will be the prime motto of future libraries and here comes the concern for quality. Libraries offering quality services will survive the threats of the day.

Quality is an elusive term that cannot be defined precisely. It changes according to the person or institution dealing it. It is a serious matter to every body that pays something to a product or service. It is not a serious matter when the product or service is provided free of charge. In the field of library and information service the concept of quality is not seriously considered due to many reasons. It may be due to either the free nature of service or its specific nature of non-measurability. But there are glimpses of changes in the outlook of library authorities and professionals in this regard. Special libraries have already started to discuss quality and many of them have acquired ISO Quality Certification also. However quality is less considered in Public and Academic Libraries with certain exceptions. It is a serious matter to the *funders, users, parent body* and *library and information professionals* of these days. Therefore, the concept of quality is seriously discussed than before.

Quality of a library can be perceived either from the organizational level or user level or both. The level of perception of the organization may be different from that of users. The organization may perceive its services very high than the level perceived by the actual users. Modern service organizations believe that customers are the apt judge for deciding the quality of the products and services marketed. As the library stands for the benefit of the users it is important and relevant to assess the quality of the library through the eyes of the users. SERVQUAL is an internationally recognized tool used in marketing research to assess the quality of products and services based on customer expectations and perceptions. Here comes the role of SERVQUAL in measuring the service quality of future libraries.

2. SERVQUAL

SERVQUAL is a multiple item scale for measuring customer perceptions of service quality and not a tool for improving service quality. It is based on the premise that service quality is the difference between customers' expectations and their perceptions of the service received. It was developed by Parasuraman et al, a marketing research team, in 1985[1] and further modified in 1988[2], 1991[3] and in 1994[4].

SERVQUAL enables an organization to compare expectations and perceptions of customers' overtime. The SERVQUAL scores can be compared with the scores of competitors and understand the service quality of the organization with other similar organizations. It can be used to understand the category of customers who are regular customers for a long period.

SERVQUAL instrument uses 22 pairs of 7-point Likert scale statements to measure the five dimensions of service quality, namely *Tangibles, Reliability, Responsiveness, Assurance* and *Empathy*. The first 22 statements are designed to measure customer expectations while the next 22 are intended to measure the perceived level of service provided by a particular service firm. The level of service quality is determined by subtracting the perceived service score from the customers' expectation score for each of the statement.

The twenty-two statements used to show the expectations in SERVQUAL are: (E stands for Expectations)

E1. They should have up-to-date equipment

E2. Their physical facilities should be visually appealing

E3. Their employees should be well dressed

E4. The appearance of the physical facilities of these firms should be in keeping with the type of services provided

E5. When these firms promise to do some thing by a certain time, they should do so

E6. When customers have problems, these firms should be sympathetic and reassuring

E7. These firms should be dependable

E8. They should provide their services at the time they promised to do

E9. They should keep their records accurately

E10. They should not be expected to tell customers exactly when services would be performed

E11. It is not realistic for customers to expert prompt service from employees of these firms

E12. Their employees do not always have to be willing to help customers

E13. It is okay if they are too busy to respond to customer requests promptly

E14. Customers should be able to trust employees of these firms

E15. Customers should be able to feel safe in their transaction with these firms' employees

E16. Their employees should be polite

E17. Their employees should get adequate support from these firms to do their jobs well

E18. These firms should not be expected to give customers individual attention

E19. Employees of these firms cannot be expected to give customers personal attention

E20. It is unrealistic to expect employees to know what the needs of their customers are

E21. Employees of these firms know what the best interests of their customers are

E22. They should not be expected to have operating hours convenient to all their customers.

The other twenty-two statements used to assess the customer perceptions about a service are (P stands for Perception):

P1. My firm has up-to-date equipment

P2. My firm's physical facilities are visually appealing

P3. My firm's employees are well dressed and appear neat

P4. The physical appearance of the physical facilities of my firm is in keeping with the type of services provided

P5. When my firm promises to do something by a certain time, it does so

P6. When I have problems, my firm is sympathetic and reassuring

P7. My firm is dependable

P8. My firm provides its services at the time it promises to do

P9. My firm keeps its records accurately

P10. My firm does not tell customers exactly when services will be performed

P11. I do not receive prompt service from my firm's employees

P12. Employees of my firm are not always willing to help customers

P13. Employees of my firm are too busy to respond to customer requests promptly

P14. I can trust employees of my firm

P15. I feel safe in my transaction with my firms' employees

P16. employees of my firm are polite

P17. Employees get adequate support from my firm to do their jobs well

P18. My firm does not give me individual attention

P19. Employees of my firm do not give me personal attention

P20. Employees of my firm do not know what my needs are

P21. My firm does not have my best interests at heart

P22. My firm does not have operating hours convenient to all the customers.

In SERVQUAL, the service quality is measured with the help of the following formula.

$$Q = P - E$$

Where **Q** is the Service Quality

P is the Customer's Perception of the delivered service

E is the Customer's Expectations of the service

Parasuraman et al, the devisers of SERVQUAL, have suggested that the instrument can be modified to suit the specific service environment of an organization. Accordingly, many researchers have used this tool with modifications to measure the service quality of different kinds of service organizations or services including library service quality. Niteki (1996)[5], Hernon and Calvert (1996)[6], Niteki and Hernon (2000)[7], Abdul Majeed and Bavakutty[8] etc. had used this tool to assess the quality of library resources and services. LibQUAL, a tool for measuring library service quality, and WebQUAL, a tool for measuring the service quality of websites, are developed from SERVQUAL.

3. LIBQUAL

On the line of SERVQUAL, the Association of Research Libraries (ARL), United States has already developed a specific tool, called LibQUAL[9], for measuring the quality of their member libraries. For the last few years, ARL is forcing its member libraries to measure their service quality using LibQUAL tool available online. Every year LibQUAL tool is revised to accommodate modern library products, services and facilities. It is a clear evidence of using SERVQUAL to measure the quality of computerized, digital or online member libraries of ARL.

The LibQUAL tool contains twenty-five statements grouped in to four service quality determinants/ dimensions, namely *Access to information, Affect of service, Library as place* and *Personal control* and use a 9-point Likert scale to mark user responses. These statements are:

1. Willingness to help users
2. Space that facilitates quiet study
3. Complete runs of journal titles

4. Employees who are consistently courteous
5. Making electronic resources accessible from my home or office
6. Modern equipment that lets me easily access the information I need
7. A library website enabling me to locate information on my own
8. Timely document delivery/interlibrary loan
9. Interdisciplinary library needs being addressed
10. A haven for quiet and solitude
11. Dependability in handling users' service problems
12. Easy-to-use access tools that allow me to find things on my own
13. A place for reflection and creativity
14. Giving users individual attention
15. Employees who deal with users in a caring fashion
16. Making information easily accessible for independent use
17. Employees who have the knowledge to answer user questions
18. Readiness to respond to users' questions
19. Convenient business hours
20. Employees who instill confidence in users
21. A comfortable and inviting location
22. Comprehensive print collections
23. A contemplative environment
24. Employees who understand the needs of their users
25. Convenient access to library collections

4. WEBQUAL

Similarly the British Broadcasting Corporation (BBC),

United Kingdom has developed a tool, called WebQUAL[10], for measuring the service quality of their news websites. It contains dimensions as well as statements and the quality of the website is measured by matching the user expectations and perceptions as in SERVQUAL and LibQUAL. WebQUAL can be modified to measure the quality of digital libraries and library websites. The BBC[11] has assessed the quality of its news website using 12 statements grouped under 3 quality determinants, namely *information quality, site quality* and *user quality*. These statements are:

1. Website has an appropriate appearance
2. Website provides accurate information
3. Website provides up to date information
4. Website provides relevant information
5. Website provides information which is easy to understand
6. Website provides the right level of details
7. Website provides fast navigation to what I intend to find
8. Website provides navigation which is free from errors
9. It is easy to find my way around and return to
10. It has content designed and selected for mobility
11. It has content which creates a sense of user community
12. It has interesting content.

The quality of information in a database/digital library or website can be assessed considering: accuracy; precision; currency; timeliness; reliability; completeness; volume; format and relevance. Besides, confidence/security of data; convenience of access; language; understanding; utility and integration can also be used for the purpose. It will help the library and information professionals to device a suitable for measuring the quality of digital libraries separately.

5. CONCLUSION

The above discussions show that SERVQUAL is a good tool for measuring the quality of traditional libraries, computerized libraries, digital libraries, online libraries and library websites. Those library and information professionals who are interested to measure the service quality of a library of tomorrow can modify the SERVQUAL, LibQUAL or WebQUAL and develop a similar one that is suited to their library. Now ARL is in the process of developing a specific tool for measuring the quality of Digital Libraries, called DigQUAL.

REFERENCE

1. Parasuraman, A et al, 'A conceptual model of service quality and its implications in future research', *Journal of Marketing*, 49, Fall 1985, p41-50.
2. Parasuraman, A. et al. 'SERVQUAL: a multiple item scale for measuring consumer perceptions of service quality', *Journal of Retailing*, 64, (1), 1988, p12-40.
3. Parasuraman, A et al, 'Refinement and reassessment of the SERVQUAL scale', *Journal of Retailing*, 67, (4), Winter 1991, p420-450.
4. Parasuraman, A et al. 'Alternative scales for measuring service quality: a comparative assessment based on psychometric and diagnostic criteria', *Journal of Retailing*, 70, (3), 1994. p201-230.
5. Nitecki, D.A. 'Changing the concept and measure of service quality in academic libraries'. *Journal of Academic Librarianship*. 22(3), 1996. p181-190.
6. Hernon, Peter and Calvert, P.J. 'Methods for measuring service quality in university libraries in New Zealand'. *Journal of Academic Librarianship*. 22(5), 1996. p387-391
7. Nitecki, Danuta. et al. 'Measuring service quality in Yale University's Libraries'. *Journal of Academic Librarianship*. 26(4), 2000. p259-273.
8. Abdul Majeed, K.C. and Bavakutty, M. Assessing the quality of information sources and information services in academic libraries. In *Information Access, Management and Exchange in Technological Age*. Ed. by Bavakutty, M *et al*. New Delhi: Ess Ess, 2002. p150-189.

9. Cook, Colleen and Heath, Fred M. 'SERVQUAL and the Quest for New Measures'. *ARL Newsletter*. 207, 1999. p12-13.

10. www.webqual.co.uk

11. Barnes, Stuart J and Vidgen, Richard T. 'Assessing the Quality of WAP News Sites: The WebQual/M Method'. *Vision* (Special Issue), 2001. p81-91.

19

The Best Practices in the College Libraries : An Evaluation

Dr. T P O Nasirudheen

ABSTRACT

A study was conducted to assess the adoption of the best practices in library and information services in the affiliated colleges in Kerala in accordance with the 'Guidelines on Quality Indicators in Library and Information Services in the Affiliated Colleges' – benchmarked by the NAAC for the effective and quality information services rendered by the college libraries in India. A questionnaire was developed for assessing the quality practices in the college libraries under four broad areas: Management of Library and Information Services, Collection and Services to End Users, Extent of Use of Services and Use of Technology and administered to 38 college librarians under Calicut and Kannur Universities to find out how far these libraries have complied with the 'Best Practices' of the NAAC. The data are analyzed and the major findings are presented along with some suggestions for the effective implementation of these Guidelines in the affiliated colleges in Kerala.

1. INTRODUCTION

Benchmarking 'Best Practices' as a means for

continuous learning through sustainable innovation is being adopted in many fields including higher education. . A practice qualifies to a 'Best Practice' status if it resulted in high-value impact on any aspect of educational activity in an institution. A Best Practice may be innovative and be a philosophy, policy, strategy, program, process or practice that solves a problem or creates new opportunities and positively impacts on organizations. Institutional excellence is the aggregate of the best practices followed in different areas of institutional activities.[1]

The Library and Information Services of higher education institutions play a central role in enhancing the quality of academic and research environments. In today's high-tech learning environment, the library as a learning resource center is taking up increasingly more academic space and time in the life of a learner. In times ahead, this will be even more so. In general, the use of technology and innovative ideas lead to evolve best practices evolving in the library and information environment.[2]

Continual review and improvement of a current practice becomes necessary to evaluate it to the status of a best practice, more so in the present scenario of fast-paced educational innovations. There is actually a view that the best practices are 'borrowed' practices in that they already stand authenticated in an institutional context. The borrowing institution, over the years of its existence, should also strive to discover what is the best practice for it to enhance institutional effectiveness.

2. ASSESSMENT AND BEST PRACTICES

The National Assessment and Accreditation Council (NAAC) strive for quality and excellence in higher education and advocates for enhancing the role of Library and Information Services in improving the academic environment. The assessment of a library, a vital sub-unit, is a key step that integrates itself with the overall institutional evaluation and accreditation.

The NAAC has recently identified the set of Best Practices in Library and Information Services, with the help of a few case presentations from a few selected libraries of the accredited universities and colleges. This is a great initiative in promoting the libraries in identifying and sharing good or best practices that can be adopted in the Indian academic environment. The NAAC evolved the 'Guidelines on Quality Indicators in Library and Information Services of Affiliated / Constituent Colleges' in the course of deliberations on the case presentations in the Workshop on Identifying Best Practices in Library and Information Services attended by the senior academic library professionals.[3] The Quality Practices are presented under four broad areas:

1. Management of Library and Information Services
2. Collection and Services to End Users
3. Extent of Use of Services
4. Use of Technology

3. OBJECTIVE

The main objective of the study is to find out how far the affiliated college libraries in the State of Kerala have complied with the 'Guidelines on Quality Indicators in Library and Information Services of Affiliated / Constituent Colleges' as evolved by the NAAC in its process of assessment and accreditation of higher education institutions

4. METHODOLOGY

A questionnaire was developed for assessing the adoption of these quality practices in the college libraries in Kerala and administered to 38 college librarians under Calicut and Kannur Universities to find out how far these libraries have complied with the 'Best Practices' of the

NAAC. The data were analyzed and the major findings are presented along with some recommendations for the effective implementation of these Guidelines in the affiliated / constituent colleges in Kerala. A copy of the questionnaire is appended.

A. Management of Library and Information Services

Library and Information Systems (LIS) management is the basic and core activity which helps the user community in identifying and accessing knowledge resources in an academic institution. As the management and administration of the library is pivotal in collection development and delivery of information products and services to the end users, adoption of best practices in this area leads to continuous improvement in overall performance. Identification and internalization of the best practices in the management would enhance the collection development process, services dissemination and use of the library. Active participation and periodic meetings of the library advisory committee, involvement of the librarian in academic activities of the college and university, standard facilities with innovative library buildings, regular flow of resource generation, skilled and qualified staff deployment with further training, capacity building in terms of information and communication technology, working hours, stock verification methods and technical processing methods.

It is noted that two-third of the libraries under the study do have a Library Advisory Committee (68%) and a defined policy for collection development, stock verification, promotion and training of staff (66%). More than three-fourth of the libraries (79%) have extended working hours before/ after the class hours and included sufficient information about the library in the college prospectus. It may also be noted that nearly three-fourth of the librarians (71%) have attended/participated in Orientation/Refresher courses/ workshops/seminars.

It may be observed that more than half the libraries have generally adapted the best practices with regard to the activities performed in relation to the library and information system management. But it also shows that majority of the libraries are not interested/serious in assessing the user satisfaction of the library resources provided and the library services rendered.

B. Library Collection Development

Collection development/management and information services generation are two important interrelated functions that facilitate the provision of the right information to the right user at the right time and thereby conformance to the five laws of Library Science is ensured. A well-defined collection development policy is to be formulated taking into consideration factors such as users and their informational requirements, subject boundaries to be covered by the information sources, documentary and non-documentary sources to be covered, methods of procurement, forms of materials to be collected or excluded, extent of duplication of materials etc.

Nevertheless, technology is changing how we collect, store and access materials. The future for libraries therefore lies in a policy of access rather than ownership, as most material will be in electronic form in future and due to economic grounds. Best practices in collection development would include a well-defined collection development policy that ensures access to peer-reviewed journals procured by individuals and a consortia approach as well as networked access to documents of all types available in other academic libraries through inter-institutional cooperation; and a well thought of weeding policy in the libraries so as to maintain an active balanced collection.

Besides print documents in their stock the respondent libraries do have a good collection of electronic information resources. But it is noted that while majority of libraries (71%) do have CDs/DVDs in their collection only one-fourth of the libraries (24%) do have electronic databases and 16% of the libraries have online journals. It may also be noted that majority of libraries (63%) provide career information to the end users for competitive examinations. While more than half the number of libraries develops collection with special materials such as audio-visual materials (58%) and book bank (50%), only 18% of libraries have rare materials. But no library has taken into consideration the needs of blind users as none of the libraries have Braille materials in their collection.

B2. Information Services to End Users

The library/information center should provide appropriate services geared to the different requirements of different user groups' students, teachers, researchers, etc. in the academic libraries. The end users will want approaches that are user-focused and will demand for customization, interactivity and excellent support. Interactive and interconnected services will be most valued. Hence collaboration among all types of libraries could lead to now solutions and now services that best address the changing needs of users. A variety of services ranging from reference to electronic information services have to be delivered both, in anticipation and on demand. Information analysis and consolidation services, appropriate orientation and information literacy training programmes, and service for the un-reached segments would be the order of the day.

A lion's majority of the libraries surveyed (95%) provide reference service to their end users. On the other hand only half the number of libraries (47%) renders referral service. It may be interesting to note that while only one-fifth of the libraries (21%) compile bibliography for their users nearly two-third libraries provide newspaper-clipping service (61%) and current awareness service (68%). More than four-fifth of the libraries (82%) display new arrivals/

notification and two-third libraries (63%) render career/ employment information services, but only one-fourth of libraries (26%) facilitate inter-library loan for their users

5. EXTENT OF THE USE OF SERVICES

Academic libraries have to play a significant role for a better and qualitative information services. The information explosion and the exponential growth of information sources require the libraries to play an increasingly significant role in evaluating resources and educating the user. New skills and approaches are required for assessing the user's specific requirements. Continuous user promotion and information literacy programmes have to be launched with novel ideas to enhance the use of library services. Besides the traditional user education and feed back of the users, there are a few user education and use measurement practices which are essential for academic libraries.

It is also significant to note that two-third libraries (66%) conduct user orientation/information literacy programme for their users and nearly half the number of libraries (42%) promote student internship/student participation in library services. It shows that a good number of libraries continue to provide the traditional library and information services.

The libraries are in low profile to provide suggestion box and timely response and to conduct user survey periodically. It may be noted that while one-third of the libraries provide suggestion box and timely response (39%) and one-fourth of the libraries conduct user surveys periodically (24%), two-third of the libraries (63%) maintain students/teachers attendance statistics

6. USE OF INFORMATION TECHNOLOGY

Information Technology (IT) has become an integral part of all aspects of the library. IT has profoundly affected library operations, information resources, services, staff skills requirements and users expectations. Today, the success of a modern library is increasingly dependent on the most effective utilization and strategic management of new technologies in libraries. It is believed that the versatility and power of IT can stand in good stead in the quest for quality and productivity in information services and products.

The college libraries in Kerala are in the forefront of computerization of in-house operation and services. A majority of the libraries (71%) have computerized their in-house jobs. While 70% of them have partially computerized, 30% libraries have fully automated their in-house jobs. Majority of them use local software for the computerization of their jobs. More than half the number of libraries provides Online Public Access Catalogue (OPAC) (58%) and Internet access (53%) to the end users for the retrieval of bibliographic information and online information.

7. SUMMARY

The study shows that majority of the libraries have computerized their in-house jobs but most of them are in the process of computerization but majority of the libraries are not interested/serious in assessing the user satisfaction of the library resources provided and the library services rendered.

It is noted that while majority of libraries do have CDs/DVDs in their collection only one-fourth of the libraries do have electronic databases and nearly one-fifth of the libraries have online journal and rare materials. But no library has taken into consideration the needs of blind users as none of the libraries have Braille materials in their collection.

It may be interesting to note that only one-fifth of the libraries compile bibliography for their users and only half the number of libraries renders referral service. It may also be noted that only one-fourth of libraries facilitate inter-library loan for their users

The libraries are in low profile to provide suggestion box and timely response and to conduct user survey periodically. It may be noted that while one-third of the libraries provide suggestion box and timely response and one-fourth of the libraries conduct user surveys periodically.

8. CONCLUSION

The college libraries in the State have started computerizing their in-house jobs and services though with local developed software in a large number of libraries. Though the overall evaluation of the college libraries in terms of their compliance to the Quality Indicators in Library and Information Service is hopeful there are a number of services and programmes in which the college libraries have to improve a lot.

The assessment and accreditation process initiated by the NAAC for the quality development of the higher education institutions in the country has started showing results in the infrastructure development of library and information system of the affiliated colleges and in the generation of quality services. But it poses new challenges for the library and information professionals and lays new responsibilities on them in the competency with other academic units of an institution.

REFERENCE

1. National Assessment and Accreditation Council. Library and Information Services: Case Presentations. Best Practice Series-2. Bangalore: NAAC, 2006. (Foreword by the Director, NAAC)
2. Ibid. p. 1
3. National Assessment and Accreditation Council. 'Guidelines on Quality Indicators in Library and Information Services of Affiliated / Constituent Colleges'. Bangalore: NAAC, 2005.

20

Librarianship in the Changing Scenario of Education

Dr. C Beena
V S Kunjumuhammed

ABSTRACT

The changing scenario of education and the new responsibilities of librarianship are discussed in this paper. The paper explores the advantages of digital libraries for e-learning. The different services offered in the web based information management system in the web based learning and teaching (E-Learning) environment is also described. How Library schools and Professional bodies can contribute to meet the new challenges of librarianship is also discussed.

1. INTRODUCTION

Technology has changed our lives in the way we cooked, the way we traveled, the way we experimented, the way we communicated. The impact of technology in our education system is very large. Higher education has undergone important paradigm shifts including the shift from teacher -centered to a student -centered learning, and the replacement of a traditional practice of learning over a specified period of time by the concept of life long learning. ICT is today playing an important role in productive and relevant learning.

The growth in e-learning, in which education is delivered and supported through computer networks such as the internet, has posed new challenges for library services. E-learners and traditional learners now have access to a universe of digital information through the information superhighway. New information and communications technologies, as well as new educational models, require librarians to re-evaluate the way they develop, manage and deliver resources and services.

Change in librarians' roles in support of e-learning in the information age appear throughout the literature: librarians "must assert themselves as key players in the learning process thereby changing their roles from information providers to educators" (Cooper and Dempsey, 1998), and they have been transformed from "information gatekeepers" to "information gateways" (Haricombe, 1998). Lippincott (2002) advocates librarian involvement in learning communities: "The librarian can shift the focus from explaining library resources to meeting the ongoing information needs of the students in the broad information environment".

2. E-LEARNING

Different terminologies have been used for e-learning, a fact that makes it difficult to develop a generic definition. Terms that are commonly used include "online learning", "internet learning", "distributed learning", "networked learning", "tele-learning", "virtual learning", "computer-assisted learning", "web-based learning", and "distance learning". All of these terms imply that the learner is at a distance from the tutor or instructor, that the learner uses some form of technology (usually a computer) to access the learning materials, that the learner uses technology to interact with the tutor or instructor and other learners, and that some form of support is provided to learners. This paper will use the term "e-learning" throughout.

3. DIGITAL LIBRARY AND E-LEARNING

In the e-learning environment, digital libraries are considered as a federation of library services and collections that function together to create a digital learning community.

3.1. Collection Development for e-learners

The range of supported materials includes, digital contents developed by the experts, class room lectures, conference reports, interactive sessions, lectures delivered by an Expert, video conferencing etc in the different formats of Text, Audio, Video, Image, such as PDF, MPEG-2, Motion JPEG, H323, MP3 etc.

3.2. Features of Digital library in E-learning

- Great Potential and Dynamic
- Easy to access, disseminate, store, retrieve, archive, copy, transmit...
- Ubiquity of the Net / Web
- Information - Any time / anywhere / anyone
- Access by a wide spectrum of Users
- Easiness of access - Plug & Play

A digital library can link e-learners to:

- Library catalogues, (OPAC)
- Licensed journal databases (E-Journals)
- Electronic book collections
- Selected internet resources
- Electronic course contents
- Reserves and tutorials
- Forums for communication
- Digital repository

Reference services offered to e-learners are:

- E-mail
- Chat technology

- Reference services using SMS
- Give links to the knowledge portals
- Download resources from the Vibrant Repository

Advantages are:

- Provide a 24x7-learning environment to supplement regular Information
- A central portal to integrate content from various sources
- A course planning and management tool
- Efficient management of course material
- Having a paper less library service
- Assignments and Tests online
- A collaborative learning environment
- Familiarize students to an IT enabled library service

Technological changes have been the dominant force reshaping library services. Instilling a culture of sharing, motivation, equity, and active partnering encourages library staff to respond positively to the changing roles, responsibilities, and skills that the integration and use of technology requires. A well-designed ongoing training program enables library staff to upgrade their skills to their new assignments, and helps them to understand and control fear of change.

4. PROGRAMS TO BUILD INSTITUTIONAL CAPACITY

- Develop or enhance curricula within graduate schools of library and information science.
- Develop or enhance courses or programs of study for library, museum, and archives professionals in the creation, management, preservation, presentation, and use of digital assets.
- Develop or enhance courses or programs of study related to the development of critical thinking skills,

such as organization leadership and research methods.

Broaden the library and information science curriculum by incorporating perspectives from other disciplines and fields of scholarship, such as, technology, Personal management, software skill, and instructional design.

4.1. Continuing Education:

- Develop or enhance programs of continuing education and training in library and information science for librarians and library staff.
- Develop or enhance programs to enable librarians and library staff to improve services to audiences with special needs such as youth at risk, seniors, and those with language, physical or other barriers to service.
- Develop or enhance programs to promote collaboration between educators and librarians employed in educational institutions.

5. CONCLUSIONS

In summary, digital library services are an essential component of a quality e-learning system. As access to internet-based courses grows, an increasing number of e-learners are dispersed around the globe, often in parts of the world where physical access to the collections of large academic and research libraries is impossible. These learners are largely dependent on the quality and academic usefulness of services that the digital library can offer. The strength of digital libraries and digital collections depends on the relationships that the libraries develop and maintain with the creators, publishers, and aggregators of e-resources, as well as with those who use, learn from, and evaluate these resources. Providing ongoing technical, reference, and instructional support to e-learners requires that libraries redefine their values and services, collaborate with their users, and approach their tasks creatively.

REFERENCE

1. Cooper, R. and Dempsey, P.R. (1998), "Remote library users; needs and expectations", Library Trends, Vol. 47, No. 1, pp. 42-64.
2. Haricombe, L.J. (1998), "Introduction to Library Trends", Vol. 47, No. 1, pp. 1-5.
3. Hemlata Talesra, Wasef, Marashdeh and M.L Nagda, 2005, Web based learning, Authors press.
4. Lippincott, J.K. (2002), "Developing collaborative relationships: librarians, students, and faculty creating learning communities", College Research Libraries News, Vol. 63 No. 3, pp. 190-2.
5. Marc J Rosenberg 2003, "E-learning; strategies for delivering knowledge in the digital Age", McGraw Hill, New York.

21

Tacit Knowledge Organization Methods and Techniques for Future Librarianship

Mehaboobullah. K
Abdul Gafoor Manningachali

ABSTRACT

Knowledge can be divided in to two broad categories i.e., Explicit knowledge and Tacit knowledge. Traditional librarianship was mainly concentrating on the organization and dissemination of explicit or codified knowledge since it is highly structured. Even now, the organization and dissemination of tacit knowledge was unexplored by the library community. Tacit knowledge is the personal knowledge used by individuals to perform their work and to make sense of their worlds. It is learned through extended periods of experience and doing a task during which the individual develops a feel for, and a capacity to make intuitive judgment about the successful execution of the activity. Valuable knowledge acquired by the organization overtime can be lost through the exit of experienced staff. The difficulty of retaining knowledge lies in the fact that part of the knowledge is tacit in nature and is highly, if not totally, inarticulate. Since we are living in knowledge based competitive society, the exploration of tacit knowledge is highly significant and rewarding. In this context, the paper deals with the various approaches and techniques for managing tacit knowledge for future librarianship. It also explains knowledge transfer process, role of librarian in managing tacit knowledge and various methods and techniques of tacit knowledge conversion.

1. INTRODUCTION

Tacit knowledge refers to the undocumented and unarticulated (but nevertheless important) knowledge held by practitioners of a profession or work. It is also known as "inarticulate intelligence," "collective wisdom," or "elusive knowledge." The phrase "tacit knowledge" was coined by Polanyi (1966), an influential philosopher of epistemology, but in recent years it has been used by management theorists as a key piece in the process of knowledge management. Tacit knowledge is contrasted with explicit knowledge, which is expressed knowledge that is communicated to others. When explicit knowledge is documented, it becomes "codified." Codified knowledge is usually quite structured and appears in written reports, databases, and other media. Conversion of tacit knowledge in to explicit knowledge is one of the upcoming challenges of future librarianship.

2. KNOWLEDGE: EXPLICIT AND TACIT

Knowledge can be divided into two categories, Explicit Knowledge and Tacit Knowledge.

2.1. Explicit Knowledge

Explicit knowledge is systematically documented knowledge in any kind of format, which guides the users to gain the knowledge and to expand the base further. It is articulated knowledge. The word we speak, the book we read, the reports we write, and the data we compile are explicit knowledge. Explicit knowledge is objective, rational and technical. It is a rule-based knowledge.

2.2. Tacit Knowledge

Tacit knowledge is the " know how" acquires by persons. It is presented in intuitions, emotions, values and beliefs. It is the knowledge acquired and possessed by a person through his/her experience, which cannot be easily articulated. All information that goes unrecorded like the values inside and the judgment is stored with the individual falls in the category of tacit knowledge. Tacit knowledge is subjective, cognitive and experimental in nature. Tacit knowledge may exist in any of the two forms:

Embodied Knowledge : The knowledge, which cannot be detached from its knower, is known as embodied knowledge. It is difficult to articulate.

Embedded Knowledge : The Tacit knowledge, which resides in the things created by individual may be known as embedded knowledge. It may reside in the product as well as in process.

3. NEED AND IMPORTANCE OF ARTICULATING TACIT KNOWLEDGE

There are many reasons why articulating tacit knowledge (making it explicit and codifying it) is crucial to the success of any organization. Organization of tacit knowledge saves organization in wasting its money and energy for solving same problems over and over. If the tacit knowledge is converted in to explicit, the "owner" of a particular piece of tacit knowledge does not have to be present and available in order to share this information. Once tacit knowledge is converted to explicit knowledge, the organization is in less danger of losing its "knowledge capital" when employees leave the organization. Explicit knowledge gives permanence to previously impermanent knowledge, and it can more easily be shared, stored, combined, and manipulated in a variety of ways.

Information is more easily accessible when tacit

knowledge has been converted to explicit knowledge. It helps different parts of the organization communicate with each other more easily, and it promotes competence and efficiency in individual employees. The purpose of the codification of tacit knowledge is not simply to facilitate retrieval of information, although this certainly is important. Beyond access, however, is the reuse of knowledge in new ways that entails reflection, criticism, learning, and ultimately the creation of new knowledge than had previously existed.

4. THE KNOWLEDGE SCHEMA

The knowledge scheme consists of various elements, namely, linguistic, formal, professional, societal and the know-x. These categorizations are not mutually exclusive; however, they are distinct. This schema acts as a tool and guideline to map various types of knowledge existing in individuals and organization. Descriptions of these categories are given in the following Figure.

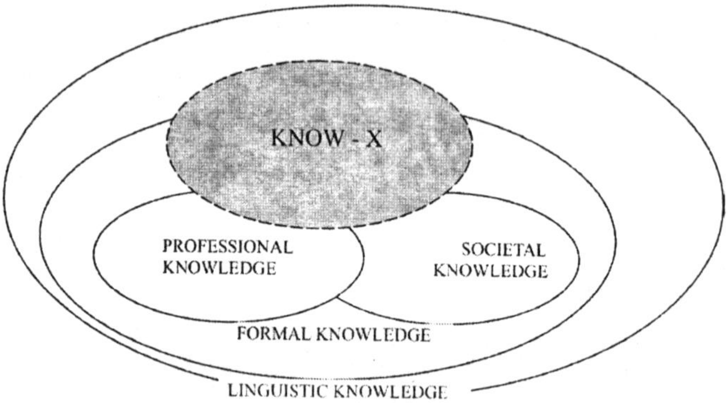

Fig.1. Knowledge Schema

4.1. Linguistic Knowledge

Knowledge of a language (English, French, Japanese, etc.) is essential for communication. A command of the language is required for the extraction of information contained in books, technical manuals, catalogues and the like, and to communicate to others.

4.2. Formal Knowledge

This is the knowledge that is acquired and learned in the classroom, library or laboratory during the individual's formal education programme.

4.3. Professional Knowledge

Knowledge that is required when carrying out the duty of a particular position in an organization can be regarded as the professional knowledge. Usually, this is learned progressively from the time a person takes up a position in an organization.

4.4. Societal Knowledge

Societal knowledge includes the awareness of the individual about the various levels of societal impact of the knowledge in application. Knowledge picked up in the daily life outside the classroom also forms part of the societal knowledge. All the societal knowledge is acquired partly on the job and partly from life experience, augmented by formal knowledge.

4.5. Know-x

The knowledge of what information/knowledge to be used where and when, why the particular information/knowledge is used and how it can be applied to achieve the design objectives is referred to as 'know-x'. The 'x' represents the 'what', 'where', 'when', 'why', 'who' 'which' and 'how' that are imposed on the design tasks by their objectives. Articulation of know-X is more challenging as well as fruitful in a highly competitive knowledge society.

5. CHARACTERISTICS OF TACIT KNOWLEDGE

Tacit knowledge possesses certain properties or characteristics that cause it to be extremely difficult, if not impossible, to articulate. It includes:

Judgment facilitating : This refers to the capability of tacit knowledge in the formation of an opinion about completion of certain task.

Estimation and envisioning capability : This is regarded as the provisioning of the best guess in certain situations. This requires the envisioning ability of foreseeing the potential problems and realizing possible outcomes if certain measures were to be instituted.

Physical maneuvering : This involves physical body movement and co-ordination. Preparing sketches, controlling hand or machine tools and so on are tasks that require tacit knowledge to control the body to move at the right time, with the appropriate amount and along the proper orientation in order to achieve the task.

Efficiency enhancing : This knowledge means the understanding developed from old experience about the sorting out of some kinds of problem in more efficient fashion and with less time because of the possession of knowledge in the learned in the previous exposure.

Image formation and recognition : Image recognition is a state of mind that utilizes inarticulatable knowledge. example of 'somebody can recognize a face among a thousand, or million, but cannot tell how he recognizes it' illustrates the tacit characteristics of the knowledge concerned. As a result, tacit knowledge is in action when we need to formulate or recognize images.

Handling of human relationships : This concerns the knowledge used in dealing with people and the realization of human factors in various circumstances.

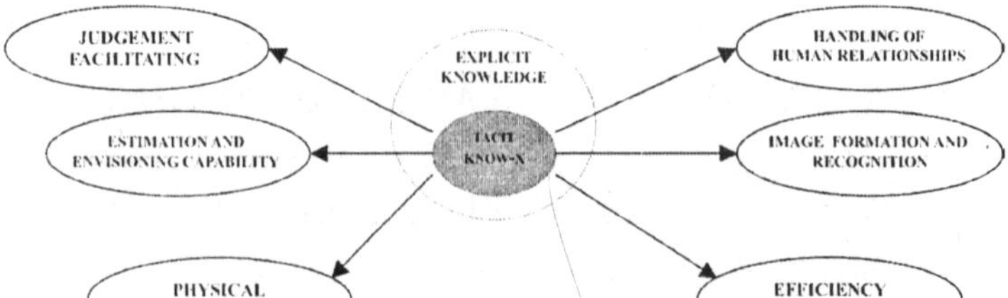

Fig. 2. Characteristics of Tacit Knowledge

6. KNOWLEDGE CONVERSION PROCESS

The knowledge transfer process including the following sequence of steps:

1. Tacit to tacit (often called "socialization," which occurs through apprenticeship, mentoring, or collegial relations; this step has also been described as "implicit learning" or "learning by doing").
2. Tacit to explicit (often called "externalization" or "articulation;" this step includes knowledge that is usually written down or communicated in some permanent or semi-permanent way; stories, narrative, multi-media presentations, group reflection, conversations, e-mails, and memos are all examples of this type of knowledge transfer).
3. Explicit to explicit (often called "combination," usually through a standardized and systematic procedure; an example would be a computer database or an expert system).
4. Explicit to tacit (often called "internalization," which results in the distribution of knowledge throughout the organization and beyond; this often comes through active participation and repetition).

7. METHODS AND WAYS TO ENCOURAGE KNOWLEDGE CONVERSION (TACIT TO EXPLICIT)

In the above discussed knowledge transfer process tacit to explicit is more difficult and complex. There are several ways to encourage knowledge conversion within an organization. One method of promoting knowledge transformation is to engage employees in "reflexive practice," which is "the activity of thinking about one's own actions and analyzing them in a critical manner, with the purpose of improving a professional practice".

Formal interviews are a useful method of making tacit

knowledge explicit. Outside observers can assist in the knowledge conversion process by asking employees a series of structured questions.

Interaction with others, as opposed to isolation, is important if knowledge conversion is to take place. A psychologically healthy environment is crucial to a successful knowledge conversion program. An obvious prerequisite to successfully formalizing tacit knowledge is identifying who the people are who have the tacit knowledge.

According to knowledge management theorists there are generally three separate but related steps in codifying knowledge once it has been made explicit. First, the organization should create "warehouses" of explicit knowledge, a process known as internal codification. These materials can be collections of paper documents, links to Web pages, rough drafts in electronic form, e-mail messages, or notes from discussions or interviews. Second, the organization should create mechanisms that will refine the collected explicit knowledge, extract valuable content, and turn it into a more usable form. This step will add value to the knowledge through a taxonomy that will include controlled vocabulary and appropriate cross-referencing. Third, the organization must provide for appropriate technologies that will support this entire process. This "delivery platform" must be able to push and pull content (through subscriptions and through searchable databases) for various groups in the organization. These three steps turn raw knowledge into refined knowledge. Developing databases of experts and timely revision of the same using the application of modern Information and Communication Technology (ICT) also promote the conversion of tacit knowledge in to explicit one.

8. BARRIERS TO KNOWLEDGE ARTICULATION

There are a number of difficulties in making tacit

knowledge explicit. Tacit knowledge is both complex and subjective. It is often embedded in an individual's intuitive personal experience, and thus is hard to formalize or communicate. It is almost impossible to observe or measure tacit knowledge, since it is in "the realm of the non-expressed". In addition, there are often personal issues that may get in the way of articulating tacit knowledge. Employees might believe that their personal knowledge is not worth expressing. They may think that expressing their knowledge may endanger their position with the organization, either because they know too much or they do not know enough. There may be language barriers to articulating their knowledge, or they may have forgotten what they once knew .

The organizational political problems present a barrier to knowledge articulation. Sharing knowledge may not be part of the "corporate culture" of an organization. The tyranny of the local environment over the overall objectives of the organization may act as hindrance in knowledge sharing. In addition the basic nature of organizational culture i.e. informal, competitive, and ceremonial, which also form obstacle in knowledge conversion.

The process of knowledge articulation is not always a pleasant one, since sometimes-content experts are not willing to share their knowledge with others. Each individual in the organization must recognize that he/she is a stakeholder and that he/she is responsible (in some way, however small) for his/her role in the process of organizational knowledge creation.

9. CONCLUSION

The codification of knowledge has been promoted in recent years by the expanding capacities of information and communication technologies (ICTs) to assist in the accumulation, storage, processing and transmission of

.information. As a result, the current period is witnessing a strong drive to codify knowledge. The nature of tacit knowledge has attracted the interest of many researchers in various disciplines. Growing concerns have also been shown by the business and organizational sector, which realizes that tacit knowledge, plays an Important role in many business and management activities. The loss of tacit knowledge through the loss of employees becomes an alarming issue for the organization, which are keen to maintain its competitive advantage. Realizing these issues, information professionals should use modern technology for articulating tacit knowledge in to explicit one and to organize and disseminate it for uninterrupted flow of all types of knowledge. Obviously it will be the big problem and opportunity before the future librarianship.

REFERENCE

1. Polanyi, 'The Tacit Knowing', London, *Rougledge and Kegan paul*,1966
2. Myers and K.David, 'Tacit Skills and Performance at Work',*Applied Psychology an International Review*,1993.
3. A.Aurora, 'Contracting for Tacit Knowledge,The Provision of Technical services in Technology Licensing Contracts', *Journal of Developmental Economics*,1996.
4. I.Nonaka, 'A Dynamic Theory of Organisational Knowledge Creation', *Organisational Science*,1994.
5. R.W Imre, 'Tacit Knowledge in Social Work Research and Practice', *Smith College Studies in Social Work*, 1985.

22

Information Technology Based Access and Services in Libraries A Study

Amulraj S
Selvakumar R
Thenmozhi R
Sathya A

ABSTRACT

Information Communication Technology (ICT) has got strong impact on library and information services of the day. Advanced library and information services can be provided even by small libraries and rural libraries with the help of ICTs. This paper is an attempt to disclose what are the suitable tools for improving the information and service base of libraries?

1. INTRODUCTION

The development of Information Communication Technology has an impact on Libraries. The growing users demand and the technological changes have revolutionized the methods of organizing, disseminating and managing knowledge. The application of IT in the digitization of information has made digital format a viable means for scholarly communication.

The Internet acts as a platform for sharing resources, which include bibliographical and full text databases, directories, table of content journals, reports, data archives, newsgroups, library catalogues etc.,

2. INFORMATION RETRIEVAL

A typical digital library implementation may employ variety of information retrieval techniques including Meta data searching, full text searching and content searching or combination of two of all of them. Information retrieval is made more effective and user's friendly by preprocessing digital document to extracts additional metadata before storing them in a database. The database is then configured to generate indices from selected fields including authors, titles, abstracts, etc., or may also be configured to generate indices from the full text articles with a predefined stop work list.

An effective and efficient access mechanism that allows a user to browse, search and navigation digital resources becomes necessary as electronics resources of a collection grow in number and complexion. The access and services infrastructure for a digital resource consists of webOPACs, multi webOPACs for library catalogues, specialized collection web sites for specialized image-based local collection, portals or subject gateways for web resources, Institutional Repository and a search and browse interface for local collections.

3. SEARCH AND BROWSING INTERFACES

The search interface provides a visual window for users to search relevant information stores in a digital resource. Designing interfaces for digital resources involve use of principles and practices of information management with rapidly evolving technological developments. The interfaces should maximize the interaction with information resources and minimize the attention to the system itself. Moreover, a web-based interface should support both browsing and searching strategies.

Some of the important features that most digital library implementations provide in their search interfaces include

1. Distinct option for browsing / Searching the digital contents;
2. Searching the digital library contents with one or more of the following restriction provided as radio buttons / section boxes / combination boxes:
   - Range in terms of number of yeas;
   - A predefined collections / category of documents or all documents;
   - Searching a given digital library or search the Internet for a given subject;
   - Select maximum number or hits desired; and
   - Sort results (by author, title Journals, etc.)

4. MULTIMEDIA PRESENTATION SERVICE

- Audio Video Presentation

5. MODIFIED WEB BASED LIBRARY SERVICES

- OPAC to Web OPAC
- CDROM to Web databases
- Manual to Digital reference service
- Manual to real-time digital
- Reference service
- Manual to Electronic
- Document Delivery Service

6. NET / WEB-BASED LIBRARY SERVICES

- Virtual Library Tours
- Library Web Sites
- Library Portals

- Web-based user Education
- FAQ
- Library Calendar
- Web forms
- Bulletin Boards, Discussion forum and List serves

7. DOCUMENTARY SERVICES

Some of the important Electronic Document Delivery Services

Uncover	http://uncweb.carl.org/uncover/subtitle.html
Articles in Physics	http://ojps.aip.org/
Bio-line Publication	http://bioline.bdt.org.br/journals
Bio-Medicine Net	http://biomednet.com/lobrary/
Chemport	http://www.chemport.org/
Science Direct	http://www.sciencedirect.com/
OCLC	www.oclc.org/
Northern Light	www.northernlight.com/

8. VIRTUAL LIBRARY TOURS

Several library web sites facilitate virtual guide to the physical facilities including collections, services and infrastructure available in the library through their web sites. The combination of the following three web-based interfaces are used to facilitate the virtual library tours.

- Library Maps and floor plans
- Library departments /Units/Services/facilities
- Photographic views

9. LIBRARY WEBSITES

Academic libraries in developed countries started using web technology to create home pages as starting points or as gateways for searching information about the library.

A home page reflects characteristics of an academic institution. It provides an opportunity to the library to propagate its services and facilities to the academic community worldwide. The home page of libraries are increasingly used as an integrated interfaces designed to deliver detailed information about a library as well as to provides access to all computer-based services offered by a library.

10. SUBJECT GATEWAYS OR LIBRARY PORTALS

A subject gateway can be defined as facility that allows easier access to web-based resources in a defined subject area. The simplest type of subject gateway is sets of web pages containing list of links to resources. Some gateways index their lists of links and provide a simple search facility. More advanced gateways offer a much-enhanced service via a system consisting of a resource database and various indexes, which can be searched and / or browse throughout a web-based interface.

Subject gateways are also known as Subject-based Information Gateways (SBIGs), subject -based gateways, subject index gateways, virtual libraries, clearing houses, subject trees pathfinders and other variants thereof. Subject gateway is an important component of a library web site designed for the library users so as to help them discover high-quality information on the Internet in a quick and effective.

Some of the Major portal sites or gateways that provide access to electronic resources on the Internet are as follows:

WWW Virtual Library http://www.edoc.com/

Internet Public library http://www.ipl.org/

Michigan Electronic Library http://mel.lib.mi.us/

Penn Electronic library http://www.library.upenn.edu/resources/

BUBL Information Service http://bubl.ac.uk/

Argus Clearing House http://www.clearingghouse.net/

Internet Index http://sunsite.berkeley.edu/internetindex/

12. FREQUENTLY ASKED QUESTIONS (FAQ)

Most library web sites have FAQ along with their answers. Some libraries have databases-driven FAQs along with search interface. These FAQs are generally on the services and facilities that the library provides. These FAQ generally do not include reference questions.

13. LIBRARY CALENDAR

The library calendar lists events or show information for forthcoming events. Library calendars have improved look and functionality with JavaScript or special software.

14. CURRENT AWARENESS SERVICE

The following services are provided electronically apart from the manual service:

- Daily received of journals list and Latest Issues of journals are being putting on Library Home page on daily basis.
- Daily received of Preprint/Reprint is putting on Library Homepage.
- List of IUCAA preprints. IUCAA Publication, thesis, CD-ROMS, Audio/video are being put on library homepage for user information.

15. NETWORK BASED SERVICES AND ITS USERS

- E-Mail
- WEBS access service to users
- Content page service to remote users
- Web services based on Library homepage

16. INSTITUTIONAL REPOSITORY SERVICES

Archiving facility for the research community is one of the new services, using the GNU EPrints or software developed at the University of Southampton or dpace. This service enables the Institute community to archive their preprints, post prints and other scholarly publications. In keeping with the objectives of the EPrints movement and the Free Online Scholarship (FOS) movement, we expect this service to facilitate the Institute researchers in self-archiving and long-term preservation of their scholarly publications, provide easy access to these publications world wide and improve impact of their research.

17. ELECTRONIC THESES AND DISSERTATIONS

This service facilitates the research community to self archive their theses and dissertations. The service has been set up using DSpace, a BSD distributed licensed open source software, developed jointly by the MIT Libraries and Hewlett-Packard (HP). This service complements the self-archiving service for research publications.

18. CONCLUSION

One of the biggest technological events of the last two decades was the invasion of digital media in an entire range of everyday activities. The libraries also have stocked the digital audio/video image and multimedia documents. These digital data can be transmitted in a fast and inexpensive way through data communication network. The digital libraries of these days are network-based distributed systems, with individual servers responsible for maintaining local collections of digital documents. The electronic libraries help to expend access, increase usability and effectiveness and establish new ways for the individuals to interact with information.

An effective and efficient access mechanism that allows

a user to browse, search and navigate digital resources becomes necessary as electronic resources of a collection grow in number and complexion. The access service infrastructure for a digital resource consists of Web OPACs, multi web OPACs for library catalogues, specialized collection web sites for specialized image-based local collection, portals or subject gateways for web resources, Electronic theses and dissertations, open archives in provide efficient services to user community for local collections.

REFERENCE

1. Jagdish, Arora (2001). Web-based digital resources and services: Trends and Innovations. CALIBER-2001. Pune: 185-211.
2. http://gateway.lib.ed.ac.uk/
3. http://www.google.co.in/search?hl=en&q=new+Technology+services+in+libraries&meta

23

Information and Knowledge Management

Babita Garg
Salek Chand

ABSTRACT

Information management and knowledge management is a matter of discussion among library and information professionals. They are the combinations of many subjects including library and information science. This paper is discussing these two managements in detail

1. INTRODUCTION

Information management has been around for more than two decades. Many authors date its beginning back to the Paperwork Reduction Act of 1980 in which U.S. federal agencies were forced to introduce information resource management. Regardless of its exact origins, there was a substantial growth in literature dealing with this topic at the beginning of the eighties. In the second half of the nineties, the term knowledge management became more popular and majority of Information professionals have been changing their working culture from information management to knowledge management.

2. WHAT IS "INFORMATION MANAGEMENT"?

This interdisciplinary field draws on and combines skills and resources from librarianship and information science, information technology, records management, archives and general management. Its focus is information as a resource, independently of the physical form in which it occurs. Books and periodicals, data stored on local or remote computers, microforms, audio-visual media and the information in people's heads are all within its scope. Some of the main topics practitioners are concerned with are:

- classification and coding
- subject indexing
- construction and use of thesauri and controlled vocabularies
- cataloguing and indexing by names, places, and events
- database design and data structures
- physical storage of books and records, in paper and electronic form
- storage of photographic and digitized images
- information audits: reviews of an organization's information resources
- documentation of museum objects, both for management purposes and as a resource for scholarship.

"Information Management describes the means by which an organization efficiently plans, collects, organizes, uses, controls, disseminates and disposes of its information, and through which it ensures that the value of that information is identified and exploited to the fullest extent." As quoted by Barbara Laffan.

According to the above definition, the word Information Management is a very broad term which consist many interrelated terms and it is not possible to know the clear concept of Information Management without knowing these terms. These terms are:-

Library management system (LMS) : Library management systems provide a complete solution for the administration all of a library's technical functions and services to the public. This ranges from tracking the assets held by the library, managing lending, through to supporting the daily administrative activities of the library.

Digital imaging system : Digital imaging systems automate the creation of electronic versions of paper documents (such as PDFs or TIFFs) and are used as an input to records management systems. By creating electronic resources, they can be manipulated directly by the records system, eliminating the need for physical filing.

Learning management system (LMS) : Learning management systems automate the administration of training and other learning. This includes registering students, managing training resources, recording results, and general course administration. Learning management systems are designed to meet the entire needs of professional trainers and other educators.

Learning content management system (LCMS) : Learning content management systems combine the capabilities of a content management system (CMS) with that of a learning management system (LMS). This allows them to manage both the content of the training materials, and the administration of the course itself.

Information Management basically divided in to two types. One is Technology-Oriented Information Management and another is Content-Oriented Information Management.

Technology-oriented information management : The general purpose of information management is to make available the right information at the right time and at the right place. For technology-oriented information management, computer-based information systems are the primary means to this end. Information management from this angle stresses the importance of information technologies. This is justified by the high degree of IT integration, the complexity of its application, and its strong consequences for an organization.

Within technology-oriented information management, the following aspects can be distinguished:

- Data management,
- IT management, and
- Strategic use of IT.

Data management

Data management can be defined as all organizational and technical tasks concerning the planning, storage, and provision of data, both for computer personnel and end-users). Its goal is to maximize the quality, usability, and value of the data resources in an enterprise. In the literature, often two components are suggested for data management: data administration and database administration). Data administration primarily serves a planning and analysis function. It may be responsible for data planning, accountability, policy development, standards setting, and support. One of the major tasks includes the design of the data architecture of an organization. Database administration provides a framework for managing the data on an operational level. Its role may include performance monitoring, troubleshooting, security monitoring, physical database design, and data backup.

IT Management

Information infrastructures provide means for all possible types of data processing open to different use (e.g., computers, networks). They constitute the basis for the information systems that, in contrast, support specific tasks of an organization. The information systems provide, in particular, the means for information use and exchange. The main role of information systems management is the management of the development and operation of an organization's information systems. Information management from this view can be defined as the planning, organization, and control of information use, information systems, and information infrastructure in an organization.

Strategic use of information technology

A strategic orientation should go along with an increased valuation of information processing in an organization. This should be met by the creation of a new post at strategic management level: the chief information officer. The main purpose behind this is to ensure that information processing is coordinated with corporate objectives.

Strategic aspects play an important role in nearly all concepts that are concerned with the management of information technology. For instance, the title of the book by Synnott indicates the significance of strategic aspects in his approach.

Content-oriented information management : Authors in this area of information management usually have a background in library and information science, records management, or a closely related discipline. Contrary to technology-oriented information management, these approaches focus on information content.

Publications can be classified here as follows:

- records management,
- provision of external information,
- human-centered information management, and
- Information resources management.

Records management

The records management is described as a discipline which is concerned with the management of document-based information systems e.g The Information Management Journal

The main goals of records management are:

- to furnish accurate, timely, and complete information in order to enable efficient decision making processes;
- to process recorded information as efficiently as possible;
- to provide information and documents at the lowest cost;
- to render the maximum utility to the users of documents;
- to dispose of records which are no longer needed.

Records management deals less and less with documents recorded on paper. The management of electronic documents has become more central instead using support systems like intranets, electronic imaging systems, and workflow management systems.

Provision of external information

The provision of external information is an important part of information management.

Human-centered information management

Human's play a much more important role in content-oriented management approaches to information management does not centre on information technology or formal theories but on how humans handle information in reality. While it is typical for technology-oriented information management approaches to model information systems in a very formal way (entity relationship diagrams, data flow diagrams, etc, content-oriented concepts use much less formalistic methods

Information resources management

IRM is grounded in the following assumptions:

– recognition of information as a resource;
– an integrative management perspective;
– management of the information life cycle;
– a link with strategic planning.

One important feature of information resources management consists is that it is a framework that seeks to integrate different information professionals and functions under one umbrella

3. WHAT IS KNOWLEDGE MANAGEMENT

Knowledge Management (KM), the latest entity conjured up by the consultancy "witch doctors", is the subject of vociferous debate. In the computing, management and library literatures, its proponents laud it with hyperbolic praise as the "...key to information management woes" and a means of"... revolutions the way companies overcome info glut". In contrast, it is subject to dyspeptic criticism as a "catchphrase", "..the worst sort of here-today-gone-tomorrow business fad" and "voodoo". Nothing, however, including the lack of valuation metrics, warnings about an impending "trough of disillusionment" or the confusion described above, stymies the billion dollar investment in KM. Descriptions of private sector projects involving hundreds of databases and threaded discussion groups and tens if not hundred of thousands of document are not uncommon. From the perspective of marginalized and chronically under resourced public sector information service providers, these descriptions read like dispatches from a parallel universe where there a few constraints on resources or skilled staff and where the information politics are very different from the confused, fractious and reductive style not unknown in government

4. COMPARATIVE STUDY

The results of knowledge are theories the effort to establish relevant relationships or connection between facts, and information in some coherent form and to explain the reasons for these generalizations.

Fritz Machlup, the well known scholar in this field, says that information is a process, a flow of messages involving, the act of telling or being told, and knowledge is a state or sense of knowing, and\ accumulated stock. So we talk of flow of information and stocks of knowledge.

The distinctions between information and knowledge are summed up below as described by Fritz Machlup.

Information	*Knowledge*
Is piecemeal, fragmented, particular	Is structured, coherent and often of enduring significance
Is timely, transitory perhaps even ephemeral and Is flow of messages	Is a stock, largely resulting from the flow, inputs of information and May affect the stock of knowledge by adding to it, restructuring it or changing it on any way

None of these distinctions relate to practical usefulness; neither information nor knowledge needs to be useful or valuable in all contexts.

5. MODULES OF KNOWLEDGE MANAGEMENT

The knowledge management system is primarily based on eight vital modules such as (1) Information (2) Expertise (3) Collaboration (4) Team (5) Learning (6) Intelligence (7) Knowledge transfer and (8) Knowledge mapping.

- *Information* the most important bezel acts as an instant access to update and customize information
- *Expertise* connects in real time experts in an organization to members who yearn assistance and even the tacit knowledge can made explicit

- *Collaboration* plays an important role to facilitate on line brain storming sessions and preserves information
- *Team* ensures efficient and systematic management among shares skills
- *Learning* abridges skill gap with the help on line sessions.
- *Intelligence* deals mainly with the explicit knowledge raise.
- *Knowledge transfer* in a structured electronic form according to William saffady relates to (a) Machine readable data files (b) Various on line databases and CD-Rom information products (c) Computer storage devices in which information resides in the shape of optical disks juke boxes or magnetic tape autoloaders and (d) Computerized networked systems
- *Knowledge mapping* identifies the body of knowledge within the organizations, which is primarily concerned with mute knowledge base and makes a repository of all skills and expertise in the organization.

Knowledge Management enables sharing of information by the people by overcoming the limitations of geographical boundaries.

As viewed by I.K.Ravichandra Rao, Knowledge Management is the broader spectrum and information management is the inner spectrum in the process.

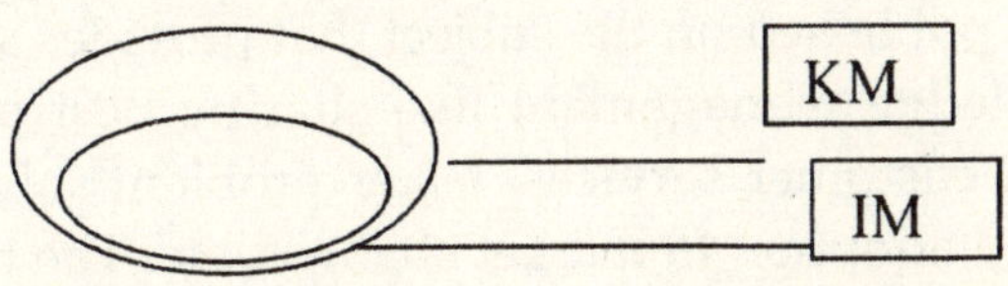

Information Management deals with information available sources, whereas Knowledge Management deals with not only information content but also knowledge present in users and employees brains. The concept of producing quality services resulted in the emergence of new concepts called information management and knowledge management.

Information management brings together and makes available hardware, software, control mechanisms and online learning resources but knowledge adds human expertise through Human Resources Development and Knowledge management is almost a step ahead of information management. Information seems to be a subdivision of knowledge management. Knowledge is an audit of intellectual assets that highlights unique sources critical functions and potential bottlenecks, which impedes knowledge flow to the point of use. Whether it is knowledge or information management, the attractiveness of the organizations arose out of three major forces.

- Knowledge is considered as the basis for organizational effectiveness
- Knowledge is the most dynamic in an organization than any other component
- It is not able to serve the organization without information/knowledge.

6. REQUISITES FOR SUCCESSFUL KNOWLEDGE MANAGEMENT

The last five years have seen a rapidly growing interest in the topic of knowledge management. Several articles and books are published on the subject that provides strategies for knowledge management like sharing best practices, improved customer services, faster problem solving and more rapid adoption to market changes, etc. The recurring success factors for knowledge management include.

- Support from top management, who recognizes the value of information or knowledge as a resource.
- Identification of the link between knowledge and the new measures of performance

- A knowledge leader who can actively drive the knowledge agenda forward with commitment
- Policies that drive the agenda forward
- Creation of an environment or work culture that supports innovation, learning and knowledge sharing

REFERENCE

1. MLIS-01 : Information communication and society p.5
2. Babita Garg : Application of knowledge management, Library and information Networking NACLIN 2003; p. 229, 234.
3. K Satyanaryana : Strategies for knowledge Management in Libraries, Library and Knowledge Management Networking NACLIN 2003 p. 294.
4. www.willpower info.co.uk :
5. James Robertson : Definition of information management terms. CMB 2004.

24

Digital Library Initiative

Johnson David
R. Balasubramani

ABSTRACT

The paper discusses the concept of digital libraries, embarking on why it is essential to adopt digitization in the present information intensive era. It's also discusses the Initiative of Digital Library in DSI Library, process of digitization of resources, identification for resources and requirement for digitization.

1. INTRODUCTION

The idea of converting library materials into digital formats for creating digital collections has advanced rapidly in the last few year, thus leading to the concept of a virtual library or a library without walls. Making the concept functional involves the use of hardware and software for capturing and converting an item into a digital format. Further, it is to be matched by developing a set of methods for describing and retrieving the digital information. The collections, services and information needs in DSI library are different from other types of libraries. The information required for R&D work, Engineering, dental, Nursing, Arts and Science faculty members and students are normally available in books, journals, technical reports, patents, standards, theses, databases, institutions websites etc., in various places and also in various format and media. These users are require the latest information for the time bound for them study. It is vary difficult for a single library to acquire all these resources and provide them to their users, yet, at the same time, it is the duty of the librarian to provide the required latest information, wherever available and in whatever form and whenever required.

Universally, librarians are being urged to digitize information in anticipation of the advantages. Even if this new technology does, indeed turn out to be revolutionary, one should be cautious keeping in mind the limitations, it is important to find out the various patterns in digital applications that enable effective and creative use in the traditional library functions of collecting, reserving, and making information accessible That is before the process of digitization, it is better to study patterns that can help one access "if and when technology will be able to meet expectations for improvement of traditional library services; when it cannot, and when it may do so, but not in a cost-effective manner." So the Dayananda Sagar Institute Central library is fully computerized and equipped with latest technology, barcode circulation, online electronic databases, i.e ASCE Journals, ASME Journals, IEE/IEE Electronic Library online, ACM Digital library.

2. CURRENT LIBRARY FACILITIES AND TRENDS

The current library system and services at DSI ranks amongst top 10 institutions in Karnataka state. The Library has computerized all its housekeeping activities using software developed in-house that is being maintained and updated regularly.

Our first priority is to enhance the collection by using power and efficiency of digital library. By adding more digital resources, the faculty members, Research Scholar, students will immensely benefit in their academic pursuits. It is proposed to strengthen the Digital Library in phase.

More than 100 P-V systems are connected to TFT LCD monitors. Online accessing of e-books, e-journals and e-news are the services extended to the users. Other services are also made available for the users like downloading to floppies, light pen's, CD's and printouts. Dedicated qualified staffs are place to help students in accessing the data base subscribed by the library.

A separate wing is totally devoted for the Audio Visual and Video Conferencing purposes. At a time, 80 participants can take part in discussion or in debate.The interested users can view educational films on the subjects. There is also a scope for personality development, communication skill and power point paper presentation

3. WHAT IS DIGITAL?

Traditionaly, digital means the use of numbers and the term comes from digit, or finger, Toady, digital is synonymous with computers.

Digital means original. The 0s and 1s of digital data mean more than just and off. They mean perfect copying. When information, music, voice, and vide are turned into binary digital form, they can be electronically manipulated, preserved and regenerated perfect at high speed. The millionth copy of a computer file is exactly the same

4. WHY DIGITIZE?

Arguments for digitizing resources include:

1. It is not only the availability of digital technology that is important but the point to be stressed is its affordability with each significant improvement in the technology driven by market forces.
2. Digitized materials that can be easily searched and retrieved will definitely augment their use.

3. Resources digitized could be easily shared among members of the library network or consortia. If each library does its bit to digitize even a part of the collection, the ultimate result will be considerable for sharing among different members.
4. Even if full text is not available outside the intranet or to members of the consortium, the search and inventory facilities over the Internet themselves will significantly enhance the image of the library and improve visibility among other similar facilities.
5. Less likely to be damaged than print counterparts, as they have no physical form to yellow and decay with age, and loaning out a copy does not relinquish the original (Weisser & Walker, 1997).
6. Require less space for storage and hence reduction in the building space required.

5. BASIC FUNCTIONS INVOLVED IN SETTING UP A DIGITAL LIBRARY

- Identification and collection of content to be digitized.
- Classification and digitization of these contents.
- Editing, formatting and storage of the contents.
- Designing search engines to selectively search and access the contents.
- Publishing contents digitally for end-user access.

5.1. Digitization

- Scanning at the highest resolution at an appropriate level of quality to avoid rescanning and re-handling of the originals.
- Creating and storing a master image file.
- Using system components that are non-proprietary.
- Using image file formats and compression techniques that conform to industry standards.

- Creating backup copies of all files on a stable medium.
- Creating meaningful metadata for image files or collections
- Storing media in an appropriate environment.
- Monitoring and recopying data as necessary.
- Outlining a migration strategy for transferring data across generations of technology.
- Anticipating and planning for future technological developments.

Since the different steps in digitization listed below must be identified and a workflow carefully designed and executed by each library, it is only possible to highlight the major challenges under each of the steps here. Deciding on appropriate formats for incorporating the contents into CD or on the Web will be dependent on the presence of different software required, and the means to support any extra systems needed as well as the size and features of materials to be digitized.

5.2. Building-up digital collections

The most important component of a digital library is the digital collection it holds or has access to. Viability and extent of usefulness of a digital library would depend upon the critical mass of digital collection that it has. A digital library can have a wide range of resources. It may contain both paper-based conventional documents or information contained in computer-processible form. Information contents of a digital library, depending on the media type it contains, may include a combination of structured/unstructured text, numerical data, scanned images, graphics, audio and video recordings. Different types of resources need to be handled differently in digital library.

Rusbridge (1998) divided resources for a digital library in four distinct categories, i.e., Legacy, Transition, and New.

Legacy resources, according to Rusbridge, are largely non-digital resources, including manuscript, print, slides, maps, audio and video recordings. Inspite of the fact that large investments are being made in the process of digitization of resources, vast majority of existing legacy resources will remain outside the electronic domain for many years to come. These legacy resources are the major resources of existing libraries.

Transition resources, primarily designed for another medium (mostly print), are those which are being or have been digitized, making the transition into the digital world. Such resources are converted for increased access and to reduce reliance on physical libraries. The transition resources are either digitized images or images that are converted to text by the process of Optical Character Recognition (OCR).

New digital resources are either expressly created as digital or are created in parallel to print. Data files created in the process of electronic publishing are used for generating outputs suitable for the Internet and the web. These datafiles are converted into SGML, HTML, PostScript and PDF. While HTML and PDF (sometimes PostScript) is posted on the web, the SGML version which is a rich archive format is used for preservation.

6. LIMITATIONS

Some of the key issues facing digital libraries today:

- Technological obsolescence: Hardware and Software
- Cost of Content refreshing: Digital preservation will be an ongong operation that requires considerable recurring expense.
- Rights Management: It is vary easy to copy, replicate, message and distribute digital information. Enforcing copyright in digital environment is a major issue
- Network bandwidth: With the exploding number of

users, multimedia content, websites and applications (e.g, chat, games), bandwidth available for accessing digital libraries is going t be a serious issue.

7. PURPOSES OF THE DIGITAL LIBRARY INITIATIVE IN DSI LIBRARY

- To collect, store and organize information and knowledge in digital form.
- To promote economic and efficient delivery of information.
- To leverage the considerable investments in computing/communications infrastructure.
- To strengthen communication and collaboration between research, project and educational communities
- To contribute to lifelong learning opportunities.

7.1. Infrastructure for Digital Library in DSI Institute

Infrastructure is an umbrella term for many activities. Digital Library infrastructure is usually considered with respect to its main areas such as computer hardware and software, telecommunication and networking. The DL infrastructure in DSI Library is as follows.

Hardware

a) For Digital Library Activities

S.No.	*CPU Detail*	*Qty.*	*CPU Speed*	*RAM*	*Hard Disk*
1	Server	3	Dual Core	1 GB	80 GB
2	Nodes	100	Dual Core processor	512 MB	80 GB

7.2. Backup devices

Optical disk/High density flat bed scanner - (HP Scanjet 6300C)

Fujitsu 3097 Getc, Minolata PS3000, Ricoh IS420

Sheet Feed Scanners - Kodak, 500S Drum Scanners (juno CP – 4000, Scan Mate 5000, color Getter)

Digital camera (Minolta PS 3000, OmniScan 3000, Canon)

Laser/Ink Jet Printer

Fax

OS Linux

SW Digital Library Software: Dspace

Publishing: Adobe acrobat including Adobe capturing, MS-Word

Multimedia tools-Photoshop, Flash, Imaging

Library software with cataloguing and searching digital resources – SIS

Searching documents created in various file formats – Dtsearch

WEB Server: Microsoft IIS, Java, Apache

OCR software – TextBridge, Omnipage

Imaging Capturing/Scanning Software _Itris, Optix, Power Office, FileNet, Data

Data Scan, OmniDoc, data Compression software

Database:	MS-SQL Server, Oracle
Formats:	Files txt, doc, html, xml, sgml. Pdf – postscript
Images:	tiff, .bmp, .jpg
Network:	High speed LAN/Intranet/Internet connectivity
Protocol:	TCP/IP

7.3. Database and E-Journals:-

DSI Institute has been selected for the implementation of the electronic resources like INDEST-AICTE, J-Gate, BITES, DELNET which provides access to database of books, current periodicals, periodical articles and CD-ROM databases.

E-Journals have almost all the characteristics of the printed journals (p-journals) and would be available either online or offline (CD, DVD) or both. Publishers like ASCE, ASME, IEEE/IEE, ACM Digital library etc., offer subscription.

Advantages of subscribing to full-text journals/contents pages

The following are the advantages of subscribing to full-text journals/contents pages:

* Access to latest information earlier than the printed version
* Access to contents page of journal free of cost
* Allows search using several attributes/data elements
* No need to create and maintain the database locally
* These journals can also be subscribed through consortium. Subscribes have to pay an extra percentage over and above the cost of the printed version. Members of the consortium have online access to full-text journals subscribed by participating libraries.

7.4. Digitizing Resources Produced/Published Internally in DSI Institute

- R & D works
- Project Reports (BE, M.Tech., MCA, MBA, Pharmacy, Dental etc.,)
- Articles published on other national/International journals
- Newsletter of the institution
- Annual reports
- Technical reports (Consultancy/Sponsored., etc) generated in-house

- Regular course materials
- Lectures
- Video/audio clippings, explaining working of some instruments, facilities, etc available
- Publications/services from the library likes CAS, SDI, select bibliographies on certain topics
- Newspaper clippings - recent and relevant information published in newspapers.
- Internally created files (correspondence, communication, circular, office order etc) available in various file formats such as ascii, txt,.pdf,.xls, etc.
- Internally created records using databases such as foxbase.

7.5. Barriers

The main drawback is the cost of digitization and preservation of files. In this aspect one can justify the cost of digitizing of a unique collection such as the collection of DSI library especially when it leads to increased access and usage of under-utilized collections. The disadvantage of digitization are:-

- Scanning the original documents of the entire collection
- IPR Issues
- Authenticity and credibility acceptance of the digital resources
- Require special skills to set up and maintain the DL
- Require special training.

8. CONCLUSION

The Central Library of DSI is fully computerized and has well maintained infrastructure. Computerization has provided high quality of reproduction, compact storage, speed of communication and online access, more accurate and better services to their users. As the Central Library has access to Internet, the task of bridging the digital divide became much easier. Internet has become the key term of today's digital age, Central library, DSI also stepped in to be at par with the latest trends. Digital library, Subject Gateways, E-reference desk and E-resources are the latest addition on the website of DSI library to provide better service to our users.

REFERENCE

1. Association of Research Libraries. (1996). Definition and purposes of a digital library. Retrieved on December 6, 2000, from http://sunsite.berkeley.edu/ARL/definition.html.
2. Bishoff, L. (2000). Interoperability and standards in a museum/library collaborative: The Colorado Digitization Project. First Monday 5(6). Retrieved from http://firstmonday.org/issues/issue5 6/bishoff/.
3. Digital Divide: an overview in – Indian context. By Padma V. Udayaya, MIM Manipal, Proceeding of the national conference on Recent Advance in Information Technology Conference : theme-Digital Asset Management held at IIT Madras, - Chennai on September 2001.
4. RUSBRIDGE (Chris). Towards the hybrid library. *D-Lib Magazine,* July / August, 1998. *http://www.dlib.org/dlib/july98/rusbridge.html*
5. Srinivasan, P. (1997). Digital library projects in the United States. DESIDOC Bulletin of Information Technology, 17(6), 15–21.
6. Weisser, C. R., & Walker, J. R. (1997). Electronic theses and dissertations: Digitizing scholarship for its own sake. The Journal of Electronic Publishing, 3(2). Retrieved from http://www.press.umich.edu/jep/03-02/etd.html.

25

Digital Library Information Resources and Services

Naresh Chandara Verma

ABSTRACT

Digital library has emerged as one of the most important applications in Information Technology in knowledge of information revolution. The digital library information collection, resources and services further facilitates on-line searching of national and international library knowledge facilities. On-line digital libraries are also accessible to daily users and update continuously by different national and international libraries. A digital library is also known as a distributed text based computerized information system and services. In this system, computer or electronic equipments are used for acquiring, storing, organizing, searching, distributing and displaying materials for geographically distributed. This paper discusses the advantages and disadvantages of digital library information knowledge resources and services in Indian libraries.

1. INTRODUCTION

Today digital world is connected with creating, sharing and using information in digital form because the right information available to the right person at the right time is the aim of modern library services. The digital library is an electronic library where the information is acquired stored and retrieved in digital form. A modern digital library is a media server connected to high speed networks. Unlike a conventional library where users are provided with physical materials from many sources, a digital library is a group of distributed repositories that users see as a single repository in a digital form.

Digital library provides such information services in which all the resources are available in computer process able form and the functions of acquisition, storage, preservation, retrieval, access and display are carried out through the use of digital technologies. Data accessible through the digital library system in addition to full text information also include non-text information like photographs, drawing, illustrations, artwork, numeric data, cosmological data, digitized sound, moving virtual images and 3-D representation. Digital library can disseminate its knowledge information across a network and users can retrieve the available information.

Dr. D. Shivalingaiah (2002). The digital or electronic libraries can be virtual libraries if they exist only virtually – that is, the library does not exist "in real life". For example, a virtual library can consist of material from a variety of separate libraries that are organized in a virtual space using computers and computer networks. The terms such as 'electronic library', 'digital library', 'virtual library', 'web-library', or 'on-line library' have been used synonymously to represent the same concept.

1.1. Definitions of Digital Libraries

According to the Larson (1985) "Digital libraries are not single, standalone and repositories of digital data. Instead, they are a heterogenous collection of network-based repositories using a variety of products for user's interaction, data encoding and transmission".

According to the Berkeley digital library project University of California (1990) "The digital library will be a collection of distributed information sources. Producers of information will make it available, and consumers will find it perhaps through the help of automated agents"

According to the Griffin (1992) "An organized collection of multimedia data with information management methods will represent the data as useful information and knowledge to people in a variety and organizational contexts".

According to the Dr. R. Rama Raj Urs (2002) "Digital library is a global virtual library- The library of thousands of networked electronic libraries"

1.2. Features of Digital Library

The various features identified for digital library

- Provide access to very large information collection.
- Focus on providing access to primary (or complete) information, not merely surrogates or indexes.
- Support multi-media content.
- Provide user friendly interface, to access the information.
- Enable 'link' representation to local/ external objects (hypertext)
- Provide client-server architecture.
- Support advanced search and retrieval of information
- Linkage with other national and international digital library system.
- Support-advanced search and retrieval.
- Support traditional library missions of collection development, organization, access and presentation.

1.3. Advantages of Digital Libraries

- Accessibility from any where home, school, libraries,

during travel, hotel etc.

- The e-books and e-journals provide keywords, subject and various other searches.
- It is a best tool for preservation of heritage.
- Archival of resources.
- Contain multi-media information.
- It saves the space that is required for physical documents.
- It saves the cost and manpower required for publishing and bringing out new editions.
- Several libraries can form a consortium and access bibliographical data base/ full text journal online by spending only a nominal amount.
- Resources sharing among libraries.
- Remote access to expensive and rare material, and
- Greater opportunity for publishing.

1.4. Disadvantages of Digital Libraries

- Intellectual Property Right (IPR) issues: Library authorities have to discuss with publishers and authors on their aspects to evolve some mechanisms to make it beneficial for library users, publishers and the authors. [.
- Security is another problem, which include the piracy of data bases virus invasion, and parallel satellite networking stress.
- Technological changes are also coming very fast in which every one is expected to be the shortcoming for implementing various programmes. So it is not feasible to change all the resources into digital forms by the common libraries.
- There is also a lack of expertise as only limited suppliers are there for digital libraries over the whole world.

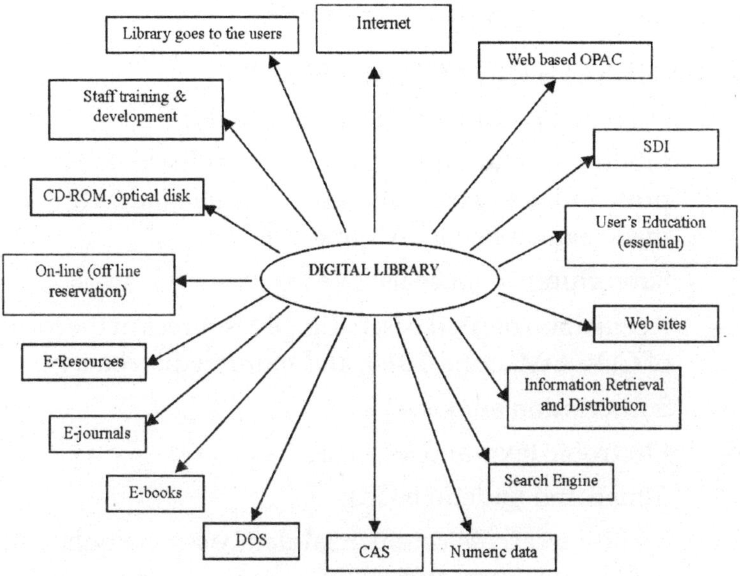

Digital Library

2. COLLECTION OF DIGITAL LIBRARY

- Metadata describing the data and having facility to provide links to other related databases;
- Open communication protocols (client-server) for information retrievals;
- Information access tools like; browsers, display and search engines;
- Electronic publishing tools;
- Data compression;
- Digital storage devices;
- Scanning and conversion technology;
- Multimedia for integration technologies;
- Privacy and security;
- Inter-operability over the libraries;
- Advanced information retrieval tools like indexing routing and filtering of information; and

- Intellectual property Rights (IPR)

3. RESOURCES OF DIGITAL LIBRARY

- High bandwidth internet connectivity;
- Library should create the bibliographic database of print and non-print materials and such database to be made available via LAN and WAN.
- Subscription e-journals;
- Acquisition of need based digital resources in the form of CD-ROM, optical disk and multimedia version;
- Subscription e-books;
- Electronic texts and journals;
- E-mail and bulletin board;
- Facility to access commercial databases via online in the related areas; and
- Internet/web.

4. SERVICES OF DIGITAL LIBRARY

The literature on digital library facilitates to develop a framework for a modern digital library. A modern digital library would provide the following services to its users regardless of their geographical location.

- Circulation of books, photocopying of articles etc.
- Inter Library Loans
- Database searches
- On-line / Off-line reservation
- User services such as membership, query
- Reference support for subject searches
- A liaisons librarian
- User education and training programmes
- Current awareness services
- Assistance in using computer facilities

- Access to library catalogues, databases, internet
- Publisher awareness service
- List of new publications received
- Electronic reference desk
- Assistance with bibliographic packages
- Flexible methods of submitting requests, e.g. via telephone, facsimile, e-mail, www, post
- Electronic delivery to requesters workstation, where possible.

5. LOCATION OF KNOWLEDGE IN LIBRARY

Every modern library has internet and external knowledge resources for their users. Internet Knowledge resources can includes librarians and staff, books and journals, in house developed databases, CD-ROMs, Encyclopedias, Projects. External knowledge resources can include experts and libraries of other libraries, online Journals and books; users, suppliers, membership of other library and Information Centers.

6. BARRIER OF KNOWLEDGE SHARING IN LIBRARIES

The following are the barriers for sharing Knowledge:

- Lack of Communication skills.
- Fear in asking questions and gives ideas.
- Lost of knowledge - Any organization cannot record everything. Knowledge is a product of human experience and reflection and "A great deal of useful knowledge is normally lost when people leave their organizations or they feel that there in no incentive for them to share what is rightly there (Al. Hawamedeh, 2002)."

7. INTERNET AND ITS USES

Internet is an inter connection of thousands of

networks to from a single network. Internet is global information network of networks. The internet spans across the globe making it a very powerful communication, business, research and educational media. Majority of information available for the internet is free. The information on the internet is made available by various organizations like government agencies, educational institutions, commercial and non-profit organizations.

The major uses of internet are:

- Send and receive electronic mail anywhere in the world.
- Conduct international business
- Download software, text, image, sound and video files.
- Access and retrieval of information on a variety of subjects and topics
- Login to a remote computer to use its resources
- Disseminate information on the www.
- Participate in a real time video conferencing.

8. CONCLUSION

The advent of the digital libraries is too important to wait for the opportune time to take advantage of the knowledge resources. Using the internet and its resources for providing information services only requires reorientation of traditional skills of university Librarianship. With the available infrastructure in the university we can make a beginning in exploiting the digital library knowledge resources on the Internet for better and newer services. The digitized media is a supportive too, for searching and locating the information faster to the targeted and users.

Finally, the digital library is inevitable large components of research materials are becoming digitized. We need to embrace change although it can be chaotic and unsettling. We must master the paradoxes presented by managing in a time of transition. We must remember that our greatest beyond that, look at who we are and the tools of the trade now in our grasp.

REFERENCE

1. Al-Hawamdeh, S. Knowledge management : re thinking information management and facing the challenge of managing tacit knowledge Information Research, 2002, 8(1), Paper No. 143
2. Berkeley Digital Library Project University of California, 1990.
3. Griffin use of Information Technology in Library & Information Science, 1992.
4. http://www.crossref.org
5. http://www.sunsite.Berkely.edu.
6. http://www.sunyconnect.suny.edu
7. Kohl, D.F.: Resource Sharing in Changing Ohio Environment: Library Trends 45(3); 1997; 435-447.
8. Larson Electronic and Digital Libraries, 1985.
9. Raj Urs, R Rama. Digital Library Networks, 2002.
10. Shivalingaiah, D. Use of Information Technology in Library & Information Science, 2002.
11. Singh S. (2001). Web Enabling a Bibliographic Database of India Biomedical Journals: Ind, MED (MS Dissertation) Pilani: Birla Institute of Technology and Science.

26
Future Librarianship

Dr. B. Mini Devi

ABSTRACT

The article explores the future of library and librarianship in general. In the changing environment librarian can act as an information specialist, information fitter, information literacy instructor etc. The different thoughts about the future of librarianship are also discussed in detail.

1. INTRODUCTION

Libraries and librarianship faced great changes from time to time. Librarians have a long ancestry of adopting technology to enhance services. From the book keepers, librarians are now in a dynamic environment in which technology, resources, information needs and user expectations rapidly changes. Even though some of the traditional roles of librarians may be disappearing, there are plenty of opportunities for proactive information profession in the new information environment. Now a day, a growing body of citation, full-text, numeric, and databases are available to the user without entering the hallowed confines of a library building. The wanted information is pushed to the writing table from the desktop of the PC of the user. The whole world is under the magic wand of cyberspace, to just think of information, no opening or closing hours; no missing or lost, or misplaced information and no due date. Librarians do not exist in a vacuum, but the changes towards the future will strongly influence the future of librarianship.

2. CHANGING ROLE OF LIBRARIAN

In the early days librarians were keepers of books. From there with changing social culture, librarian and library became an essential and respectable part of the society. Now the Internet and ICTs (Information and Communication Technologies) force librarians to wear new promising dresses to adapt the virtual environment. They are:

2.1. Information Specialist

Even though, through Internet there is an information flood users do not know how to access the specific information they needed. We librarians help our users search for, locate, and obtain documents and information. Librarians are communicators of knowledge, possessing the skills and abilities to share the users the tools to access, evaluate, analyze and synthesize information into a knowledge base.

The content of the library became a commodity and libraries role will become increasingly pedagogical. "Content means all forms of information, and without limitation include: text, formatted text such as HTML pages, interactive and/ or dynamic Web pages such as those generated from data files and databases, images, animation, video and sound files. It may also include software, Web-based output from software applications and web-based input (i.e. transactions)" [1]. As Ranganathan said 'every book its reader', in modern times, every piece of content has a use to experience its lure.

In our current information environment, the Web is a vast disaggregated vault of information. In it is available the best of information and the worst of information. Users are the best searchers and the worst searchers. By understanding the deeper currents of change in our society, we become empowered to deliver solutions that rise above the mere management of content. The Web-oriented environment serve as a wonderful foundation for managing content and the user interface - virtual and face to face. The traditional libraries context is different in a world of virtual libraries, e-learning and distance education, portals etc. Information specialist should be well versed in software and Internet applications.

2.2. Information Literacy

Information Literacy became a focal theme for future librarianship. Librarian should spend more time on bibliographic instruction and information literacy and less time on computer training.

2.3. Collaboration with intelligent software agents

The software agents can automate many of the more tedious and intricate library operations. Hence librarian can concentrate on other important jobs. In many areas such collaboration will make higher results beyond our expectation. Some of the areas are:

Meditation between searcher and information

- assistance with database and Internet site selection;
- automated searching and retrieval of information-based on users' queries from the Internet, online databases, and/or corporate data warehouses;
- assistance with query structuring (e.g., matching users' terms to controlled vocabularies, subheadings, and thesaurus terms, suggesting similar concepts/ terms)
- assistance with strategy modification; and,
- assistance with the interpretation and sorting of search results.

Virtual/automated reference

- good for all-hours reference service;

- useful for serving geographically distant library customers;
- helpful for users who may be unable physically or unwilling to approach a librarian in person;
- provide automated, context-sensitive creation and presentation of frequently asked reference questions;
- guided tutorials (e.g., database searching, learning and using applications), and,
- indexing and abstracting; assigning index terms (automated matching to thesaurus/controlled vocabulary) and abstracting (identifying key sentences).

Automating serials processing

- recommendation of titles for acquisition;
- updating databases when titles change or cease;
- identifying missing serials issues and generating claims; and,
- processing statistics and generating reports.

Interlibrary loan processing

- identifying the best source(s) for requested documents;
- routing document request to source;
- updating and notifying document delivery staff of the status of open requests;
- archiving close requests; and,
- generating reports (e.g., document delivery statistics)

Acquisitions

- recommending acquisitions based on budget, reviews, size and type of institution, history of purchases and rejections, etc;
- assignment of vendors to items selected for acquisition;
- automation of copy cataloging (and able to handle

diverse formats), and

- advisory function for human cataloging (e.g., ensuring rule compliance, eliminating duplicates, automatic identification of main entry terms, cataloging tutorials).

Circulation

- checking items out to users;
- generating overdue notices;
- processing renewals;
- generating circulation statistics and reports; and;
- generating invoices for overdue/lost materials.

Digital libraries

- indexing and classifying documents and searching and retrieving documents.

Personal Information Gathering and Sorting

- customized current awareness services;
- automatic, customized searching (sometimes in cooperation with other subject-expert agents)
- generation of personal newspapers and Web sites (e.g,)
- customized search engines;
- e-mail filtering and sorting programs;
- custom recommendations of sites/items of interest, and,
- translation of documents from other languages [2].

2.4. Information Filters

Information filtering is a process in which a filtering agent reads every document in an information stream and compares it to a set of interest profiles. If a document matches a profile, the filter sends it to the appropriate user's inbox or stores it somewhere for the user. The rest of the documents are filtered out. In the digital age librarian acts as an information filter. In addition to filtering information, librarian can package, repackage, create, find and classify information for the users.

3. ARGUMENTS ABOUT FUTURE LIBRARIANSHIP

Librarians are anxiously looking forward about the future of their profession. The Internet and cyberspace have had big impact on these anxieties. Some advocates the complete disappearance of library as a physical institution. "Librarians or the competence of librarians, transformed into something slightly different or nearly similar, in the future will be of interest to all kinds of information or knowledge industries and activities - public or private. However, the institution or department which is called the 'library' can take to a much more insecure future" [3]. One of the most threatening views of the future is put forwarded by Charles Martell in his two-part essay "The Disembodied Librarian in the Digital Age". He points out for a revolutionary, not evolutionary, change. "The common view among librarians is that the changes in their profession are following an evolutionary, rather than a revolutionary, pattern. From this perspective, relatively few adaptations will be required of them. However this vision is too narrow"[4]. Martell believes that the digital age will completely alter what it means to be human, both conceptually and consciously. He foresees the change coming in the dichotomies between time and space, mind and body, real and virtual, and humans and technology. Martell's writing is heavily influenced by William Gibson's 'Cyberspace' in his scientific novel Neuromancer. According to Martell cyberspace has huge implications for the library profession.

Books are more tightly connected to their readers, authors are building books out of Google's content. Book prices are dropping, open access keeps increasing librarians are helping to discriminate between good, bad, lousy and lousier materials. "When everything is digital, you're paying people to help you not need bad stuff". Librarian becomes censors – less judgemental and polarizing term 'filters'.

Some argue that all users jump into this 'digital love fest'. Digital won't make print go away – it never will. Putting digital materials online increases book circulation. Libraries have never been just about stuff". They are about service. They doesn't change when collections are digital.

Some are of opinion that library is an institution about learning and information, not limited to type of material. It is a manifestation of how to organize and access information, whether it works with digital or print artifacts. There will be a 'pushing down' of librarianship into some institutions (like schools) and a pushing up into businesses – but pain will be in the middle. That's where the impact of Google will be.

1. Who will take the responsibility for ensuring that books themselves continue to exist?
2. Will they be lost in the digital shuffle? Librarians still have a lot to learn about Google and Google still has a lot to lean about libraries.

Borger's strange view of information and disinformation bewitches Borges's librarians view serves as a text for today's librarianship i.e. between order and disorder, between information and disinformation, between poverty and surfeit. The vastness of current information flood has made librarians madly pursuing the technologies of data.

When think about the future of librarianship, it is not to dream about riding up an escalator to the structural tapping of profession hood. It is wise to think about the evolution of librarians work and to ask what the consequences of that evolution might be for the occupation. Knowledge commodity is under the control of the relevant human experts. Likewise librarian's control of the vast panoply of reference tools is a clear example.

The future of librarianship hinges on what happens to

the perpetually changing work of the profession in its 3 contexts: larger social and cultural forces, competing occupations and competing organizations and commodities. To these complex contextual forces, librarianship responds with varying policies and internal charges. The social force influencing librarianship is the technological change. Online databases, catalogues, visual and multimedia equipments will not endup replacing librarians themselves. Some fear the elimination of librarians as brokers between users and data.

Another argument is that the search services offered by large commercial companies such as Google, Microsoft & Yahoo replace the need for libraries.

It is an information market, if libraries let that happen if their services are sufficiently powerful and obiquitous, then people will go there if the millions of searches going to them came to us. People think the sponsored links in commercial search engines are better because they are sponsored and the difference between commercial search engines and library search we are going to let them win or are we going to start building community and search.

As new technological development is applied, it has its impact on libraries and information centers, where it is of direct application; development of more rapid communications by high speed networks. Library being major elements in the chain of information flow are usually more affected than effecting in relation of these change. Apart from changed education environment, library infrastructure has also undergone change. The convergence of telecommunication and computer technologies in the context of libraries led to such an explosive development. The networking of libraries has now given rise to information networks, information databases and information infrastructure. The information environment has changed the infrastructure, the scope, the services and the goal of a library. The whole world as well as the library field is working today towards a Global information infrastructure.

Library has powerful competition from other directions, from Amazon to Google Book search. Whether libraries provide an important service is irrelevant if they provide it in a manner that drives their users away, particularly the users who vote. Many of the libraries hate email courtesy notices. But users shout 'treat me well- 21st century style', tells librarians to hurry up please, it's time to group the importance of embracing comfort and life management services, or be prepared for extinction. Google has almost no competition and is the 'king' of search of engines. Every six months many more humans are introduced to Google and to the magic of full-text searching. This feature continues to widen the usability gap between how our library operations works and the conceptual models our users bring to our tools.

Gone are the days when the physical building was the centre of the library. In the digital age, the virtual space created in cyberspace by librarians will become central. All library services will be virtual, making current service philosophies marginal. Librarians will have to move from a value-neutral approach to service, to a value-added approach [5].

Martell believes that his approach to future librarianship is revolutionary. It ultimately sounds very much like the Googleizers' approach to modern librarianship. He believes that keyword searching will make the traditional controlled-vocabulary search irrelevant, although "whether users will be more successful in retrieving relevant information as a result of these changes is unclear" [6]. However, like the Googleizers, he is not overly concerned with the quality of the information gathered, but rather the user's ability to access information. He sees three trends conspiring to make access the central issue in librarianship:

1) the erosion of funding to libraries; 2) the rapid growth of electronic information, and 3) the increasing utility of this information for teaching and research. As librarians provide access to electronic information, they will free themselves from the physical world of the library, and start to enter into the disembodied world of cyberspace [7]. And, he cautions that "if librarians are unable to find comfortable roles in cyberspace with new value-added products and services, it will be difficult to maintain the relevance of librarianship as it exists today"[8]. Librarians in the future must anticipate the needs of their users by compiling user profiles and use information. This value-added librarianship actually tramples on one of the core values of modern librarianship: the right of users to have their privacy protected [9].

"The development of the Internet challenges traditional conceptions of information rights including freedom of speech, copyright, universal access, cultural, and minority, diversity, and privacy. The discourse surrounding these rights typically deals with each in isolation. As well, these discussion strive to adapt long established understandings of each right to the new technological environment." [10]

They believe that the only way to properly address the challenges of the Internet is to address the needs of information freedoms with the human-rights framework of the right to communicate.

"A library is a growing organism," allows room for the right to communicate in modern librarianship. If the concept of library is taken to mean more than simply a physical building, then this value can eclipse the other nine to make room for a new set of values based on the right to communicate. Concern about the future of the physical library is what fuels much of the Resistors' defiance of the realities of the Internet. In "What is a Library Anymore, Anyway?," Keller, Reich, and Herkovic [11] worry that once the local content of the library is replaces with the global content of the Internet, the library, as it is currently conceived, will cease to exist. They want librarians to continue to be information gatekeepers: "Librarians need to be deliberate about what we gather, control carefully what we do gather, and even more deliberate about discarding information" (12). How then do librarians move from being information gatekeepers to communications advocates?

William F. Birdsall discussed his belief that librarianship would become the paradigm profession of the Twenty-first Century. He states that the traditional values of librarianship were no longer enough to sustain the profession because they were based on the concept of an informed citizen exercising his or her democratic rights with information supplied by government and the broadcast media. Birdsall believes that the concept of an informed citizen should be replaces with the concept of a communicative citizen, or a citizen who is active in the communicative process of democracy, and not a passive recipient of information and content. The library, both as a physical place and as a concept, is the perfect social institution for people to exercise their right to communicate. The primary resource of the library would cease to be the books and other information packages, and become the staff. He outlined three steps that librarians should take to become communications advocates:

Librarians should help to develop the definition of right to communicate;

Librarians must re-examine their values under the view of the right to communicate;

Librarians must take the lead as advocates for the right to communicate

3. CONCLUSION

The position of library and librarians are under debate.

The role of library in our society and the esteemed and valued function of librarians are understood. But in today's digital information society, the library and the librarian are no longer enjoying such consensus about their value.

There are so many questions arise:

1. If libraries exist in the new developments in ICTs, what will these organization look like?
2. What future will there by for librarians?
3. Will the traditional library functions disappear and will they be placed by new ones?
4. Will libraries disappear or a new generation will start?

The future of the library will be characterized by four aspects:

1. Library will be a gateway to information.
2. With the increasing complexity of information landscape, library will be a centre of expertise.
3. There will be a need for preserving library as a physical entity, not only as place for scholarly communication, but also for advanced study facilities with adequate user support.
4. Library will not lose its dignity as a centre for printed literature.

For the survival librarian has to meet the demands regarding profession knowledge and skills. He must have good organizational, active, communicative and contractual qualities. New opportunities and responsibilities will wait for librarians who are able to take this account.

The status of information within our organization is undergoing a profound transformation. Many of our users foresee that in the future the availability of quality information will be a necessary contribution to their professional competence and to the competitiveness of the organizations that they belong to.

In this context, we have to examine the following points.

- The effectiveness of library schools - what they should and shouldn't be teaching and doing.
- Technology education which library schools doing enough?
- We have to prepare librarian for leadership in the new age.
- Technology should become an integral part of LIS (Library and Information Science) education.

Librarian can add to the virtual environment as a coach, mentor and information advisor.

REFERENCE

1. www. Murdoch.edu.au/cwisad/glossary.html. accessed on 12.2.07
2. Zick, Laura. 1999. Artificial intelligence and libraries: A primer for librarians at http://wlc.doch/com/doc index.html accessed on 21.2.2007.
3. Bakken, Frode, 1998. The possible role of librarians in the digital future. Libri. Vol 48.No.2.p.82.
4. Martell, Charles.2000. The disembodied librarian in the digital age. College and Research Libraries. Vol.61.No.1 (January).p.12.
5. Martell, Charles. 2000. The disembodied librarian in the digital age. College and Research Libraries. Vol.61.No.2 (March).p.98.
6. Ibid.p.105.
7. Ibid.p.111
8. Ibid.
9. http://www.ala.org/ala/olf/statementsspots/corevaluess tatement/ corevalues.htm//privacy.accessed on 2.2.07.
10. Melver, William J., Bridsall, William F., and Rasmussen, Merrilee.2003. The internet and the right to communicate. Vol.8.No.12 (December) at http://www. firstmonday.org/issues/issued 8_12/melver/index html, accessed on 21.2.07.
11. Keller, Michael A., Reich, Victoria A., and Herkovic, Andrew C. 2003. What is a library anymore, anyway? Vol.8.No.5 (May) at http://www.firstmonday.org/issues/issues_5/keller/index.html accessed on 8.2.07.
12. Ibid.

27

Skills for Library and Information Science Professionals in Future Libraries

K.S.Sivakumaren
T.Elanchezhiyan
B. Jeyaprakash

ABSTRACT

Advances in technology have changed the library and information field drastically. There should be a corrending change in the knowledge and skills of library and information professionals also. This paper is illustrating what are the additional skills and knowledge required for managing future libraries.

1. INTRODUCTION

Advances in technology have changed virtually every aspect of our lives. These changes have dramatically impacted how we communicate, manage information, use our time, and complete simple and complex daily tasks. Technology is also reforming how information is accessed and processed. Electronically, the users are able to visit various websites to access the information in any where in the world, in a variety forms, for their studies and research activities. The library and information science professionals strive to keep abreast of current research and best practice in teaching and learning to meet student and community educational needs.

2. CHALLENGES FOR LIBRARY AND INFORMATION SCIENCE PROFESSIONALS

The libraries have experienced a reduction of their physical space and print materials as virtual resources and services expanded with desktop delivery of information directly to the user. It is creating an exciting opportunity for library growth and development for both the collection and the staff.

- Organizing information resources to meet the specific needs and interests of users
- Monitoring trends in publishing and computing to effectively select and organize materials for their users
- Managing staff, programs, information systems and databases
- Computer and technical ability
- Instructing users in research skills, techniques and systems
- Negotiating contracts for resources, services, materials and equipment
- Preparing and managing budgets
- Directing the daily activities of the library
- Communication skills such as written, verbal and listening

3. CORE SKILLS

- Identifying and meeting the information needs of the users
- Identifying, accessing, organizing, interpreting and

evaluating knowledge and information

- Interpersonal and communication skills;
- Professional development, including updating IT-related skills;
- Generic management skills
- Credibility with academic staff, teaching and training

4. LEADERSHIP SKILLS

The librarians frequently hold positions of leadership that extend beyond the sphere of their primary responsibilities, academics are also involved in administration of information technology, contribute administrative expertise across the organization. Moreover, successful librarians understand that the demands of a changing information environment require that they actively apply their knowledge, expertise and skill to analysis issues facing professionally. There are significant challenges to expressing leadership. These challenges disproportionately affect the library professionals that

- Institutional bias that does not recognize the versatility of the information professional
- Perceived lack of value of the professional activity on the part of the institution
- Many library professionals would like to be more active in their professional associations, but find that the rigors of their job responsibilities, or the lack of support from their institutions.
- Ensuring that adequate educational opportunities exist to train new information professionals in the expanding requirements of leadership
- Encouraging experienced librarians to develop or update their own leadership skills
- Encouraging library leaders to develop leadership skills in all levels of staff members

- Encouraging employers of librarians to see the value in professional contributions and continuing education
- Fostering meaningful leadership opportunities for our younger generation librarians

5. MANAGEMENT SKILLS

The staff who is required to adopt the skills and techniques of sound management practice will depend largely on organization and structure of the service. It is essential that librarians acquire the skills that will enable them to operate effectively in large and increasingly competitive organizations. There is a range of factors, which suggests that managerial responsibilities need to be more widely adopted. These include

- The gradual breakdown of hierarchical staffing structures
- Increasingly participative decision-making models
- Greater emphasis on accountability and service of individual performance
- Ability to negotiate effectively with institution
- Greater emphasis on teamwork
- Recognition of the importance of flexibility in working arrangements
- The devolution of responsibilities and budgets
- The importance of individual time management

6. TEACHING AND TRAINING SKILLS

The librarian's educational role forms the central plank on which his or her other duties and responsibilities are built. According to Fielden Report that the librarians understand teaching and training skills to fulfill academic needs.

- To provide effective user education for large group of users or small group of users

- To understand how students organize their studies and how they go about learning. In this way, library programmes may be tailored to majority needs and styles of learning
- To be familiar with a wide variety of teaching and learning methods including coaching, facilitation, workbooks, joint or group teaching and increasingly nowadays the opportunities provided by the electronic classroom
- To be aware of the problems of non-traditional students such as those studying part-time, distance learners, and overseas and disabled students
- To prepare to innovate and take risks whenever the opportunity presents itself
- To help academic staff to design and develop course material. This may be particularly helpful where open and distance learning conducted

7. ICT SKILLS

It is information technology, which generates the most vigorous debate in relation to the changing role of the librarian. The technological advances continue to ask questions of the support services, including the library. The Library services examined on the balance between collection development and the accessing of information electronically.

- To keep up to date with subject-based knowledge and accompanying IT developments
- To play an advisory role in guiding students and staff through the diverse range of electronic sources, formats and services
- To train library staff and users
- To access to electronic sources of information including for various academic activities

8. IT MANAGEMENT SKILLS

- Word processing
- Desktop publishing
- Use of bibliographic software packages
- Spreadsheets
- Graphics packages
- Bulletin boards
- Maintaining WWW files
- Library Automated systems
- IT troubleshooting
- Familiarity with different operating systems
- Elearning Education
- Search Techniques
- Digital Library and Digital Library Software
- Digital Repositories
- Information Literacy
- Web designing, Web portals
- Network Technology
- RFID Technology

9. INNOVATIONS AND COLLABORATION

Innovation will be key to the very survival of the librarian in the future. The Librarians will need to find innovative solutions to the "economics of physical things it means that digitizing a collection, using all electronic sources including online journals, or on databases, services, providing research and training, web management, knowledge management, archive management and competitive intelligence.

- Access to online journals
- Links to the Hidden Internet

- Access to the archives
- Internal experts
- Vendor databases
- Internal articles, papers
- Online catalog
- Training videos
- Elearning Education

10. PROFESSIONAL COMPETENCIES FOR LIBRARY AND INFORMATION SCIENCE PROFESSIONALS

10.1. Managing Information Organizations

Information professionals manage information organizations ranging in size from one user several hundred users. These organizations may be in any environment from corporate, education, public, government, to non-profit. Information professionals excel at managing these organizations whose offerings are intangible, whose markets are constantly changing and in which both high-tech and high-touch are vitally important in achieving organizational success.

- Extensive development of self-access to collections and processes
- Assessing and communicating the value of the information organization, including information services, products
- Establishing effective management, operational and financial management processes and exercises in decision-making.
- Contributing effectively to management strategies and decisions regarding information applications, tools , technologies, and policies for the organization.
- Building and leading an effective information services team , professional and personal development of users

working within the information organization.

- Marketing information services and products, both formally and informally, through web and physical communication, presentations, publications.
- Collecting the best available evidence to support decisions about the development of new service and products, the modification of current services or the elimination of services to continually improve the array of information services offered.
- Advising the organization on copyright and intellectual property issues and compliance.

10.2. Managing Information Resources

Information professionals have expertise in total management of information resources, including identifying, selecting, evaluating, securing and providing access to pertinent information resources. These resources may be in any media or format. The information will be recorded digitally and resources will be available in electronic forms.

- Creation of publications resulting from information packaging and repackaging, in response to users needs rather than to the academic vanity or personal interest of the librarians
- Innovation leading to the creation of new information products and versions of those already existing to contribute to knowledge dissemination to increase the value of primary sources and catalogues
- Managing the full life cycle of information from its creation or acquisition through its destruction. This includes organizing, categorizing, cataloguing, classifying, disseminating, creating and managing taxonomies, intranet and extranet content, thesauri etc.
- Building a dynamic collection of information resources based on a deep understanding of users information

needs and their learning, work and/or business processes.

– Demonstrating expert knowledge of the content and format of information resources, including the ability to critically evaluate, select and filter them.

– Providing access to the best available externally published and internally created information resources and deploys content throughout the organization using a suitable of information access tools.

– Negotiating the purchase and licensing of needed information products and services.

– Developing information policies for the organization regarding externally published and internally created information resources and advises on the implementation of these policies.

– Reading / paper = reader + document and in future it will be electronic reading = reader +electronic device + reading devices which will require three elements to access information

10.3. Managing Information Services

The library of future will focus on helping the users to access information both remotely and independently. This will require direct and indirect services, which, without necessarily being present to support all the possibilities of a library and to give access to knowledge by means of electronic devices. The lending and reference services will be available in future library also

– Remote information services so that information may be accessed from different academic, social and domestic environments

– An extensive global online library and information network

– Videotexts (telecommunication + informaics +

television); teletext (television network); interactive videotexts (telephonic network)

- Multimedia information sources
- Information distribution by mobile communication technologies
- Multiple and accurate interface among libraries and all kinds of information suppliers and users
- A great variety of gateways and access keys to information
- Information offered by and accessible from libraries as well as being available from outside the library, together with information collection, organization and analysis
- Quality control of processes and services to facilitate the flow and efficiency of information exchange, access and use
- Quality will be a top priority in the libraries
- Variety of help programs so users will have self access to the desired information

10.4. APPLYING INFORMATION TOOLS AND TECHNOLOGIES

Information professionals harness the current and appropriate technology tools to deliver the best services, provide the most relevant and accessible resources, develop and deliver teaching tools to maximize use of information.

- Assessing s, selects and applies current and emerging information tools and creates information access and delivery solutions
- Applying expertise in databases, indexing, metadata, and information analysis and synthesis to improve information retrieval and use in the organization
- Protecting the information privacy of clients and

maintains awareness of, and responses to, new challenges to privacy

– Maintaining current awareness of emerging technologies that may not be currently relevant but may become relevant tools of future information resources, services or applications

11. ROLE OF LIBRARY AND INFORMATION SCIENCE PROFESSIONALS

The library will no longer be thought of as a monolithic institution but as a distributed institution that facilitate information access to all its users, regardless of their category and location. The library will no longer be a building and concentrated collection, but a main or central office with access station to other sources of information such as that coordinated and found in local library networks. The role and activities of library professionals will be as

– Education by designing and applying teaching programs to simplify access to the varied informative commercially available resources

– Information search processes that will be perfected and simplified because in most cases they will not be run directly by the user but through communication technologies

– Index and database creation that will be a priority in order to offer analyzed information for very specific interests

– Inclusion of full texts, which will increase, their usage will depend on users needs and the demands of he subject matter.

– Ability to search information from various electronic sources

– Promote elearning education

– Provide information at their desktop in the networked environment

12. CONCLUSION

The library and information science professionals have to learn the new technology to provide effective service to the users. The information resources are available in a variety of forms. The users also need specific information related to academic activities. In order to satisfy the requirements of the users, the library staff should have ability to access information from various sources like online sources, databases etc. In future, the user will depend on library for information where as the librarian has to play a vital role to direct or to connect the users to resource electronically in networked environment.

REFERENCE

1. http://www.emerald -library.com

28

Knowledge Management and The Librarian : An Overview

Subrata Sur
Sujata Sur

ABSTRACT

Present day library is not limited within the four walls. In the knowledge era, the library will become a treasure house of human knowledge, participate in knowledge innovation. It is, therefore, pertinent on the part of library professionals to acquire new skills required for developing and managing knowledge. The paper covers the overview of KM, key steps in KM; critical success factors; discuss application of KM in library and explains the changing role of librarian to address and solve the problem that raised at the time of managing digital library.

1. INTRODUCTION

While people have criticized knowledge management as the same old thing using different words, a well-developed knowledge management system would stimulate the creative of each employee by providing exactly the knowledge that employee would be optimally creative. Knowledge Management must be an enabler to achieve strategic business objectives. Knowledge strategy must evolve from business strategy and again contribute to achieving business results. It also suggests measures of KM success that are linked to achievement of real business results.

2. DEFINITION OF KNOWLEDGE

"Knowledge has become the pre-eminent economic resource more important than raw materials, more important, often, than money. Considered as an economic output, information and automobiles, oil, or any of the products of the industrial age." (Thomas Stewart, 1998)

"Knowledge in the capacity for effective action." (Argyris, 1993)

2.1. What Exactly is Knowledge Management?

Knowledge Management is the discipline that helps spread knowledge of individuals or groups across organizations in ways that directly affect performance.

Knowledge Management is 'the process of capture, refinement, aggregation and sharing of data and information between employees, departments and partner organizations to achieve a position of knowledge-based competitive advantage'.

Knowledge can be divided into two categories: Tacit knowledge and explicit knowledge.

Tacit Knowledge : It is the "know how" acquired by persons. It is intuitive. It is subjective, cognitive and experimental in nature.

Explicit Knowledge : It is articulated knowledge. Explicit knowledge is objective, rational and technical. It is rule -based knowledge. It is systematically documented records in any kind of format, which guides the users to gain the knowledge, and to expand the knowledge based further.

Knowledge management is thus explained as "a collection of processes, technologies and principles that serves to promote a learning environment supportive of the search community goal." (Srinivasan)

Knowledge Management envisions getting the Right Information within the Right Context to the Right Person at the Right Time for the right business purpose.

2.2. Objectives of KM

The objectives of KM include the following:

- To support the achievement of strategic business objectives.
- To create knowledge repositories.
- To improve knowledge access or to facilitate its transfer.
- To manage knowledge as an asset and to recognize the value of knowledge to an organization.
- To improve customer service and efficiency.
- To facilitate better, more informed decisions.

2.3. Critical Success Factors for KM

The three key components of KM are:

People: Those who produce and those who use knowledge that will be the basis for action. The component "People in the KM in digital environment are thus required to develop full competencies which include:

- Ability to use e-resources effectively;
- Ability to evaluate e-resources;
- Ability to search databases;
- Knowledge of document preparation and production in digital environment;
- Knowledge of networking, web-page designing and web-security;
- Knowledge to select, acquires, process and shelves e-resources.

People have been recognized as the most important enablers of KM success. Change management of traditional mindsets and culture is being achieved through awareness programs and global case studies. Motivation is provided through recognition, visibility and incentives.

Content : The flow of data, information and knowledge that will be the success of the business. "Contents" needs to be in digital format to enhance its flow in a more effective way.

Technology : Another component "Technology" for the digital environment should cover the entire new ICT infrastructure for success in KM. It enables the captures, storage and delivery of content to those who need it and when they need it.

Environment needed to maximize gaining and sharing of Knowledge:

- Learning and changed environment.
- User-friendly technique and technology environment.
- Interaction and reflection environment.

Pre-Requisites for Effective KM

- Know your needs-Be clear about what is wanted.
- Check the **Knowledge Map**- Knowledge map acts as a blue print for a building.
- Have a check with technology.
- Take a stock of where you are.
- Be prepared to fill the **Knowledge Gap**.

2.4. KM Process

Knowledge management technology should support the collaboration of people to create, capture and share knowledge. It should also provide people with access to a variety of data, information and knowledge. It should support each of the phases of knowledge creation, knowledge capture, knowledge organization, knowledge storage and retrieval, knowledge diffusion and knowledge presentation and maintenance.

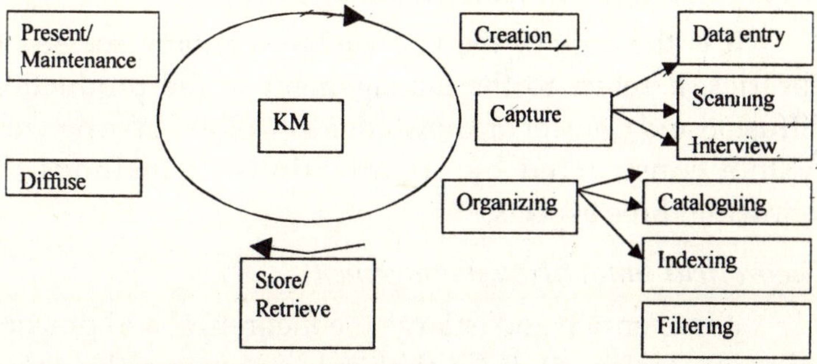

2.5. Knowledge Performance

Knowledge performance carries a high weightage on performance appraisal systems- often as high as service-quality or business development. Knowledge Performance has three aspects:

- Knowledge contribution/ sharing
- Knowledge application/ re-use or implementation based on knowledge contributions by others.
- How others have re-used or benefited from your contributions.

For best results, a combination of recognition, reward is necessary. Measures to motivate knowledge performance could include:

- Incorporating knowledge performance in employee performance appraisals.
- Introducing awards both at the individual and organization level to encourage knowledge sharing as well as application/ re-use.

3. KNOWLEDGE MANAGEMENT IN LIBRARIES

The role of KM in libraries will become more and more important along with the development of knowledge economy. In my opinion, KM in libraries should include such respects as follows:

3.1. Knowledge Innovation Management

It is the core of the knowledge economy society. In libraries, it refers to the management of the production, diffusion and transfer of knowledge as well as of the network system constructed by organizations. It includes the following three aspects:

Theoretical innovation management

It is to enrich and enlarge the theoretical and practical research fields of LISc through pursuing the latest development trends in library science the world over.

Technical innovation management

It is to manage the network systems that relate to the technical innovation.

Organizational innovation management

It is to create a set of effective organizational management systems adaptable to the requirements in the e-library era to support and strengthen KM activities, by optimizing the functional departments and operation procedures of libraries.

In these systems, it firstly requires that leaders to formulate the management plans and co-ordinate all knowledge management activities. Secondly, it requires special leading groups of knowledge flow for accomplishing all tasks. Electronic resources committees to take charge of evaluating of evaluating, procuring and creating the electronic resources, and co-ordinating activities on the one hand, as well as providing services on the other hand.

3.2. Knowledge Dissemination Management:

Knowledge creators do not have much time and energy to look for knowledge users. Therefore, libraries use diverse media and channels to disseminate various new knowledge and acquiring information (like internet).

Libraries follow some guidelines:

- continuously raising the quality of libraries' staffs and strengthening continuous engineering education of working staffs;
- uninterruptedly strengthening the creation of libraries' own document resources;
- making a comprehensive utilization of all media to ensure security of operation of networks, and prevent online criminal activities.

3.3. Human Resource Management

HRM takes it as its basic starting point to train high quality specialized talents and to revitalize the library undertaking. We should pay full attention to diversity and variation of library staffs' requirement; applying contingency approach. That is,

- to some people, rigid management method is applied; supervision, quality and procure are made clear;
- and, to the rest of people, more flexible management method is applied to let them participate in decision-making.

Librarian's Role

Many librarians and information professionals already have been "transformed" into knowledge professionals.

David Skyrme and Debra Amidon listed the roles for knowledge professionals based on their observations:

- **Knowledge Engineer** : represents or maps tacit and explicit knowledge to enable its classification and dissemination.
- **Knowledge Editor** : refines explicit knowledge into formats, which makes subsequent access and use easier.
- **Knowledge Analysts** : acts as a link between the

customer and the knowledge bare.

- **Knowledge Navigator :** understands where the repositories of knowledge are within the organization. Acts as mentors to new knowledge analysts.
- **Knowledge Managers :** Tools of KM consists 70% of services and 30% of Technologies. Librarians provide these 70% services. This indicates the role of librarians as knowledge Managers. Where their functions are:
  * Sharing of information and understanding of user needs.
  * Analyzing documents, classifying and sorting them for easy retrieval.
  * Building the index, etc.

4. GUIDELINES FOR IMPLEMENTATION OF KM

- KM should be integrated into the culture, so that everyone becomes a "knowledge leader".
- An organization must develop a framework of capturing knowledge to avoid losing it.
- Information System must be made accessible and easy to use.
- Technology should be "human centered".
- Knowledge must be quickly created, capture and transformed across internal boundaries in order to increase the pace of innovation.
- Time and resource must be provided for knowledge sharing.
- Understanding among staff.
- Keeping track of the process of workflow in the organization.

5. CONCLUSION

Knowledge is power; it is the backbone of any

organizations. KM is emerging as a predominate force in overall strategies of organizational management. The objective of knowledge management is to support the achievement of business objectives. Both knowledge-contributions/ sharing as well as re-use need to be encouraged and recognized at the individual employee level as well as the organization level. This is best done by measuring and rewarding knowledge performance. Measures used to evaluate success in KM must be related to business results. With a concerned effort, KM will help to increase libraries operational efficiency and cater to the ever-increasing needs of our clientele.

REFERENCE

1. Awad (Elias M.) and Ghaziri (Hassan M.). Knowledge Management. Delhi: Pearson Education, 2004,456p.
2. Mahapatra (P.K.) and Chakraborty (B.K.). Knowledge management in libraries. New Delhi: Ess Ess, 2002,288p.
3. CFAI Journal of Knowledge Management 1(b), 2003, 1-90.
4. Binwal (J.C.). Knowledge management. IASLIC Bulletin 46(2) 2001,65-78.
5. Rao (Madanmohan). Leading with knowledge. New Delhi: TMG, 2001,p73.
6. Rusbridg (E Chris). Towards the hybrid library. D-Lib Magazine July/Aug 1998.
7. Singh, Pramod Kumar- Knowledge Management Application in Libraries and Information Centres-DRTC project-2, 1999-2001.
8. Ahmed, P.K., Lim, K.K. & Loh, A.Y.E (2002) learning through Knowledge Management Oxford: Butterworth-Heinemann.

29

Knowledge Management System's Life Cycle : A Study

Nagappa V. Bakkannanavar
Suryanarayana Sastry B H

ABSTRACT

This paper deals with data, information, knowledge, types of Knowledge Management (KM), steps involved in it, KM life cycle, challenges in building in KM system, Implementing KM system, Quality Assurance, etc.

1. INTRODUCTION

Knowledge Management is the solution for realizing the firm's technical capabilities to create the knowledge that drives the firm forward. The new and unpredictable business environment puts a premium on innovation and creativity much more so than it has in the past. This emphasizes the need for the present working to be smarter, not harder. It is obsoleting what you know before others obsolete it and profit by creating the challenges and opportunities others haven't even thought about.

2. DATA, INFORMATION & KNOWLEDGE:

Data are unorganized and unprocessed facts. They are static. The word information is derived from the word "inform", which means, "to give shape to", information means shaping the data to arrive at a meaning in the eyes of the perceiver. Information is an aggregation of data that makes decision making easier. It is also facts and figures based on reformatted or processed data.

Knowledge has different meanings, depending on the discipline where it is used. In this text, knowledge is "human understanding of a specialized field of interest that has been acquired through study and experience". It is based on learning, thinking, and familiarity with the problem area in a department, a division, or in the company as a whole. The focus is on "sustainable competitive advantage". Knowledge is not information, and information is not data. Davenport and Prusak (2000) define knowledge as a fluid mix of framed experience, values, contextual information, and expert insight that provides a framework for evaluating and incorporating new experiences and information.

3. TYPES OF KNOWLEDGE

Knowledge is classified into different types. When considering KM, the knowledge developer should be familiar with each type and know how to tap into it during knowledge capture.

3.1. Shallow and Deep Knowledge

Shallow or readily recalled surface knowledge indicates minimal understanding of the problem data. Deep knowledge is the knowledge acquired through years of experience.

3.2. Knowledge as Know-how

Knowledge based on reading and training is much different from knowledge based on practical experience that spans many years. Knowledge based on know-how, or accumulated lessons of practical experience, is what is needed for building expert systems. The problem with practical experience is that it is rarely documented. Capturing such experience requires special tools. Know-how is not book knowledge; it is practical experience. It can be expressed as rules or thumb or heuristics if one were to build a knowledge base for knowledge sharing within the organization.

3.3. Common Sense as Knowledge

Common sense is another type of knowledge that all human beings posses in varying forms and in varying amounts. It is a collection of personal experiences and facts acquired over time and type of knowledge that humans tend to take for granted.

3.4. From Procedural to Episodic Knowledge

Procedural Knowledge : It is an understanding of how to do a task or carry out a procedure. It is the knowledge contained in the application of a procedure.

Declarative Knowledge : It is the information that experts can easily discuss. Unlike procedural knowledge, it is "awareness knowledge"' or routine knowledge of which the expert is conscious. It is shallow knowledge that is readily recalled, because it is simple, uncompleted information.

Semantic Knowledge : It is a deeper kind of knowledge. It is highly organized, "Chunked" knowledge that resides in long-term memory. Such knowledge may have been there in years and may have been used so often that the information systems like second nature. Semantic knowledge includes major concepts, vocabulary, facts, and relationships.

Episodic Knowledge : It is the knowledge based on experimental information, or episodes. Each episode is chunked in long-term memory. In general, the longer a human expert takes to explain it or verbalize his or her knowledge, the more semantic or episodic it.

3.5. Explicit and Tacit Knowledge

Tacit knowledge is the knowledge embedded in the human mind through experience and jobs. Coined by Hungarian Medical Scientist Michael Polanyi (1891-1976), it includes intuitions, values, and benefits that stem from years of experience> It is the knowledge used to create Explicit Knowledge and is best communicated personally through dialogue and scenarios, with use of metaphors. Therefore knowledge is not private but social. Socially relayed knowledge becomes part of the real-life experience of the knower.

In contrast, Explicit Knowledge is the knowledge codified and digitized in books, documents, reports, white papers, spreadsheets, memos, training courses, and the like. Explicit knowledge can be retrieved and transmitted more easily than Tacit knowledge. Because it is the knowledge learned directly from experience, tacit knowledge (also referred to as whispers in the ears) is difficult to share across space and time.

3.6. Chunking Knowledge

It is the knowledge stored in an expert's long-range memory as chunks. Knowledge compilation or chunking enables experts to optimize their memory capacity and process information quickly. Chunks are groups of ideas or details that are stored recalled together as a unit. Chunking promotes expert performance. The more chunking a person does, the more efficient is his or her recall.

3.7. Human Thinking and Learning

Because knowledge is the focus of Knowledge Management, knowledge developers need to understand how humans think and learn. Humans do not receive and process information in the same way that machines do. For instance, humans receive information via sensing - seeing, smelling, tasting, touching, and hearing. This system of receiving external stimuli promotes a kind of thinking and learning that is unique to humans.

As humans acquire more and more knowledge, they generally experience little interference with the recall ability or the quality of information in memory. In other words, as people learn new facts, they integrate them in some way with what they think is relevant and organize the resulting mix to produce valuable decisions, solutions, or advice. Such learning ability is the basis of accumulating knowledge, experience and expertise.

3.8. Learning by Experience, Example and Discovery

Trial and error or reworking problems is used to acquire experience in the problem solving. An expert uses experience to explain how a problem is solved. Specially constructed examples or scenarios are used to develop the concept(s) the student is expected to learn. In knowledge capture, the human expert uses a scenario to explain how a problem is solved. This is an undirected approach where human explore a problem area with no advance knowledge of what their object is.

4. WHAT IS KNOWLEDGE MANAGEMENT (KM)?

KM is a newly emerging, interdisciplinary business model that has knowledge within the framework of an organization as its focus. It is rooted in many disciplines, including business, economics, psychology, and information management. It is the ultimate competitive advantage for today's firm. KM involves people, technology, and process in overlapping parts.

5. STEPS IN KM

- Using accessible knowledge from outside sources.
- Embedding and storing knowledge in business processes, products and services.
- Representing knowledge in databases and documents.

- Promoting knowledge growth through the organization's culture and incentives.
- Transforming and sharing knowledge through out the organization.
- Assessing the value of knowledge assets and impact on a regular basis.

KM is the process of capturing and making use of a firm's collective expertise any where in the business - on paper, in documents, in databases (Called Explicit Knowledge), or in people's heads (Called Tacit Knowledge). KM is the fuel or raw material for innovation - the only competitive advantage that can sustain a company in an unpredictable business environment.

The goal is for an organization to view all its processes as knowledge processes. This includes knowledge creation, dissemination, upgrade, and application towards organizational survival.

6. KM LIFE CYCLE

KM goes through a series of steps, making up an ongoing life cycle. The process includes gathering, organizing, refining, and disseminating.

The capturing phase deals with knowledge capture and includes e-mail, audio files, digital files and the file. After the capturing phase, captured data or information should be organized in a way that can be retrieved and used to generate useful knowledge. One can use indexing, clustering, cataloguing, filtering, codifying, and other methods to do the organizing. Speed, user-friendliness, efficiency of access, and accuracy are important elements to consider throughout the organizing phase. After organizing the information, it should be refined. Data Mining can be applied in this phase. Data Mining takes explicit knowledge found in databases and transforms it into tacit knowledge. Data Mining software is used to find patterns in data, predict behavior and warn against future problems based on the data supplied in data warehouses.

6.1. KM Systems Life Cycle

Rapid Prototyping Process

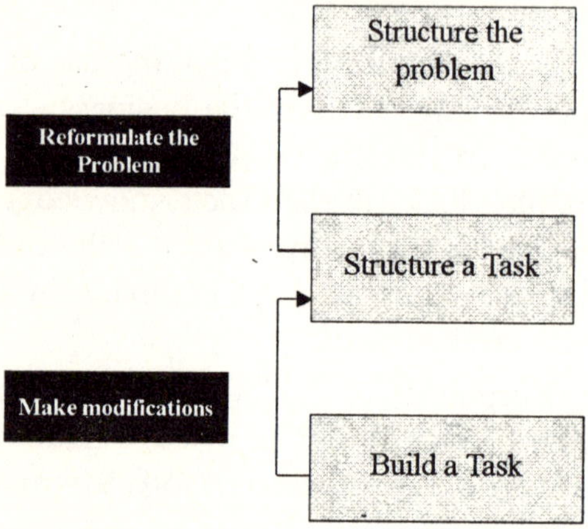

7. CHALLENGES IN BUILDING KM SYSTEMS

At this juncture, we must need to discuss some major challenges the KM is facing. They are:

1. Culture : Changing the organizational culture is not an overnight exercise. The number one challenge is getting people to share their knowledge rather than hoarding it. To do so means changing people's attitudes and behaviors. The company that develops the right combination of incentives for employees to collaborate and share their knowledge will go a long way towards ensuring a successful KM System.

2. Knowledge Evaluation : An organization, which tackles the evaluation issue, will have both a head start on the employee incentive problem and an edge on refining KM processes for maximum profit. Assessing the worth of information is a crucial step if an organization wants to refine its methods or create a reward system for employees who have generated the best knowledge. Unfortunately, estimating the worth of knowledge is complicated. Reliable materials have yet to be made available.

3. Knowledge Processing : Many organizations do not recognize the importance of the human element in KM. Effective KM Systems must allow the organizations not only to store and access information but to document how decisions were reached as well. Specifically, techniques should be identified that will capture, store, process and distribute the kind of knowledge that cannot be readily tabulated in rows or columns.

4. Knowledge Implementation : When comes to KM, every organization must commit to change, learning and innovating if it is to realize leadership in the market place. Technology has already made it possible to implement knowledge collaborations regardless of time and place. One of the important tasks in KM is extracting meaning from information that will have an impact on special problems or missions.

8. EVALUATING EXISTING INFRASTRUCTURE

The basis for a KM system is satisfying a need for improving the productivity and potentiality of employees and the company as a whole. To do so, we need to gain familiarity with various components making up the KM strategy and supporting technology. So that, identifying and evaluating the current knowledge environment makes it easier to point out the critical missing gaps and justify the formation of a new KM environment.

As part of this, we focus on system justification, scoping the evaluation, and determining feasibility.

8.1. System Justification

The goal of this step is for the knowledge developer to justify whether it is worth undergoing the kinds of changes and investment that ensure top management support. KM system justification involves answers to specific questions:

1. Is current knowledge going to be lost through retirement, transfer, or departure to other firms?
2. Is the proposed KM system needed in several locations?
3. Are experts available and willing to help in building a KM system?
4. Does the problem in question require years of experience and cognitive reasoning to solve?
5. When undergoing knowledge capture, can the expert articulate how the problem will be solved?
6. How critical is the knowledge to be captured?
7. Is there a champion in the house?

8.2. The Scope Factor

When deciding how large the KM system should be, it is important to know the scope of the project. The term "Scoping" means limiting the breadth and depth of the project with the financial human resource, and operational constraints. The project should be small enough for the knowledge developer's capability, especially if it is the organization's first attempt at developing a KM system.

As part of the scoping factor, several areas must be included:

1. Readiness of the organization's current technology including Intranet, local area networks, extranet, decision support tools and other information technology tools.
2. Identification of gaps and areas needing improvement in current technology to see how well such technology will match the technical requirements of the proposal KM system.
3. General review and understanding of the benefits and

limitations of KM tools and components that become part of the feasibility study.

8.3. The Feasibility Study

The first phase to consider is feasibility. A feasibility study should address the following questions:

1. Is the project doable? Can it be completed within a reasonable time?
2. Is it affordable? Do the system's potential benefits justify the cost of development?
3. Is it appropriate? How frequently would the system be consulted and at what cost?

8.4. Importance of User Support

At this stage of development life cycle, a knowledge developer needs to address a no. of questions.

1. Does the intended user know the new KM system is being developed? How is it perceived?
2. How involved should the ultimate user be in the building process?
3. What user training will be required when the KM system is up and running?
4. What operational support must be provided?

8.5. Form the KM Team

After the evaluation of organization's existing infrastructure is complete, a KM team should be formed; this team stays with the building process until the final installation. Forming a KM team means:

– Identifying the key units, departments, branches, or divisions as the key stakeholders in the prospective KM system. Each stakeholder unit has certain knowledge requirements and one or more experts who could represent the unit on the KM team.

- The KM should consist balanced no. of experts in each area to collaborate on the multi-dimensional nature of the KM system building process.

Team success mainly depends on a number of factors:

- Caliber of team members in terms of personality, communication skills and experience.
- Team size.
- Complexity of the project.
- Leadership and team motivation.
- Promising more than can be realistically delivered.

8.6. Knowledge Capture and Transfer Through Teams

In KMSLC, knowledge capture takes on several directions and meanings. Briefly, explicit knowledge is captured in repositories from documentation, files and then media. In contrast, tacit knowledge is captured from company experts and from knowledge stored in databases for all authorized employees. Ata Mining also enters the picture in terms of using intelligent agents that analyze the data-ware house and come up with new findings that could lead to new products or services. The following diagram will give the better idea about the knowledge capture and transfer:

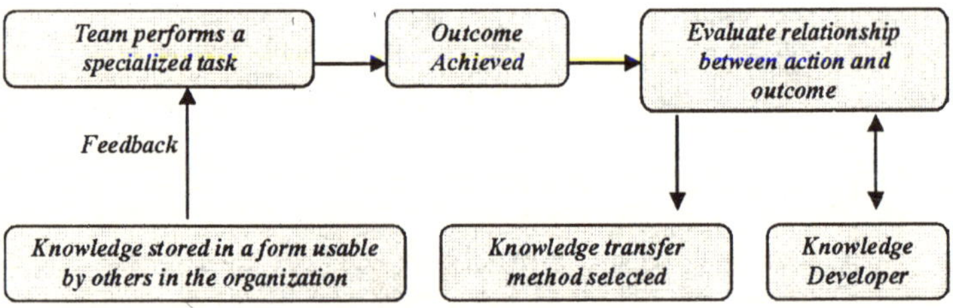

8.7. Role of Knowledge Developer

The knowledge developer is an important player in the KMSLC. He or she is the architecture of the system. This one person identifies the problem domain, captures the knowledge, writes and tests the heuristics that represent the knowledge, and coordinates the entire project from beginning to end.

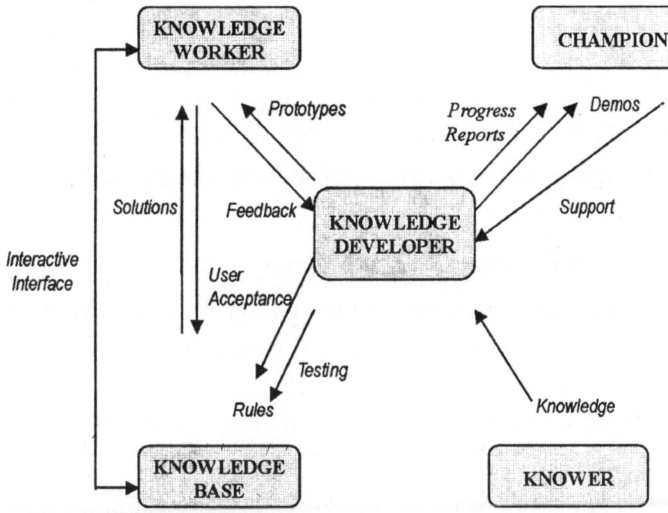

8.8. Design the KM Blue Print

This phase is the beginning of designing the IT infrastructure and the knowledge management architecture. The KM team relies on such a blue print to proceed with the actual design and deployment of the KM system. A KM blue print referred to as the KM system design, addresses several important issues. Once created, the next step is to actually put together the KM system.

8.9. Test the KM System

The testing phase involves 2 steps: A Verification Procedure and a Validation Procedure. A Verification procedure ensures that the system is right that the programs do what they are designed to do. The internal makeup of the systems is checked to see that the right knowledge is available when needed in the format needed and that any rules will fire when they are supposed to fire. In this way, technical performance of system is evaluated.

The second procedure is called "Validation Procedure". This test ensures that the system is the right system that it means the user's expectations that it is user friendly and that it will be usable and scalable on demand. Validation provides assurance that the solutions or advice derived from the KM system comes close enough to that of the human expert. In other words, the validation process checks the reliability of the KM system.

8.10. Implementing the KM System

Once the appropriate knowledge has been captured, encoded in the knowledge base, verified, and validated, next task of the developer is to implement or deploy the proposed system on a computer or a server. Implementation means converting a new KM system into actual operation. Conversion is a major step in implementation. The other steps are post-implementation review and KM system maintenance. Another way of looking at implementation is that it is the transformation of a precise representation of knowledge into a machine-executable equivalent – a specific program or software package.

8.11. Role of Quality Assurance

Quality Assurance is the development of controls to ensure a quality KM system. This feature is actually emphasized in every stage of the system development process. The goal is to have as error-free and reliable a system as possible. Knowledge developers under time and budget constraints could compromise quality, especially during knowledge capture. The chief knowledge officer (CKO) has the responsibility to ensure that every step in KM is error-free.

There are several kinds of errors to look for in knowledge base design:

- Reasoning Errors
- Ambiguity
- Incompleteness
- False Representation

8.12. User Training

A major part of the implementation phase is training organization employees on the new KM system. The level and duration of training depends on the user's knowledge level and system's attributes. Users range from novices to experts. A novice is generally a casual user with limited knowledge of I.T. An expert is someone with prior IT experience and who keeps abreast of the technology.

9. CONCLUSION

An essential criterion of knowledge and learning is memory. Learning by discovery is less understood than learning by experience or by example. A knowledge base is a critical component of knowledge management. Knowledge developers need to understand the theory and meaning of knowledge early in the knowledge capture phase and become familiar with the unique kinds of knowledge available in the corporation under study. It should be pointed out that an expert's knowledge is not limited to information or complex procedures. Knowledge embraces a wider sphere than information. Likewise, a knowledge base is not the same as a database. A database has a predetermined structure; a knowledge base is a set of facts and inference rules for determining new information and "smarter" knowledge for decision-making.

The most critical word in KM area is *Knowledge.* Unfortunately, there is a continuing myth that knowledge resides only in books, reports, or documents. What do we mean when we talk about knowledge? Two key issues are distinguishing between knowledge and information and determining how they are interrelated. Knowledge is neither data nor information, although it is related to both. The terms are not interchangeable, and knowing what is needed often determines organizational success or failure.

The building of Knowledge Management can be viewed as a life cycle that begins with a master plan and justification ends with a system structured to meet KM requirements for the entire company. A knowledge team representing the thinking of the firm and a knowledge developer with expertise in knowledge capture, knowledge design, and knowledge implementation ensure a successful system. Lack of planning, structure, and order can invite disaster.

The most critical phase of the KM systems life cycle is identifying the immediate, intermediate, and long-term needs for the prospective system. This means reviewing the knowledge core of existing employees; conducting a cost/ benefit analysis to determine the justification for the potential benefits of the candidate system; and determining the tools and the procedures to ensure completeness, accuracy, integrity, and operational success of the installation.

REFERENCE

1. Knowledge Management by Shelda Debowski, Australia: John Wiley & sons, 2006.
2. The knowledge management field book by Wendi R. Bukowitz and Ruth L. Williams, Delhi: Pearson Education Asia, 2000.
3. Knowledge Management tools & techniques: Practitioners and experts evaluate KM solutions Edited by Madanmohan Rao, New Delhi: Elsevier India, 2005.
4. Knowledge Management: A new dawn Edited by Ratnaja Gogula, Hyderabad: ICFAI University, 2002.
5. Knowledge Management in organizations: A critical introduction by Donald Hislop, New Delhi: Oxford University Press, 2005.
6. Knowledge Management by Warier E. Sudhir, New Delhi: Vikas Publishing House, 2003.

30

Knowledge Management Course Curricula for Indian LIS Schools

K. V Satyanarayana
Seema Nair
Shubhada Apte

ABSTRACT

This paper provides background of Knowledge Management (KM) and attempts to identify the core skills required in the KM field. It surveys the library science curriculum available in India and, and suggests possible curricula changes required to enable new library professionals graduating from Indian library schools to perform wide ranging and multiple KM roles in organizations.

1. INTRODUCTION

Technological advances, particularly with growth of the Internet, have changed the role of librarianship and posed serious questions for libraries. Knowledge Management (KM) is one such relatively new area that emerged in the early nineties. It is now widely accepted that KM is a key factor in the success of the organization. There are several definitions available for KM and they all vary based on the tradition or practice they belong to, bringing out the multidisciplinary nature of the field. A broader definition of KM includes activities that will facilitate creation, capture, organization, access, and application of knowledge.

In general, it is agreed that KM has relevance to the library and information profession, however the relationship between KM and the library profession is not yet clear. By looking at number of activities involved in KM, it is clear that KM activities go well beyond library and information services and library professionals alone will not play the leading role. While KM represents new opportunities for library professionals, it also acts as a threat to library professionals. If library professionals are unable to gain new skills required and involve themselves in organizational KM activities, their relevance and importance to the organization will reduce and other professionals from other industries will find more employment in KM rolesfields.

KM projects in libraries tend to focus more on capturing and sharing knowledge. A few other roles that library professionals can play in their organization are development of taxonomies, content management, providing information for the Intranet, providing competitive intelligence, creation of best practice databases, and creation of knowledge expert's directory, identifying and acquiring internal information sources and designing of information architecture.

Rise in the importance of KM in organizations leads to many academic departments starting the courses in KM with taking different views on the nature and scope of Knowledge Management. In general, we can find Knowledge Management modules in schools and departments of library science, computer science, business and management, education, etc. Contents and focus of the courses vary, depending on which department is having the programme. A few examples of library schools offering Master's degrees in knowledge management include Loughborough, London Metropolitan University and a few others like RMIT, State University of New Jersey offer KM as the subject.

University	*IT topics*	*KM topics*
Bharati Vidyapeeth Deemed University	IT basics	
Delhi University	IT basics, ICT, Advanced computer applications in LIS	
Documentation Research & Training Centre (DRTC)	IT technology & systems design, IT transfer and dissemination, Application of AI to Library and information, Programming languages	DLsDigital libraries
IGNOU	IT basics, computer knowledge, library automation, information network, intellectual organization of information, subject indexing, information storage & retrieval, automated libraries and information systems.	
Mumbai Bombay University	Computer application to library work, IT to librarians	
Osmania University	IT - basics, computer software, software for libraries, Introduction to programming languages,	KM concepts, content management, virtual library, E-libraries, document management, citation analysis, networking library automation
University of Madras	Introduction to Computers	Knowledge management, Information Society, Knowledge organization
University of Mysore	Fundamentals of IT, IT skills, practical	Virtual Libraries, DLs, Economic and

	knowledge (hands-on with Microsoft Word, Excel), data communication and networking	legal issues - copyrights and IPR
University of Pune	Basics of IT- Networking, library automation, networking, Telecommunication	Concepts of KM-, introduction to AI and digital library

TFPL Report, a hall mark study for identification of roles and skills required for effective implementation of knowledge management, found that information professionals' involvement in KM implementation at a strategic level was extremely rare. This is because these professionals lacked business understanding, experience, mindset, risk-taking ability and initiative. It also found that information professionals are more concerned with external information. Morris survey found that industry experience, team and leadership skills, communication skills, and project management skills are key skills required for KM professionals.

Choi and Rasmussen identified Technical, Library-Related, and Other Managerial Competencies as three broad categories of digital library competencies. Technical knowledge competencies include Digital Library (DL) architecture and software, technical, and quality standards. Library-related competencies include cataloging and classification, digital archiving and preservation, identifying user needs. Special managerial competencies include communication skills, project management and leadership skills, and the ability to handle legal issues.

Current library school programs incorporated some of the core elements of KM but there is also need to train students in business and management competencies.

2. INDIAN CONDITION

In India, there is a sudden rise in job advertisements for KM roles for last two years. Many of these job advertisements included need for practical knowledge management experience or understanding of the importance of knowledge to the development of an organization. Chief Knowledge Officer, Knowledge Architect, Knowledge Manager and Content Manager Positions are available in organizations. In a few instances, librarians occupied these roles.

Through Internet research, we examined the curriculum of nine library science schools in India. We found that many of these programs are not sufficient to meet the KM role requirements. The institutes covered are University of Pune, University of Mysore, Bombay University, Osmania University, Delhi University, Bharati Vidyapeeth, Pune, DRTC, Bangalore and University of Madras. Less than 50% of these institutes have topics related to KM and digital libraries and most of them deal with the basics of KM and digital libraries.

Hence based on surveys conducted worldwide by various authors and needs of knowledge organizations, we suggest a broad framework of curriculum for Indian library schools to include under following categories:

1. Foundations : includes theory and practice of knowledge management, sources of knowledge, knowledge organizations, intellectual property, and business impact

2. Technology : KM architecture, open source digital repositories, markup languages, collaborative technologies including social networking, electronic document management, KM technologies and systems including Business Intelligence systems

3. Library related skills : codification, classification, search and retrieval, external and internal source identification, competitive intelligence, data analysis or data mining, and identification of user needs

4. Application : applying of KM in organizations, KM strategies, case studies

5. Management skills : Project management, change management, team building, oral and written communication

6. Industry skills : basic understanding of business process and value chain of knowledge intrinsic industries and functions, e.g., Financial services, Insurance, Pharmaceutical, R&D

7. IP laws : basic understanding of legal aspects of all intellectual property assets, e.g. patents, copyright, trademarks, service marks

Collaboration with business and management, computer science, law departments in their institute or university and linkages with industries for guest lectures and networking with industrial and professional associations will provide necessary faculty for all these categories. Without the collaboration from other academic departments and industry experts, it is unlikely KM teaching will be successful.

We expect such broader framework will provide starting point for library schools to further discuss, elaborate and include in their curricula in near future.

REFERENCE

1. Terry L Weech. Competencies needed for digital Librarianship. *In* Digital Library for the Magreh workshop, Rabat, Morocco. 25-27 Jan 2007
2. Sharat Fergusar and Philip Hider. Knowledge Management education in Australia. In Education for Library and Information Services, p. 89-104
3. Sajjad Ur Rehman and Abdus Sattar Chaudhry. KM education in LIS programs. In IFLA 2005: World Library and Information Congress

31

The Components of Knowledge Management

Gireesh A. Ganjihal
Santosh A. Navalur
Pratibha S. Kumbargoudar

ABSTRACT

Knowledge management seeks to understand the way in which knowledge is used and traded within organizations and treats knowledge as self-referential and recursive. This recursion means that the definition of knowledge is in a state of flux. Knowledge management treats knowledge as information within some context. Knowledge in this context consists of information augmented by intentionality (or direction). The main objective of knowledge management is to ensure that the right information is delivered to the right person just in time, in order to take the most appropriate decision. In this paper we made an attempt to point out various activities of knowledge management under three major components namely ***knowledge generation*** *which includes all activities, which brings to light knowledge that is "new" to the individual, to the group, and to the organization,* ***Knowledge codification*** *which is the representation of knowledge so that it can be "reused" either by an individual or an organization and* ***Knowledge transfer*** *which is the "Movement of knowledge" from one location to another.*

1. INTRODUCTION

The move from an industrially based economy to knowledge or information-based one in the 21st Century demands a top-notch knowledge management system to secure a competitive edge and a capacity for learning.

Globalization and other rapid changes in technologies increasingly require organizations to generate new knowledge in order to remain competitive. In order to innovate successfully, firms must generate knowledge faster than their rivals. So to be competent in the competitive environment and to able to grow according the objectives of the organization the transfer of that knowledge, as a form of capital among the people of the organization is most important, so successful knowledge transfer involves neither computers nor documents but rather interactions between people.

2. KNOWLEDGE MANAGEMENT

2.1. What is Knowledge?

Knowledge is what is known. Like the related concepts truth, belief, and wisdom, there is no single definition of knowledge on which scholars agree, but rather numerous theories and continued debate about the nature of knowledge.

"Knowledge is the awareness and understanding of facts, truths or information gained in the form of experience or learning (a posteriori), or through introspection (a priori). Knowledge is an appreciation of the possession of interconnected details which, in isolation, are of lesser value." [1].

"Knowledge is a fluid mix of framed experience, values, contextual information, and expert insight that provides a framework for evaluation and incorporating new experiences and information." [2].

"Knowledge is the right information put into use in the right way at the right time, whereas information is merely the amalgamation of various data sets within a specific context." [3].

2.2. Basic Types of Knowledge

– Tacit Knowledge; and

– Explicit Knowledge

Tacit Knowledge

It is highly personal and hard to formalize, making it difficult to communicate of share with others. Subjective insights, intuitions and hunches fall into this category of knowledge. It is deeply rooted in and individuals' actions and experience as well as in the ideals, values, or emotions he or she embraces. Personal qualities which make it hard to formalize and communicate. It 'indwells' in a comprehensive cognizance of the human mind and body. Japanese view knowledge as being primarily tacit, something not easily visible and expressible.

There are two dimensions to tacit knowledge:

* Technical dimension, which encompasses the kind of informal personal skills of crafts often referred to as 'know-how'.
* Cognitive dimension. It consists of beliefs, ideals, values, schemata and mental models, which are deeply ingrained in us and which we often take for granted. While difficult to articulate, this cognitive dimension of tacit knowledge shapes the way we perceive the world.
  - Embedded in the human brain
  - Cannot be expressed easily
  - Requires extensive personal contact
  - Mentorship networks
  - Knowledge Maps, Video conferencing

Explicit Knowledge

Codified knowledge that can be transmitted in formal and systematic language, it is discrete or 'digital'. It is captured in records of the past such as libraries, archives and databases and is assessed on a sequential basis. It can be expressed in words and numbers and shared in the form of data, scientific formulate, specifications, manuals and the like. This kind of knowledge can be readily transmitted between individuals formally and systematically. In the west, in general, this form of knowledge has been emphasized.

- Can be easily codified,
- Embedded in procedures,
- Represented in documents,
- Transferred with reasonable accuracy.

2.3. Knowledge Management?

Knowledge management seeks to understand the way in which knowledge is used and traded within organizations and treats knowledge as self-referential and recursive. This recursion means that the definition of knowledge is in a state of flux. Knowledge management treats knowledge as information within some context. Knowledge in this context consists of information augmented by intentionality (or direction). This conception aligns with the DIKW model,

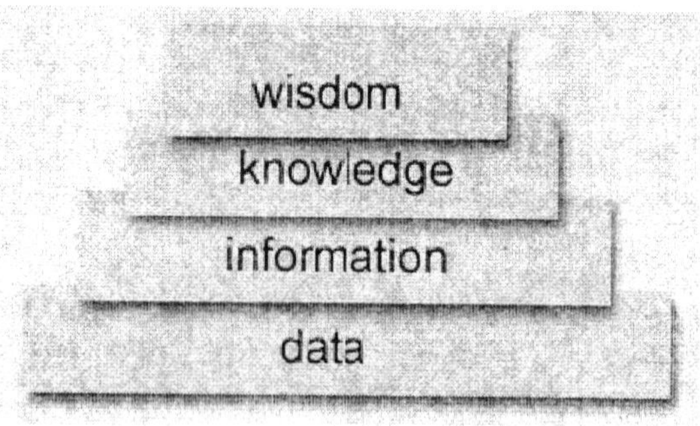

Fig. 1. The Knowledge Pyramid

which places data, information, knowledge and wisdom into an increasingly useful pyramid.

The main objective of knowledge management is to ensure that the right information is delivered to the right person just in time, in order to take the most appropriate decision. In that sense, knowledge management is not interested to manage knowledge per se, but to relate knowledge and its usage.

3. COMPONENTS OF KNOWLEDGE MANAGEMENT

- Knowledge generation.
- Knowledge codification.
- Knowledge transfer.

Knowledge generation includes all activities, which brings to light knowledge that is "new" to the individual, to the group, and to the organization. Knowledge codification is the representation of knowledge so that it can be "reused" either by an individual or an organization. And Knowledge transfer is the "Movement of knowledge from one location to another.

4. KNOWLEDGE GENERATION

Globalization and other rapid changes in technologies increasingly require organizations to generate new knowledge in order to remain competitive. In order to innovate successfully, firms must generate knowledge faster than their rivals.

* Knowledge Generation involves intentional activities of an organization
  - To acquire new knowledge
  - To create new knowledge
* Techniques include
  - Buy or rent
  - Can hire 'expert' firm or individuals

- Support external research, grants, and consortia

* Value of intellectual capital, "fair price"
  - How to keep 'purchased knowledge' intact
  - Differences in culture make hard to assimilate
  - Research and Development
* Long time to get financial return
* Value depends on how effectively applied
  - Xerox – the problem child PARC
* Most knowledge generation from synthesis
  - Combination of Knowledge from different sources
  - In unique ways so that new ideas emerge
  - Shared Problem Solving
* Leveraging diversity of people
* Different backgrounds
* Different cognitive styles
* Creative solutions
* Experience can constrain search for novel ideas
  - Creative abrasion
* People with diverse background
* But a shared vision
* Come together to solve problems
  - Adaptation
* External and internal threats
* Force need to generate new knowledge
* Apply existing resources in innovative and
* Creative ways to rethink workflows, processes,
* Business models
* When core capabilities can become core
* Rigidities
* When best practices become worst practices

Communities of Practice

- Groups of workers who share common interests and objectives, but are not necessarily employed in the same dept/location (or firm), and who occupy different organizational roles
- Bonded by a common sense of purpose
- Shared interests in knowledge sharing
- Collaboration for new knowledge creation
- Collaborate F2F, or, by phone, by email and via online Internet/web communities

5. KNOWLEDGE CODIFICATION

- Knowledge generation needs to be channeled
  * Continuous processes of classifying, categorizing, scanning, filtering, organizing and packaging knowledge
  * Codification is representation of Knowledge to make it easily accessible and transferable
- Knowledge accumulates and changes over time and so it is hard to "measure" in discrete units
  * Subjective and Context sensitivity.
  * Capturing and Coding go hand in hand
  * What is not coded is not accessible nor transferable
  * D&P's 4 basic principles for Knowledge codification

5.1. Principles of Knowledge Codification

- Business goals, importance
- Identify Existing Knowledge and goals
- Usefulness and appropriateness
- Medium for codification and distribution
- What is the purpose of knowledge codification?

- To convert corporate knowledge into accessible and applicable formats

5.2. Basic Principles

- What business goals are to be served?
- What knowledge exists in what form to accomplish the goals?
- How can it best be codified for usefulness?
- What is the appropriate medium for codification and distribution?

6. KNOWLEDGE TRANSFER

At its simplest, knowledge transfer is about starting a conversation. This may be with a colleague from a university or a chance meeting with a researcher at a professional seminar you have attended. As in all good conversations, knowledge transfer is a two way process. It's about being open to learning from others as well as sharing your ideas and experiences.

Knowledge transfer in the fields of Organizational development and organizational learning is the practical problem of getting a packet of knowledge from one part of the organization to another (or all other) parts of the organization.

'Knowledge transfer is finding the effective ways to let people talk and listen to one another'. Transfer of knowledge does not denote a full replication of the knowledge in the receiving unit. Indeed, knowledge is often modified in the receiving unit. The key element in knowledge transfer is not the underlying (original) knowledge, but rather the extent to which the receiving subsidiary receives potentially useful knowledge and utilizes this knowledge in its own operations.

6.1. Different Modes of Knowledge Transfer

According Nonaka and Takeuchi (1995) there are four different modes of knowledge transfer viz.

- Socialization
- Externalization
- Combination
- Internalization

Nanoka and Takeuchi (1995) emphasize 'beliefs' and 'justification' rather than 'truth' to differentiate them from the cognitivist tradition, in which a belief is considered more or less true based on its similarity to an external reality. Cognitivists, have generally assumed that the world consists of a number of objects or events, and that the key task of the brain (or any cognitive system) is to model these as accurately as possible. In cognitive terms, knowledge Is universal, and two cognitive systems should achieve the same representations of an object or event.

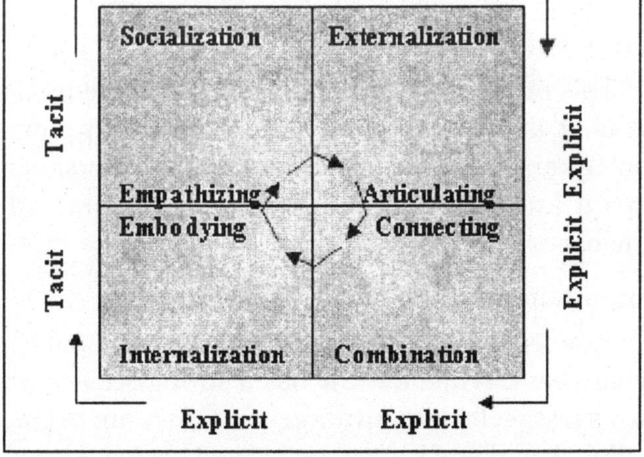

Fig. 2. The SECI model(Nonaka and Takeuchi 1995)

6.1.1. Socialization

"The process of sharing experiences and thereby creating tacit knowledge, such as shared mental models and technical skills. The key to acquire tacit knowledge is experience. Without some shared experience, it is extremely difficult for one person to project her/himself into another individual's thinking process."

6.1.2. Externalization

"The process of articulating tacit knowledge into explicit concepts. It may however be difficult to find an adequate verbal expression for a mental image trough use of analytical methods alone. Externalization is therefore often driven by metaphor and/or analogy."

6.1.3. Combination

"The process of systematizing concepts into a knowledge system, i.e. combining different bodies of explicit knowledge. This entails reconfiguration of existing information, where sorting, adding, combining and categorizing of explicit knowledge can lead to new knowledge."

6.1.4. Internalization

"This process is closely related to 'learning by doing'. When tacit knowledge is incorporated and applied in a person's or an organization's tasks. In this conversion mode it helps if knowledge is verbalized or diagrammed into documents or oral presentations."

6.2. Importance of Knowledge Transfer

Knowledge transfer has risen up the national agenda in recent years. While the UK has a strong science base, it performs less well on innovation - and if we are to compete in the global marketplace, we need to increase our knowledge transfer and collaboration to get our research into practice.

Investment in research provides much of the foundation for innovation, and the new products and services that result. The DTI Innovation Report and the Lambert Review of Business-University Collaboration both emphasized the importance of strengthening links between our research base and the UK business sector, creating benefits for universities, business and society as a whole.

For us working in the social sciences, successful innovation is about the creation and implementation of new processes, products, services and methods of delivery which result in significant improvements in outcomes, efficiency, effectiveness or quality across public, private and voluntary sectors.

The Government has firmly placed knowledge transfer as a priority for the future. In its report Science and innovation: working towards a ten-year investment framework, it highlights the many benefits to society and the economy in ensuring that research is translated into innovation in the private, public and not-for-profit sectors. It has also increased funding for knowledge transfer activities.

6.3. Number of Factors Inhibits the Transfer of Knowledge

Lack of trust, to overcome this problem, it is recommended that relationships are built through face-to-face meetings. It has been found that direct contact is essential to build rapport and eliminate the barrier created by lack of trust. To build trust, time and an adequate number of meetings are required.

Differences in culture, language and reference systems, a common ground is required through education, discussions, publications and workshops. Basically the aim is to achieve a common language between the people who share knowledge. Effective knowledge transfer is obviously easier when participants speak the same or similar languages.

6.4. Other Factors

The other factors that hinder the transfer of knowledge producing gaps in the communication process when:

- "The initiator's coding does not relate to the receiver's ability to decode the message; this occurs, when the message is not properly generated and coded due to cultural and language factors not being taken into account. Different cultures with different languages, beliefs and reference systems are real barriers to the communication of knowledge.
- The hierarchy of needs of a particular community may have been over or underestimated; and the message therefore, is alien to the values of the community. The knowledge conceived may not be relevant to the needs of the community (receiver not acknowledged); therefore the receiver may be unwilling to decode the message.
- Lack of access to a common media or medium.
- Lack of evaluation instruments for effect assessment of the transferred message.
- Wrong media used.
- Links and interactions of networks are broken.
- Knowledge transferred is not coded in a proper way. This refers to the need to code 'expertise' knowledge in such a way that recipients will be able to decode the knowledge transferred.
- The need for appropriate settings (e.g. meeting places) and adequate time for the transmission and assimilation of knowledge.
- The belief that the receiver's lack of absorptive capacity may result from a conviction that knowledge is the privilege of particular groups. This may be overcome

by encouraging non-vertical hierarchical approaches to knowledge, and the acceptance and reward for creative errors.

– Lack of consideration for the receiver's local tacit knowledge.

– Lack of absorptive capacity in recipients: Velocity and viscosity (knowledge transference characteristics) are two further factors that help to determine whether knowledge may be transferred or not." [2].

7. CONCLUSION

The power of *knowledge management* is in allowing organizations to explicitly enable and enhance the productivity of these activities and to leverage their value for the group as well as for individual. The key to being innovative is knowledge that held within the organization or country and outside it. The key is also in ensuring that knowledge is continuously generated, accessed, communicated, sustained, and exploited as a resource as much as other resources like capital and labour. Knowledge management serves to achieve the major objectives of the organization by managing the knowledge in systematic manner with three major components *like Knowledge generation, Knowledge codification, and Knowledge transfer*. These three components of knowledge management are making an attempt to provide the right knowledge to right person in right time, which will help him to be innovative as well as be competitive.

REFERENCE

1. http://en.wikipedia.org/wiki/Knowledge (Accessed on 24-12-2006)
2. Davenport, Thomas H. and Prusak, Laurence. "Working Knowledge: How Organizations Manage What They Know". Boston: Harvard Business School Press, 1998.
3. Krogh, Georg Von. Ichijo, Kazuo and Nonaka, Ikujiro. "Enabling

Knowledge Creation: How to Unlock the Mystery of Tacit Knowledge and Release the Power of Innovation". New York: Oxford University Press, 2000.

4. Ruggles, Rudy L. "Knowledge Management Tools". Boston: Butterworth-Heinemann, 1997.
5. Suresh, J. K. and Kavi Mahesh. "Ten Steps to Maturity in Knowledge Management: Lessons in Economy". England: Chandos Publishing, 2006.
6. Lehaney, Brian et al. "Beyond Knowledge Management". Hershey. USA: Idea Group Publishing, 2004.
7. Improving Research Knowledge Technical Transfer Final Report DFID Research R7171 Chapter 4
8. Polanyi, M. "The Tacit Dimension". London: Routledge & Kegan Paul, 1966.
9. Haravu, L. J. "Lecture on Knowledge management: Paradigms, Challenges and Opportunities". Bangalore: SREL, 2002. P 35-51.
10. Charles D Winslow and William L Bramer. "Future Work: Putting knowledge to work in the knowledge economy". New York: The Free Press. 1994.

32

Role of Library Professionals as Knowledge Managers in Rapidly Growing Libraries

Susanta Kumar Sahoo

ABSTRACT

The progresses of the Libraries have come at the cost of the much revered education values that alone can help the increasingly diversified libraries sustain in harmony. This paper focuses on the role of Library Professionals as Knowledge Managers in Rapidly Growing Libraries for shaping the modern libraries of the 21st century. Presents an outline of what should form of the libraries during the coming decades.

1. INTRODUCTION

Knowledge Management is introduced to help an organization of whatever nature to create, share, and use knowledge effectively because it pays off in fewer mistakes, less redundancy, quicker problem solving, better decision making, reduced research and development costs, increased worker independence, enhanced customer relations, and improved services to customers. Knowledge Management support functions are needed to implement knowledge management in an organization.

Knowledge Management emphasizes "the human aspects - cognitive, social, and cultural and organizational-aspects, in addition to information storage and retrieval. Rather than focusing on the management level of an organization, expert sharing focuses on the self-organized activities of the organization's members."(Ackerman, Pipek and Wulf)

Knowledge Management is a discipline that treats intellectual capital as a managed asset. Knowledge management is not a centralized database that contains all the information known by an organization's workers. It is the idea of sites, employees, and business partners- and cultivating that information wherever it resides. Business insight comes from capturing information and giving it greater meaning via its relationship to other information in the company. And to allay fears, knowledge management is not about making plug and play workers, dispensable because all they know is recorded for the next person who fills their shoes; it s about delivering information to knowledge workers, partnering culture, business processes, and technology to make businesses and people successful.

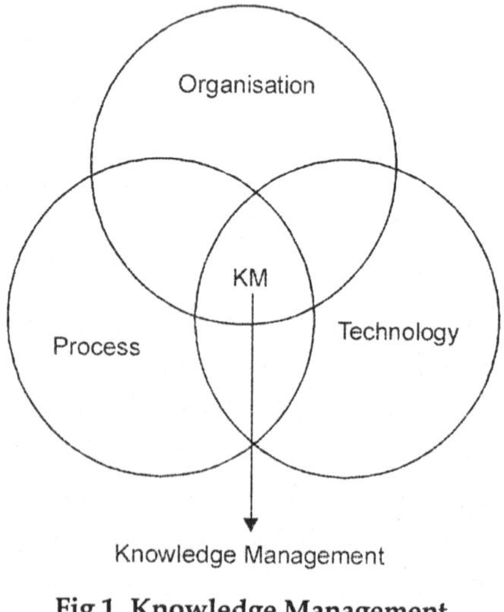

Fig.1. Knowledge Management

2. INTEREST IN KNOWLEDGE MANAGEMENT (FACTORS CONTRIBUTE)

* Organization/Companies valuations depend less or their fixed assets than on their management skills and how quickly they adapt to changing business climates. More than at any other time in history, investors value companies based on what they know.
* Trends toward leaner, meaner organizations result in employees who take what they know with them when they leave the Organization/Company. Thomas H.Davenport and Laurence Prusak call this phenomenon *corporate amnesia* in their book, *working knowledge* (Harvard Business School Press, 1998)
* A global economy in which information travels at lightning fast speeds is an important factor. In the last 50 years, economies have changed from labor-oriented, production-value added systems to intellectual and skill valued systems. In *Intellectual Capital* (Doubleday,1997), Thomas A Stewart notes that in the United States, production workers accounted for only 34 percent of the workforce in 1980, as opposed to 57 percent in 1940 and 76 percent in 1900.
* Technology itself makes a strong contribution. The ability for technology to capture data, information and knowledge has far outpaced knowledge worker's ability to absorb and analyze it. But it has also evolved to a point that allows companies to achieve Microsoft's vision of knowledge worker without limits. In this vision Microsoft's approach is to focus technology on the source of companies' knowledge: knowledge workers.
* The existing ways of doing business are constantly under attack, more so now due to rapid changes in economics. Businesses must respond more quickly. The

old ways of doing business and the old tools-such as TQM, Reengineering, and Activity Based Costing-don't cut it any more. Companies now understand that managing knowledge as well as the innovative processes is the way to remain competitive in a ruthless, fast-paced business climate.

3. KNOWLEDGE WORK CHARACTERISTICS

Knowledge management has been prominent in a range of literature from the late 1990s. A primary characteristic of knowledge management is the representation of a range of business and academic disciplines including: human resource management, information management, information technology, sociology, organizational learning and strategic planning. As a consequence there is an extensive and diffuse literature on knowledge management reflecting differing perspectives and competing claims for ownership of the area.

If knowledge organizations can be described as those competitive advantages depend on their employees abilities, then knowledge managers and their abilities are essential for organizational success. They are supposed to identify and solve difficult and complex problems, using their abilities, imagination, creativity, and high level of education (Suurla, 2002).

According to Malhotra (1998) there are a number of characteristics that are relevant to the effective working of knowledge workers in knowledge society. Fundamentally, the aim is to achieve synergy of data and information processing capacity of information technologies and the capacity and creativity of their human members (Malhotra, 1998)

The knowledge work does not have a routine and is characterized by the unpredictability and long cycles of feedback. Therefore, knowledge workers are hired for their ability to think independently; not needing to receive orders about what and when to do their duties. The nature of their work involves high level of autonomy. Knowledge workers are usually required to cooperate with co-workers from the same department, from other departments, and even with workers from different organizations (Andrews, 2003)

The knowledge professional does not repeat the same tasks everyday. He does not act according to instructions given by someone else; instead he uses his own know-how, and thinks by himself. The success in knowledge work presupposes that an individual works at his own will, not because he was given orders. A person who thinks independently uses his/her own creativity, seeking challenges and not instructions merely. The challenges of knowledge work are: insight learning, wise care, development of knowledge, skills and communication (Suurla, 2002)

In developing knowledge management systems it is necessary to take into account the following factors:

- Knowledge management does not come cheap
- Effective knowledge management requires hybrid solutions using people and technology.
- Knowledge Management is highly political, has socio-cultural and human implications.
- Knowledge Management requires development of knowledge managers.
- Accessing knowledge is only the beginning
- Knowledge Management is a never ending continuous process
- Knowledge Management requires a knowledge contract.

4. PROCESS OF KNOWLEDGE MANAGEMENT

Davenport, Thomas H (1993) explains that the

knowledge management process is about acquisition, creation, packaging and application or reuse of knowledge. Some examples of knowledge management process are:

- Knowledge Acquisition, finding existing knowledge, understanding requirements, searching among multiple sources
- Knowledge Creation, research activities, creative processes in advertising, writing books or articles, making movies and so on.
- Packaging, publishing, editing, design work.
- Reuse of knowledge for new purpose, leveraging knowledge product development processes, software development.

5. LIBRARY PROFESSIONALS AS KNOWLEDGE MANAGERS

Library and Information Science professionals are not in unanimity about knowledge management. Some commentators argue that knowledge management is nothing more than information management (Wilson 2002) or that it is no different from what librarians have done for years (Koenig 1997). Nevertheless, there is a general acknowledgement within the literature that LIS professionals have excellent information management skills in order to be significant players in knowledge management. Abell & Oxbrow state that: "A knowledge management environment needs excellent information management (IM). Although IM is not KM, knowledge is communicated through information, and the management of information creation, flow, storage and destruction is essential if individuals and groups are to share and build knowledge. The skills that facilitate the building of infostructures-the combination of information architecture, content management and information technology that enables individuals to access the right, reliable information at the right time, prevents information overload, and supports push-and-pull information delivery- are increasingly valued and sought by organizations. There are no doubt that the information profession has the theoretical basis and practical skills to provide this essential element of Knowledge Management. (Abell and Oxbrow 2001)"

The *role of knowledge management in libraries* will become more and more important along with the development of knowledge economy society. Knowledge innovation is the core of the knowledge economy society. As bases for collection, processing, storage and distribution of knowledge and information, libraries represent an indispensable link in the scientific system chain, an important link in the knowledge innovation. Secondly, libraries take part in scientific research process directly. The library work is a component of knowledge innovation. Libraries must pay attention to diffusion and conversion of knowledge. They act as bridges for turning the results of knowledge innovation into realistic productive forces. *Knowledge management in libraries* is to promote relationship in and between library and users to strengthen knowledge internetworking and to quicken knowledge flow. In the knowledge management era, libraries will carry out researches on development and application of information resources, construction of virtual libraries, protection of intellectual property rights in the electronic era etc., thus founding the base for knowledge innovation.

6. CATEGORIES OF KNOWLEDGE MANAGERS

- Information producers
- Information possessors
- Information distributors
- Information infrastructures

6.1. Abilities of Knowledge Managers

- **Information Technology Literacy :** To have an understanding of computers and telecommunication technology and how they could be applied to improve business/organizational performance or as a resource to solve problems and issues.
- **Information Technology Competency :** To have the necessary skills to apply information technology to meet information needs and improve performance.
- **Information Literacy :** Besides understanding and applying information technology, knowledge managers also need to become knowledgeable, or information literate, being able to find, analyze, and interpret information for the purpose of making better business decisions and taking action
- Knowledge management developers, working more closely with faculty and students to design, organize, and maintain a broader range of digital assets;
- Knowledge management integrators, having a more active role in the educational and research mission of university, integrating information resources and services in course and research projects;
- Knowledge management educators; teaching and training students and faculty information literacy and how to organize, preserve, and share their own information resources;
- Knowledge management researchers, applying library and information science and new digital technology to create new organizational (metadata), retrieval, and storage (preservation) options.

Librarians have always played a vital role in the field of education as Information distributors. We have formed relationships with subject specialists to build library collections to support instruction in the classroom and provided instruction in the form of classes on library skills and have conducted library instructional orientations sessions to assist students doing research in their classes. The instructional orientation sessions were usually by request only or offered as an optional course. Library collections were built around curriculum that was being taught at the time the books were published and purchased but rarely were library collection and course curriculum built simultaneously. In most cases, a librarian's role was limited and in some cases more passive than proactive in the area of instruction. A librarian's role has traditionally been more of the builder of library collections and maintainer of library collections. With the growth of the Internet and availability of vast amounts of information in an instant, a librarian's role must be one of teaching critical thinking and resource-based learning. New vocabulary in education such as: living curriculum, critical literacy, information power, information literacy, and information problem solving mandate that we re-examine our roles as professional information providers and educators. Students need to acquire the skills of evaluating information. We no longer have the luxury of having professionals in subject areas to evaluate and filter 'bad' information from 'good' information in magazines and books with clear references to experts in a field. Valid information is published on the Web daily along with opinions and rumor. This new vocabulary is bringing new challenges in library instruction.

1. Librarians assist Faculty Members and students to search out their information needs, critically evaluate the materials they locate, and use technological means to synthesize their findings into new knowledge (Brown, 1990). Librarians must become proficient in the use of the new technologies to promote them and instruct students and teachers in their use. As students become more self-directed learners, the librarian acts as a resource person in the students[1] quest for supporting information and the development of appropriate presentation strategies. Consulting duties added to an already growing schedule gives the librarian more than enough work to fill the day. In fact, without an aide to assist in the clerical duties required to circulate materials, program effectiveness will be compromised.

2. The information explosion has created far more information than one school library could possibly contain. The librarian is responsible for locating, acquiring, disseminating and tracking information resources of many types. This job might include database searching, interlibrary loans, monitoring Internet newsgroups, or maintenance of a computerized library information system. All these tasks involve managerial expertise equivalent to that required of corporate information center managers. The librarian manages the budget and evaluates and selects new materials for purchase or access.

As tasks grow in the library, the need for support staff increases. As information center manager, the librarian will supervise and evaluate the performance of technical and clerical assistants. Training of these assistants will take a significant amount of time and expertise. Since budget may be slim, some of these paraprofessionals may need to assist with duties once exclusive to professionals. Under the supervision of a librarian, paraprofessionals may become highly proficient in database searching, computer catalog maintenance, and other tasks. Student assistants and parent volunteers may also compose the cadre of workers. Different management skills are necessary to manage these two groups.

3. The mission of librarians typically is to provide access to selected information resources according to the needs of our users, to collect and preserve material, to organize it, and to deliver it to the requester. This mission statement refers to all available media and document formats and therefore is not limited to particular technologies or specific software applications. Librarians are system-independent information specialists, aiming at fulfilling the information needs of library users. Our experience indicates that user needs and expectations are very similar in the paper-based and in the electronic environment:

> Users' needs will continue to be what they long have been. Users will want information reliably locatable [...] (and) easily accessible [...]. In the electronic environment the need for access tools will be more evident [...]. Users will expect information to be available that was placed in the library's care a long time ago; and they will expect that the integrity of the information they get from the library will be assured. (Graham, 1995)

As in the paper-based environment, digital services must be *"planned, implemented, and supported"* (Hastings and Tennant, 1996), and instead of being the *"gatekeepers"* to material, librarians now follow new directions which were identified by Ching-chih Chen (1994) as follows:

- from library-centered to information-centered
- from the library as an institution to the library as an information provider, and the librarians as a skilled information specialist functioning in an all-related information environment
- from using new technology for the automation of library functions to utilizing technology for the enhancement of information access and delivery of items not physically contained within the four walls of the library
- from library networking for information provision to area networking for all types of information source providers

4. Knowledge innovation management : In these systems, firstly requires that leaders who take charge of knowledge management activities should undertake to formulate the management plans and coordinate all knowledge management related activities. Secondly, it requires establishment of special leading groups of knowledge flow for accomplishing all tasks relating to knowledge management activities. Electronic resources committees are established composed of various types of specialists to take charge of evaluating, procuring and creating the electronic resources on the one hand, and coordinating activities of business departments and spurring them on to close cooperation in such fields as procurement and organization of the electronic information resources as well as providing services on the other hand.

5. Knowledge Dissemination Management : Knowledge dissemination is of equal importance as compared to knowledge innovation. Knowledge creators do not have much time and energy to look for knowledge users. Though there are a multitude of knowledge users, it is very difficult to acquire knowledge that already exists in the minds of knowledge creators as restricted by various objective and subjective conditions. Therefore, libraries may play the part of knowledge tosser, use diverse media and channels to disseminate various new knowledge. In the 21st century, the Internet, with its mass information and extensive contents, will provide people with the main approach to searching knowledge and acquiring information. But now there emerge absurd, salacious, false and uncivil information resulting from seeking for commercial profits and political objectives on the Net.

Therefore, it is necessary to strengthen knowledge dissemination management in libraries as follows:

- uninterruptedly strengthening the creation of libraries' own document resources and deepening the development of document information resources;

- continuously raising the quality of libraries' staffs and strengthening continuous engineering education of working staffs;
- giving full play to the special role of the expert system in knowledge dissemination;
- making a comprehensive utilization of all media to ensure security of operation of networks, and prevent online criminal activities and online dissemination of inappropriate information

6. Knowledge Application Management : In the 21st century libraries should also attach importance to provision of services for people to acquire knowledge and achieve maximum functions and efficiency of knowledge information. Therefore, knowledge services based on high-speed information networks should be carried out by:

- Setting up virtual libraries or information centers for enterprises, governments, public organizations and scientific research institutions. It is difficult for an enterprise or a social organization to put sufficient manpower, material and financial resources on information gathering, organizing and developing. It is also impossible and unnecessary to spend a large amount of funds on information resources for their own use. Libraries can create virtual libraries or information centers for these organs separately according to their respective information requirements by using abundant information resources on the high-speed information networks.
- Setting up digitized knowledge services which is actually a development trend of libraries in the 21st century. This presupposes: creating step by step the users-oriented information service systems such as information dissemination, information search and

special supply of information; quickening the creation of digitized libraries; studying the methods, means and techniques of information distribution and search with the Internet as the base and WEB technique as the core.

- Digitizing libraries' resources. The electronic libraries or digitized libraries are the technical modes and development trends of libraries in the knowledge economy era. The knowledge services of libraries in the future will start with creation of databases comprising electronic journals and books in different languages that have discipline features and can operate on high-speed information networks. Great efforts should be made to transform all existing large non-electronic information resources into electronic information and integrate them into electronic libraries.

7. Information Provider : Librarians provide access to the most important information resources on the network, making use of current technologies (WWW or its successor). Electronic resources must be organized in a logical, easily understandable manner, integrating documents and services that belong logically together. The purpose of value-added services like subject-oriented clearinghouses is "not only to save the researcher time and effort in searching for appropriate sources in the vastly unordered, unstructured Internet, but also to provide him or her with a pre-assessed, semi-ordered, annotated list of sites with activatable links" (Rusch-Feja, 1997) which match or supplement the targeted group's information needs. Research

8. As Research Associate : The second aspect of our role encompasses identifying, locating and obtaining publications not owned or leased by the library. No resource, be it electronic or on paper, can be called "complete" today, and if we don't find particular information on the Internet, this does not mean that it doesn't exist. It is the librarian's duty to know which additional sources can be queried to make a search as complete as possible. Publications *"not imbedded in a formal journal context"* (Rusch-Feja, 1997) as well as electronic equivalents to today's "grey literature" need to be retrieved, which requires the librarian's experience in locating information as well as technological skills. Research assistance in this sense also includes helping our users to become familiar with handling new technologies. Various methods for providing user support for networked library services can be developed, for instance distance support (by telephone or e-mail), printed or online manuals, and on-screen instructions (Mackenzie Owen and Wiercx, 1996). Face-to-face end-user training already has become an important part of our work.

9. Collaborative System Designer : Librarians are in direct contact with users of information retrieval systems. Often users report difficulties to us which they encountered while using a system, or we recognize what needs to be redesigned while we are explaining a system to our users. When IT departments design new databases, application programs and user interfaces for us, we must be able to explain precisely to them *"how language works and how to use layout, typography and design principles"* (Moore, 1996) in order to provide the required functionality. The information flood can only be mastered with appropriate tools that are capable of matching user needs with the available information, no matter whether these tools will be operated by librarians or users in the end.

7. LIBRARY AS FACILITATING COLLABORATION

- Creation of collaboratory, both as a virtual immersive electronic environment facilitated by the Library and as a physical space
- Interdisciplinary collaboration about working with all schools; getting faculty and students to collaborate-library can be a center for this.

- Library as a Collaboratory, connecting both virtual and physical.
- Library could host events like this one on a variety of topics, with great accompanying Web sites like this one
- The Library should establish something where diverse groups can come together for aaccess to global networks and the availability of information to scientists through these networks have changed vastly how science is done today. Despite the many advantages of electronic publishing, there are still many problems to be solved. The information overload results in a need for specialists who are experienced in retrieving information and therefore can guide end-users through the jungle of available resources and technologies. In the Information Age, professional librarians are likely to be more in demand than ever problem solving.

8. CONCLUSION

We have noted that there are several groups of workers who may claim to belong the Knowledge Profession. Obviously Library and Information Science professionals also has legitimate claim to be included in the knowledge profession. The Library and Information Professional has the education, knowledge and skill to manage large collections of knowledge resources of various types including their electronic versions. The Library and Information Science professional is also knowledgeable and has the skill and experience of many decades in the processing, organization and retrieval from such sources to produce various types of information products and services desired by end users. Manual and technology based tools and techniques for accomplishing such tasks have been developed. However, Library and Information Science professionals need to: i)

Expand their horizon vis a vis their potential clientele, ii) Extend interaction and collaboration across disciplines and user groups of different interests and service requirements.

REFERENCES

1. Andrews K (2003), *"A Review of Selected Knowledge Focused Literature". Working and Learning in Vocational Education and Training in the Knowledge Era. Professional Development for the Future Project. BDO Kendals.* http://www.flexiblelearning.net.au
2. Abell, A.and Oxbrow,N.(2001): *Competing with Knowledge: The Information Professional in the Knowledge Management.LA,TFPL*
3. Brown, J. (1990, September-October). *Navigating the 90's - the teacher-librarian as change agent. Emergency Librarian, 18(1), 19-28. (EJ 415 352)*
4. Debbie (Anderson) and Janet (Gesin), *"The Evolving Roles of Information Professionals in the Digital Age".*
5. Davenport, (Thomas H. 1993),. *"Process Innovation: Reengineering Work Through Information Technology". Boston, MA: Harvard Business School Press.*
6. Davenport T and Prusak L (1998) working *knowledge: How Organizations Manage what they Know* (Harvard Business School Press,)
7. D.C.Brown (July 1990) *Research into Knowledge-based Design at WPI. Invited paper,* Proc. 5th International Conf. on Applications of AI in Engineering, Boston, MA.
8. Honeycutt (Jerry, 2000), *"Knowledge Management Strategies".*
9. Koenig, M. E. D. (1997). *...kmlis.blogspot.com/ - 35k –*
10. Malhotra Y (1998), *"Knowledge Management, Knowledge Organizations & Knowledge Workers: A View from the Front Lines".www.brint.com/interview/mail.html*
11. Mark Ackerman, Volkmar Pipek, and Volker Wulf (Editors). *Sharing Expertise: Beyond Knowledge Management.* www.questia.com/PM.qst?
12. Mackenzie Owen, J.S.; Wiercx, A. - *Knowledge models for networked library services. - Luxembourg, European Commission DGXIII, 1996.*
13. Moore, (1996), *"The future demand for information professionals in Europe" www.emeraldinsight.com/.../viewContentItem.do?*
14. Suurla R (2002), *The New Profile of a Knowledge Professional".* http://www.trainingzone.co.uk

15. Tang (Shanhong), "*Knowledge Management in Libraries in the 21st Century*".
16. Library of Chinese Defense Science and Technology Information Center (CDSTIC) Beijing, China-66th IFLA Council and General Conference , Jerusalem, Israel, 13-18 August
17. Thomas A. Stewart (1997) -*Intellectual Capital*
18. Wilson T D (2002), *Information Research, Vol. 8 No. 1, October 2002*
19. www.csdl.tamu.edu/DL95/papers/graham/graham.html
20. The Role of Librarians in the Electronic Environment, www.eso.org/gen-fac/libraries/bits-and-bytes/node10.htm
21. Source:*blog.jackvinson.com/archives/2007/01/19/a_librarians_perspective_on_knowledge_management.html* - 32k –
22. Source: *creativelibrarian.com/320/knowledge-management-and-librarianship/*
23. Source: kmlisc.blogspot.com/2006/10/knowledge-capture-librarians-role.html P.08 of 09.

33

Knowledge Management System for a Multi Campus Univertsity

Dr. M Bavakutty
Dinesan. K
Muhammed Najeeb

ABSTRACT

Knowledge society is explained and the significance of Knowledge Management (KM) in the institutions of higher learning is emphasized. K M.is the way to keep knowledge growing through sharing and it is possible in a networked environment. The multicampus features of Kannur University warrants the adoption of latest information and communication technology. Solutions for intracampus and intercampus networking and development of digital information content are explained.

1. INTRODUCTION

We are living in a society in which the quality of life, prospect for social change and economic development depend increasingly on information and its exploitation. Such a society that has an economy dependant on the creation, storage and accessibility of information and knowledge on a national and global scale is considered as a knowledge society. UNESCO's vision of a knowledge society is where every one has access to information that is relevant to them and where everyone has the opportunity and skills to use this information to meet their needs and aspirations. The seeking and acquiring information/knowledge is the way of life of human society, only that its management is what makes the difference between a civilized and modern race. Knowledge Management is also the way to keep knowledge growing through sharing and such sharing is best done either in material or human terms. The relationship between the knowledge and the social development can be understood with the help of the following flow chart:

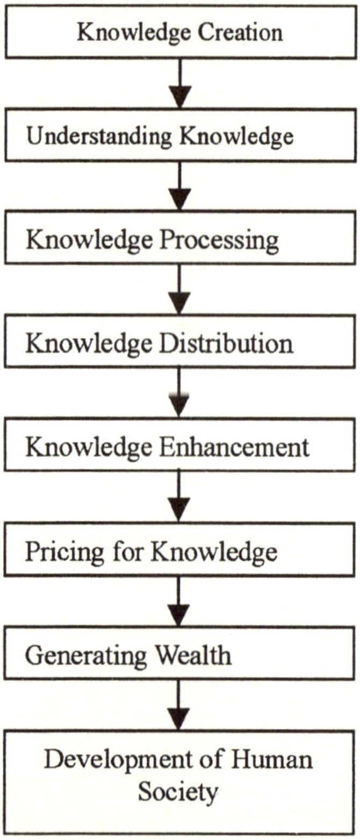

The educational institutions especially Universities, R & D organizations and other centers of higher learning generate knowledge and this knowledge in turn is used to solve social problems. The University Library plays a pivotal role in the academic activities and act as the central knowledge repository of the University, the University Library System is envisaged as a collaborator in improving access to information and knowledge supporting the institutional learning, research and operational activities of its students, the research community and the faculty. It has to be a dynamic centre of knowledge and culture serving as a conduit for recorded information in all its form.

Library network is an essential component of knowledge society. The network should identify the beneficiaries and it should be distributed in such a manner so as to decrease the digital divide. The basic components that constitute a network are the following:

1. **Technical infrastructure** : consisting of the hardware, software, equipment, communication line and technological aspect of network.

2. **Information content** : it consists of the information resources available at the network.

3. **Information services** : the activities in which users can engage and the services that users may use to complete various tasks.

4. **Support** : the assistance and support services provided to the users to make use of the network.

5. **Management** : the human resources, governance, planning and fiscal aspect of the network.

While designing a knowledge management system for a university, the geographical locations and the objectives have to be realized and a realistic plan has to be formulated. The plan should provide a flexible framework for the uninterrupted growth of the library and information system. The plan must clearly ascertain the institutional needs, the variety of users and their needs, progress of technologies applicable to information storage and distribution, equipment, human resource requirement and financial capacity.

Kannur University established in the year 1996 is unique in the sense that it is a multi Campus University with campuses located at various places under its jurisdiction. The act envisages that the University shall establish, maintain, manage and develop campuses at Kannur, Kassargod, Manathawady, Payyannur, Thallasery, Kanhankad and such other places as are necessary for providing study and research facilities to promote advanced knowledge in Science and Technology and other relevant disciplines.

At present there are twenty post graduate departments in Kannur University under sixteen schools of studies. In addition to this, there are four community colleges, three cost based courses, three teacher education centers and two information technology centers. Three campuses have been established so far at Thalassery, Mangattuparamba and Payyannur. The University Central Library is functioning in Kannur city. Thalassery Campus, the largest one where most of the teaching departments are housed has a campus Library. The other two campuses have no campus library and they have only department libraries.

The library expert committee constituted by Kannur University has recommended establishing campus libraries in each of the campuses instead of separate department libraries. It has also been recommended to network all the campus libraries and University Library in consultation with the network experts. Having built the multi campus environment, Kannur University has to set up a state-of-the-art and cost effective IT and communication infrastructure for the intracampus and intercampus communication. Those would also provide the infrastructure required for implementing office automation and also for interaction between different teaching departments of the University and administration wing Mangattuparamba Campus. This network may also be used to make use of the UGC-Infonet E-Journal consortium in the different campuses of Kannur University.

Accordingly, Kannur University has requested the help of Centre for Development and Advanced Computing (CDAC), a scientific society of the ministry of Communication and Information Technology, Govt. of India, located at Trivandrum to propose a cost effective networking solution for intra campus and inter campus communication. The Knowledge Management System for Kannur University should ensure uniform development of all locations and information from one location to any user should be provided without any hindrance as if provided from a single location. This involves adoption of latest suitable technology in computer, communication and content development. There are three aspects to be identified in planning multi campus networking, they are:

1. Campus Networking
2. Inter-Campus Networking
3. Computer System Requirements.

The following four locations may be identified for Campus networking and inter campus networking.

Mangattuparamba Campus : the present head quarters of the University with offices of VC, PVC, Registrar, FO, Seminar Hall, Guest House, School of Distance Education and the departments of IT, Physical Education and Education.

Thalassery Campus : the biggest campus of the University with the departments of English, Anthropology, Biotechnology and Microbiology, Management Studies, Applied Economics, Law, Medical Microbiology, Medical Biochemistry, Medical Laboratory Technology and Campus Library.

* Payyannur Campus with the departments of Chemistry and Physics.
* Kannur University Central Library.

The common network topology proposed for the backbone campus network is 1 GIG ring topology using Mmultimode Fibre, in view of the reliability and ever expanding demand for bandwidth. The fibre ring helps to build high link availability and link redundancy within the campus. A core Layer 3 (L3) manageable Switch will be positioned centrally to distribute 1 GIG network connectivity within the campus to the different departments. A core Layer 2 (L2) manageable switch will be positioned in the departments inside a wall mount rack. Category 6 UTP or Multimode Fibre Cable shall be drawn from the L3 switch to L2 switch depending upon the access distance. From the departmental switches access to the user PC's shall be provided using UTP cable.

More numbers of computers in each campus necessitates a logical network separation to be created in between the departments. This can be achieved by creating virtual LANs for each department and providing limited/ unlimited access to other common centers like campus library. Necessary access privileges are to be set up and proper network discipline has to be followed in each campus with the help of Core L3 Switch.

The router provide in each campus shall terminate the inter campus leased line connectivity. Each Campus router shall have facility for establishing a secure VPN tunnel with the central location to set up a site to site VPN network. The router at Mangattuparamba Campus also provides facility for the termination of the internet leased line. This is also required for access to the proposed UGC- Infonet by students and staff of all the campuses.

The available solutions for networking of different

campuses of the University are by using wired or wireless technologies. In the wired technology, Mangattuparaba Campus can be identified for setting up the network operating centre of Kannur University. A 2mbps point to point leased line from each of the campuses to Mangattuparamba campus can be considered. Interconnectivity between the campuses can be facilitated through the central router located at Mangattuparamba Campus. In the wireless technology the connectivity of the campuses may be on a star fashion. CDAC has conducted a feasibility study for wireless technology and has suggested that wireless link between Mangattuparamba Campus and Payyannur campus is feasible as these locations are almost the same height from the sea level. In order to cover the height of the peak point in between the campuses at Kuppam area mart of the height of about 24 meters at both the locations are suggested. For establishing connectivity between Mangattuparamba campus and the proposed central library at Kannur requires a mart height of approximately 39 to 42 meters. Since the altitude of Palayad Campus is also low in comparison with the terrain between Kannur and Palayad, a mart of similar height is required at Palayad Campus for establishing wireless connectivity to Palayad Campus from Central Library at Kannur. The proposed mart is guy wire supported since this is less costly than self support mart. (Layouts of Network Backbone and Distribution of each campus are given in appendix I)

The node distribution and the computer systems requirement may be assessed on the number of teaching departments, library and other offices of each campus.

2. THE INFORMATION CONTENT AND SERVICES

The information content of the system may include both printed and digital information sources. Kannur University Knowledge Management System should provide quality digital information services to the users of all the campuses. Digital information sources listed below may be accessed by the users through the network.

1. E-books published in CDs/DVDs/WWW.
2. Reference sources/Services (Dictionaries, Encyclopedias, and Handbooks etc) in CDs/ DVDs/ WWW.
3. Online scholarly/trade publications issued in CDs/ DVDs/WWW.
4. Online e-journals subscribed directly from publishers through internet.
5. Aggregated e-journals submitted through publishers/ aggregators like EBSCO or Proquest through internet as well as backup on campus.
6. Full text journals and abstracts of UGC-Infonet e-journal consortium.
7. Publications emanating from Kannur University which include Statute Act, Ordinances, Proceedings of Senate, Syndicate and Academic Council in the digital format.
8. Theses, Dissertations submitted to the University for the award of PhD. and M Phil in CDs along with hard copy.
9. Documents, audio visual material etc., relating to Malabar, its culture, folklore, art, music, sport, history etc., have to be collected and organized as "Malabar Studies" collection with proper documentation for reference to the research scholars. A database of this collection has to be created and made available through the network.
10. Once computerization of the libraries of the Kannur University are over the online catalogue of each campus can be merged to form a Union catalogue which can be edited to include the location of each book

in the library system. The Union Catalogue can be web enabled so that any user from any campus can locate any book available in the system. This will also facilitate avoiding unnecessary duplication and even the office where the bills are passed can check whether the books are really purchased and processed.

11. Rare and out of print books in the possession of the system may be digitized and hard copies of documents may be kept as reference materials so that the loss of such valuable documents can be avoided.
12. Scheme, syllabi and previous question papers of the courses of study may be made available to the users in the digital format.
13. The Website of Kannur University may be updated by incorporating the on-going research topics in various subjects and the research projects undertaken by faculty members.

The scope of the Knowledge Management System of Kannur University is not limited to library related activities. The entire activities of University, academic and administrative, can be included. The Heads of Departments of the different campuses have to travel 30 to 60 KMs for attending the meeting at the head quarters. Teleconferencing may be effectively utilized to address such difficulties and thus time and effort is saved at a greater extend. The proposed KMS will provide the ultimate platform for e-governance in Kannur University.

REFERENCE

1. Bavakkutty, M. *Kannur University Library and Information System: development plan*. Report of the Library Expert Committee, Kannur University, 2005.
2. CDAC, *Preliminary Study Report and budgetary proposal for setting up a state-of-the-art network infrastructure for Kannur University.*
3. Seema Nair. et al., *Local Information Networks: social and technological considerations*, UNESCO, 2006.

4. Kerala Library Association. *Towards Excellence in Higher Education in Kerala through IT enabled Library and Information System.* KLA National Seminar Souvenir, 5-7 May 2005, Thiruvananthapuram.

5. Cholin, V S and Karisiddappa, C R, *Study of design and development of an integrated University Library System in the digital environment". Web based information Systems,* Proceedings of the fourth International CALIBER, 2006. Edited by TVA Murthy.

6. Raman, A, Thothathri. *Knowledge Management: a resource book,* Exell, New Delhi, 2003.

7. Mritun Jayakumar, *Network Information Society: a window to library profession in 21st century. Digital preservation, management and access to information in the 21st century.* Proceedings of the 4th convention Planner 2006. INFLIBNET.

APPENDIX I

Mangatuparamba Campus – Network Backbone Layout

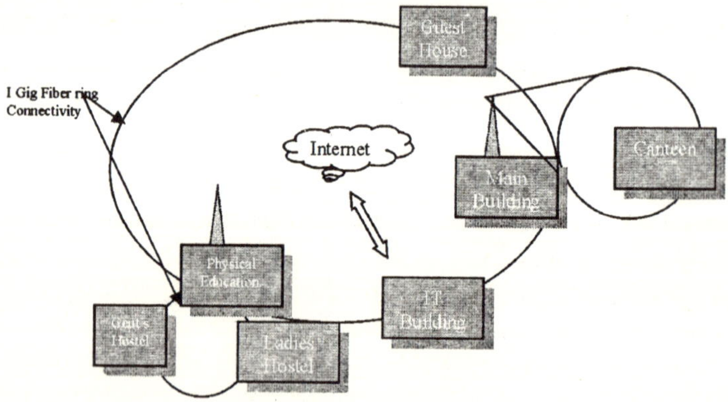

Mangatuparamba Campus Network Distribution Layout

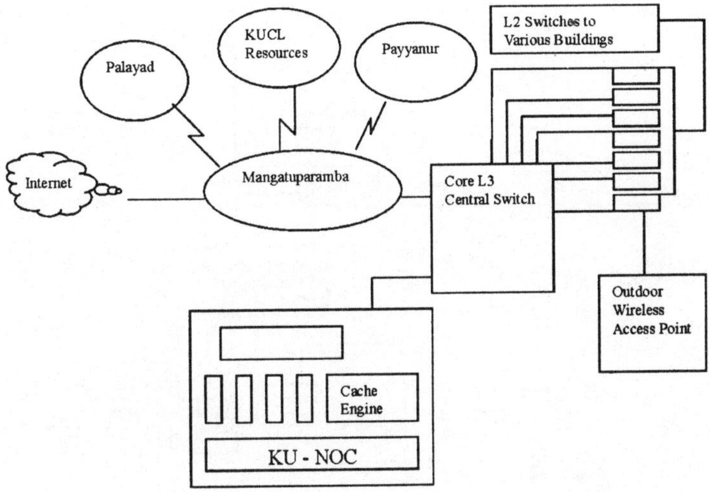

Palayad Campus Network Backbone Layout

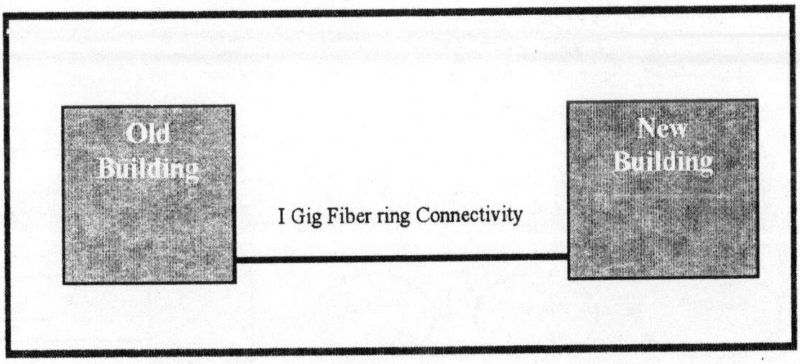

Palayad Campus Network Distribution Layout

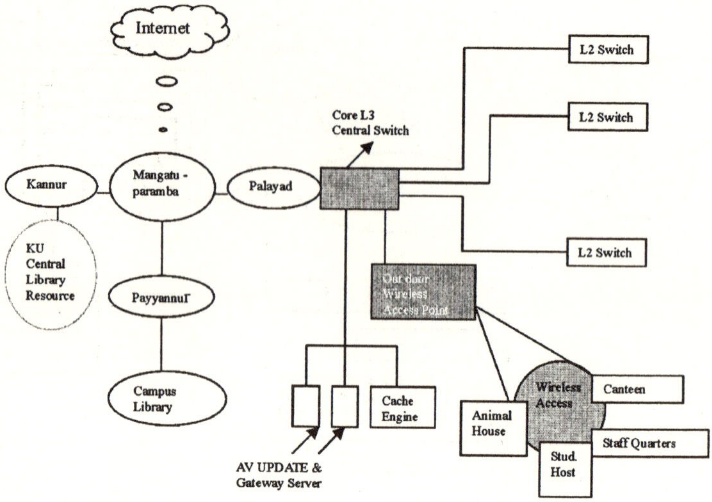

Payyannur Campus Network Backbone Layout

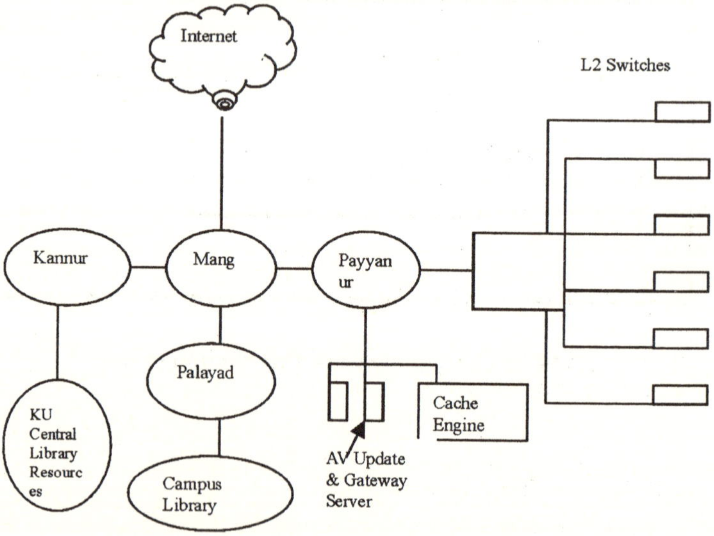

Payyannur Campus Network Distribution Layout

34

Role of Learning Styles and Methods in Learning in the Context of Knowledge Management System

M. Surulinathi
Titiksha Goswami
Dhanya P

ABSTRACT

Learning styles are simply different approaches or ways of learning. There are Visual Learners, Auditory Learners, Kinesthetic Learners. They use different Learning Methods. The paper discusses learning methods like discovery learning, Task-based Learning, and Goal-based Learning

1. INTRODUCTION

Are you having trouble learning new information in Organization? You may want to learn more about your unique learning style. Your learning style is the way you prefer to learn. It doesn't have anything to do with how intelligent you are or what skills you have learned. It has to do with how your brain works most efficiently to learn new information. Your learning style has been with you since you were born.

There is not such thing as a good learning style or a bad learning style. Success comes with many different learning styles. There is not right approach to learning. We all have our won particular way of learning new information. The important thing is to be aware of the nature of your learning style. If you are aware of how your brain best learns, you have better chance of studying in way that will pay off when its time to take that dreaded exam. Learning styles are different ways people can learn. Lesson Learning is one of the parts of Knowledge Management System.

2. LEARNING STYLES

"Learning Styles" are a way to help improve learning performance. Information about learning styles is helpful for everyone especially for people with learning disabilities and Attention Deficit Disorder. Knowing your learning style will help you develop coping strategies to compensate for your weaknesses and capitalize on your strengths.

What are Learning Styles

Learning styles are simply different approaches or ways of learning.

What are the types of learning styles?

- Visual Learners
- Auditory Learners
- Kinesthetic Learners

***Visual Learners** : learn through seeing.* Visual learners need to see the teacher's/teller's body language and facial expression to fully understand the content of a lesson. They tend to prefer sitting at the front of the discussion room to avoid visual obstructions (e.g. people's heads). They may think in pictures and learn best from visual displays including: diagrams, illustrated textbooks, overhead transparencies, videos, flipcharts and handouts. During a lecture room discussion, visual learners often prefer to take detailed notes to absorb the information.

***Auditory Learners** : learn through listening.* Auditory Learners learn best through verbal lectures, discussions, talking things through and listening to what others have to say. Auditory learners interpret the underlying meanings of speech through listening to tone of voice, pitch, speed and other nuances. Written information may have little meaning until it is heard. These learners often benefit from reading text aloud and using a tape recorder.

Tactile/Kinesthetic Learners: **learn through moving, doing and touching...**

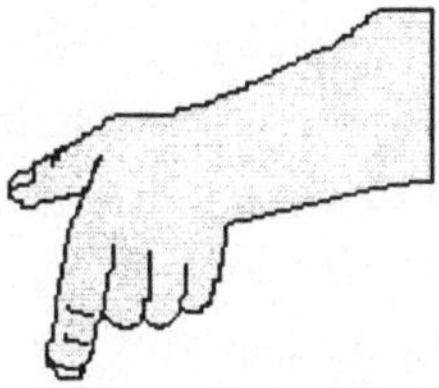

Tactile/Kinesthetic persons learn best through a hands-on approach, actively exploring the physical world around them. They may find it hard to sit still for long periods and may become distracted by their need for activity and exploration.

3. LEARNING METHODS

Discovery Learning and Constructivist Learning

Discovery learning takes place most notably in problem solving situations where the learner draws on his own experience and prior knowledge to discover the truths that are to be learned. It is a personal, internal, constructivist learning environment.

What is Discovery Learning?

Discovery learning has various definitions. At one end of the spectrum we find discovery learning in its simplest form. The tools and information needed to solve a problem or learn a concept are provided and the learner "makes sense" of them. Another definition is discovery learning as experimentation with some extrinsic intervention – clues, coaching, and a framework to help learners get to a reasonable conclusion. At the other end of the continuum is the expository teaching model of discovery learning where the learner "discovers" what the teacher decides he is to discover using a process prescribed by the teacher.

When does discovery learning occur?

Discovery learning is most noticeable in problem solving situations. The learner calls on their past experience and prior knowledge to discover the new information or skills. It is a personal, internal, constructivist-style learning environment. "Emphasis on discovery in learning has precisely the effect on the learner of leading him to be a constructionist, to organize what he is encountering in a manner not only designed to discover regularity and relatedness, but also to avoid the kind of information drift that fails to keep account of the uses to which information might have to be put." (Bruner, 1962).

Learners can work together and learn from each other's experiences.

How is discovery learning applied?

– In the development of instructional systems that cause

all users to think and work more creatively and to have a greater role in their own learning

- To encourage users to develop problem-solving strategies for confronting the unknown or unfamiliar.
- To increase the use and effectiveness of discovery learning by promoting the development of discovery learning courses, modules, laboratories and technology.

Task-based Learning

Using tasks : Users have been using tasks for hundreds of years. Frequently, in the past, the task was a piece of translation often from a literary source. More recently, tasks have included projects for producing posters, brochures, pamphlets, oral presentations, radio plays, videos, websites and dramatic performances.

What makes 'task-based learning' different?

In the model of task-based learning described by Jane Willis, the traditional PPP (presentation, practice, production) lesson is reversed. The Users start with the task. When they have completed it, the teacher draws attention to the language used, making corrections and adjustments to the users' performance. In *A Framework for Task-Based Learning*, Jane Willis presents a three-stage process:

- Pre-task - Introduction to the topic and task.
- Task cycle - Task planning and report
- Language focus - Analysis and practice.

The advantages of TBL

Unlike a PPP approach, the users are free of language control. In all three stages they must use all their language resources rather than just practicing one pre-selected item.

- A natural context is developed from the users' experiences with the language that is personalized and relevant to them. With PPP it is necessary to create contexts in which to present the language and sometimes they can be very unnatural.

- The users will have a much more varied exposure to language with TBL. They will be exposed to a whole range of lexical phrases, collocations and patterns as well as language forms.
- The language explored arises from the users' needs.
- It is a strong communicative approach where students spend a lot of time communicating. PPP lessons seem very teacher-centred by comparison. Just watch how much time the students spend communicating during a task-based lesson.
- It is enjoyable and motivating.

Goal-based Learning

Goal may be a particular job or serious of goal.

Step1..........Step2..............Step3...........Step n

Goal1... ...Goal2..............Goal3............Goal n

A goal-based scenario (GBS) is a simulation in which learners assume a major role in the pursuit of a mission or task associated with that role in the scenario. In order to achieve this goal the learner needs to acquire particular skills and knowledge in the organization. This is where the learning is taking place.

Goals in this context refer to the successful completion of the task, not the achievement of grades. A GBS serves to motivate learners and give them the opportunity to "learn by doing". As long as a goal is of inherent interest to learners, and the skills needed to accomplish those goals are the targeted learning outcomes, we have a match and a workable GBS.

4. CONCLUSION

- Human people are different in Knowledge Organization.
- More than one learning style are there.
- They would like to get services in different form from the Knowledge Management System.
- It may be useful for users to think about their strongest style and weakest style to identify how they learn.
- By thinking about their preferred style, they can try and apply this to learning new things.
- If they are able to use their natural style, they may find learning much easier and quicker.
- Knowing your learning style may help you develop to compensate for your weaknesses and capitalise on your strengths in the Organization.
- Raise awareness of personal learning styles in the Organization.

REFERENCE

1. http://www.ldpride.net/learningstyles.MI.htm# Learning%20Styles%20Explained
2. http://www.chaminade.org/inspire/learnstl.htm
3. http://en.wikipedia.org/wiki/Learning_styles
4. http://www.findarticles.com/p/articles/mi_m0FCR/is_4_35/ai_84017183
5. http://ferl.becta.org.uk/display.cfm?resID=7543
6. http://www.longman.com/teaching-tips/task-based-learning.html
7. http://coe.sdsu.edu/eet/Articles/discoverylearn/index.htm

35

Building Knowledge Management Based Organisations : New Role of LIS Professionals

N. Sureshkumar

ABSTRACT

Today, Knowledge Management seeks to make the best use of the knowledge that is available to an organization, creating new knowledge, increasing awareness/utilisation and understanding in the process. It is nothing but Capturing, organising, and retrieving knowledge and experiences of individual members and groups within/ outside of an organization and making this information available to others in the organization. But building knowledge management based organisation is a challenging task. The role of professionals in every function is in a state of transition. With the LIS function moving from its former document provider to become a TRUE Knowledge Management System manager and the need to balance its day to day responsibility with the parent organisation. LIS professionals must be very clear about the goal to achieve and how to achieve it. They should have great degree of commitment and high morale. This article guides to quickly creating high performing knowledge management organisation in the highly competition environment.

1. INTRODUCTION

In the era of information explosion, every new generation organizations are becoming increasingly competitive, dynamic, innovative and productive. It is in this context, the Library and Information Centres need to innovate new practices/services to prepare its users to meet the challenges of modern times/present day requirements and to respond with technology and work environment/ requirement.

The innovativeness in LIS profession will have to become more strategic and proactive, the magnitude of innovativeness can be measured with respect to the results, which can happen only when proper LIS practices act as a catalyst in organizational/ users operations or activities.

2. DEMAND OF USERS

LIS professionals need to develop competencies and embrace new roles as Information/ Knowledge managers, and act as service providers to both internal and external users. They need to have a comprehensive of the entire requirements / operations of his user groups not only within the organization but also to the potential users out side the organization too.

3. NEW ROLES

First and foremost, there has to be a change in the mindset of LIS professionals towards modern technological changes. LIS professionals will themselves have to undergo specialized training in order to coup with the situation. In the ever changing world, LIS activities/services are undergoing massive transformation in the job title and roles. Future LIS jobs will be internal user service, managing external user requirements, networking stakeholders, transmission of organizational goals, making bottom line consequences and building learning / Knowledge Management organizations.

4. INTERNAL USE SERVICE

Services offered to various /other departments like faculty, placement/training/ promotion division, technology/information transfer, settlement of benefits/ customer care etc. LIS professionals have to ensure just-in-type internal user service, by taking internal service tenders from the user department / functions annually and mapping out the services accordingly for implementation. Cost/ benefit of services can be calculated for the contribution to bottom line of LIS department.

5. MANAGING EXTERNAL USER REQUIREMENTS

The new generation organizations will simply transfer the operational responsibility of the organization to an external agency in many of its present day activities. It is expected that in the coming days, all the staff functions will be outsourced. An organization will be run with three departments: Operation, commercial (buy & sale) and Administration. In such scenario, The job of LIS centre would to manage / provide the necessary Knowledge/information services to not only the parent organization but to market the LIS services to the potential user companies such as identification of agency, making standard terms of reference, provide MIS services to monitoring the work and providing information about legal problems arising out of such activities etc.

6. NETWORKING WITH STAKE HOLDERS

The persons/ bodies who have stake in the organizational profit and loss are called stake holders, such as, share holders, contractors/ vendors/ suppliers, customers, employees, Administration department, Production department, marketing department, Public relation department , Govt. bodies etc. LIS department has to network with the external stake holders on a regular basis through meeting and visits, sending annual report, news letters, gifts, conducting conference and seminars, participating in exhibitions, organizing cultural programs etc. Proper networking will help in brand positioning and image building of the parent organization.

7. TRANSMISSION OF ORGANISATIONAL GOALS

Organizational goals are the targets of the institution, set at the corporate/management level. LIS department can work as liaison to transfer the goals of the management to the hands of the users/customers/ employees at different levels and functions through workshops and presentations, bulletins, newsletters etc along with conventional LIS activities.

8. MAKING BOTTOM LINE CONSCIOUSNESS

Bottom line of the parent organization is achieving its goals. Organizations calculate what is the investment and what is the return. LIS department has to make skill audit and competency mapping periodically and work out LIS programmes appropriate in each level. The coverage would be total i.e. top to bottom. Through bottom line consciousness programs, the quality and productivity will be increased and there by achieving the organizational goals of the institution.

9. BUILDING LEARNING / KNOWLEDGE MANAGEMENT ORGANIZATION

Organization of tomorrow will be staffed by knowledge employees only. There is need for developing and retaining performing employees. Organizations can be made performing institutions through knowledge- creation, knowledge-acquisition, knowledge-integration and knowledge- sharing. LIS departments have to plan purposefully, prepare carefully, process positively and pursue persistently. In the process, the organizations will be learning organizations to cope up with ever changing world.

Leading organization of the world attached the highest important to learning/ research and development, Knowledge Management Systems enabling alignment of individual aspirations with organizational plan/goals.

10. THE ROAD AHEAD

Conventional information system works logically as depicted in Fig 1. below

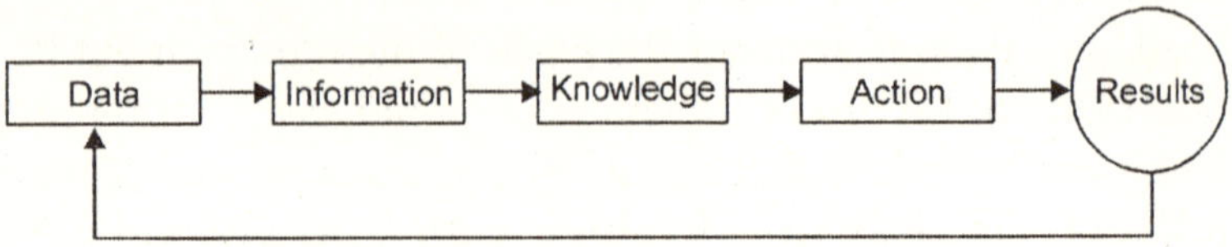

Fig. 1. Conventional Information System

Process, Computer System and people form MIS system. Collecting data, generating information to knowledge for taking an action, to create values (results) forms an MIS system. The system grows in terms of volume of useful and other data for the regular operation of the organization and the knowledge generated is not captured in the computers and over a period of time the organisation will become less depended on the MIS system and become more depended on the people rather than process and system. This makes the performance of the organization poor in customer satisfaction / organizational performance. In brief Knowledge move with people and that is not a good practice for any successful organization / research project.

Computer based knowledge management system is designed as shown in Fig 2. Actionable information is within the system rather than within the people. Knowledge to execute the actions are arrived by the people who are the main source of knowledge. From knowledge required for an action, the right information set is derived by the performing team. Then right quantity and quality of data is collected to arrive at the information as the last phase in the flow as shown in the fig 2. Action, knowledge, information and data are optimised to control the nature and quality of the system.

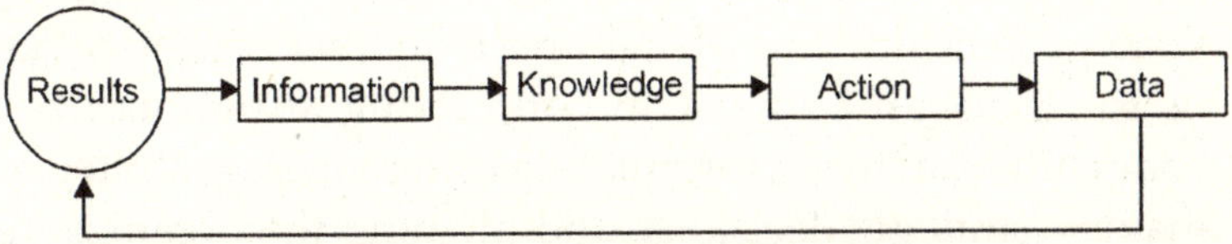

Fig. 2. Knowledge Management System

KMS is designed in reverse order of conventional MIS systems and implemented like the MIS system. Main difference is the volume of qualified data input and storing process. In the case of KMS the system will have only the right quality data for the right purpose in the system. But the conventional MIS, the required data is filtered from the huge volume of data stored in the databases.

Prime purpose is to collect right amount of qualified data and capture and reuse the actionable information and knowledge for improving the performance of the organization in the immediate future. People driven organization will get transformed into a system and process driven one.

People get an environment where they discuss, share, publish, accept, and/or learn right actionable information with right members for right purpose at the right time making everyone involved to grow in his own field of knowledge event-by-event and day-by-day of his/her stay in the organisation.

11. HIGH LEVEL DESIGN (HLD)

Knowledge networks are commonly defined as formally set up mechanisms, structures, and behavioural patterns that connect knowledge agents who were not previously connected because of functional, hierarchical or legal boundaries between organizations. Inter organizational knowledge networks provide the setting for knowledge management under cooperation. The identification of key resource capabilities or critical knowledge areas is an essential step in defining competitive forces and determining strategy. A critical knowledge area is another critical success factor that can be used in conducting situational and competitive analysis, formulating differentiating strategies, making strategic decisions, and aligning the organization infrastructure for a strategical KMS fulfilment. The consideration of critical knowledge areas in management deliberations in a variety of scenarios can enhance competitive advantage and the potential for positive performance result. The structure of an organization, its processes, systems, policies, and practices can be examined and adjusted to achieve greater leverage with the critical knowledge areas selected for KMS.

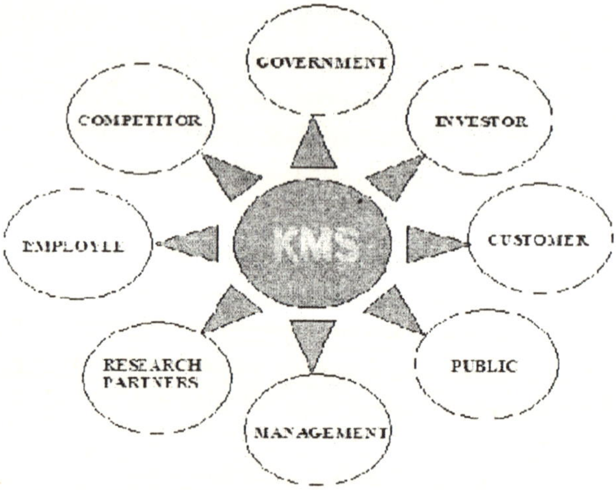

Fig. 3. KMS Design

The critical knowledge areas can also used as a benchmarking measure for comparison of practices. Asset valuation and ownership policies can be more intentionally applied to the critical knowledge areas. All of these are ways in which the identification and measurement of critical knowledge areas, that can impact management decision making and contribute to the economic value / performance of a firm / organization.

Fig. 3 shows the high level conceptual design of KMS for an organisation. The design shows the KMS server at the center of the architecture and the knowledge agents (Sources, Users or both) communicating through the KMS server.

In this design, KMS is the Knowledge Server which works 24 X 7 hours a week, helping the people in every members of the agents in capturing actionable information or data that could be transformed into actionable information and insights, storing and making that available to members for future activities in the projects or process to develop product and service for the global customers of organisation.

Secure internet connections are treated as main communication channel for members of the PUBLIC, CUSTOMER, COMPETITOR, RESEARCH PARTNERS (other research institutes, universities etc., and working with the organisation in various projects) and GOVERNMENT. Intranet of the organization creates the link between others through the KMS server.

Technical design shall be created upon approval of the HLD by the management of organisation. This will be based on the investment plan of organisation for the KMS. The hardware, software and other computer resources shall be decided for desired size and quality of the KMS system.

12. CONCLUSION

LIS professionals have to read the winds of changing the world. The days of only conventional Services and systems are numbered. The challenges before the profession are unpredictable and highly competitive in the era of Information technology. Scope for innovative ideas/ services is in abundance. The very existence is performance liked/

based. LIS professionals have to change their mind set and to take up action plans in building learning/ knowledge Management based organization for tomorrow and contribute to the bottom line. It is not enough that you innovate something. It is even more important that you know how to implement it, and you do implement it.

36

Impact of Knowledge Management on Organizational Development

Nagappa V. Bakkannanavar
Anju Govindani

ABSTRACT

This paper deals with the KM concepts, need, objectives, features, components, requisites, initiatives, impact on organizational development, value proposition in organizations, librarians role, future, etc.

1. INTRODUCTION

The Concepts of knowledge and management are old, the former means to understand the facts or skills that one gained through learning or experience while the latter is the act or skill of directing and organizing the work. However quite recently they have been put together for conceptualizing an organization as an integrated knowledge system. Man has gained skill through experience and implementing such skill by directing and organizing leads to knowledge proliferation in multifaceted and multidimensional directions. For accessing such newly emerged knowledge, it is necessary to have Knowledge Management.

Increasingly organizations world over are realizing that today knowledge is the real key to success. It is simply too valuable a resource to be left alone. In an era of discontinuous change, increased business complexity and specialization, the life cycle of knowledge is getting shorter and shorter every day. Many of the skills and knowledge gained in the past are considered outdated today. Some of the yesterday's best practices are today's worst practices. In order to maintain competitive edge in such a dynamically changing environment, organizations need to keep their knowledge on a cutting edge, deploy it, leverage it in operations and spread it quickly across the organization. Today it is imperative to devise a comprehensive knowledge strategy to translate Business Strategy into a success.

This concept has very wide applicability in all types of organization. It believes in human - centric approach to find solutions to all the problems in an organization with the perspective of improving working results year after year to an appreciable extent. It is an incontrovertible fact that the human forces undoubtedly the biggest asset in any industry / Organization, and its intuitive and tacit knowledge should be harnessed in productive ways with a view to reaping the gains at a later stage. Knowledge is power and the reservoir of knowledge that resides in employees is very important for all-round growth of any organization. A mechanism should be in place by which knowledge that lay buried not only in core professionals but also in every employee, irrespective of their cadre, is managed efficiently and leveraged into organizational assets in the long run that can be easily accessed by individuals at any point of time.

The term Knowledge Management (KM) was first applied in the profit-seeking enterprises to improve the operations to gain competitive advantage and make-profits. Now, knowledge management can also be applied to non-profit -making institutions such as Government bodies and statutory bodies as well by exploring present and future roles in the transformation of individuals, communities, government and societies at large.

It can also be used to LICs simultaneously for communicating knowledge between different levels of management and who are directly involve improving work processes as well as in service sectors. Knowledge management stimulates and manages an environment in which knowledge is created, shared and used for the benefit of the organization, its people, and its customer or users. Knowledge Management has gained significance with the advent and application of IT. KM enables sharing of information by the people by overcoming the limitations of geographical boundaries.

KM is seen as a logical extension society in that its purpose is to cope with explosion of information and capitalize on increased knowledge in workplace. One of the earliest examples of KM can be seen in the Stone Age days when people Sat around a fire in the evening and shared their experiences of hunting and gathering food. Simply put KM is all about capturing knowledge from where it is available, and disseminating to where it is required.

2. MEANING AND DEFINITION

The term "Knowledge Management (KM) has been borrowed from the corporate world which was used as a strategy to seek as well as capture the knowledge residing in people's heads and consciousness to help the environment. Corporate knowledge is at present well accepted as a decisive factor in major enterprises in advanced countries, nowadays followed by developing countries in their companies as well for achieving better results by manipulating the know-how, increasing the effectiveness and efficiency of human resources, employing limited inputs and others.

Knowledge management is the systematic process of

creating, maintaining and nurturing an organization to make the best use of its individual and collective knowledge to achieve the corporate mission, broadly viewed as sustainable competitive advantage or achieving high performance. The goal is for an organization to become aware of its knowledge, individually and collectively, and to shape itself so that it makes the most efficient use of the knowledge it has or can obtain. By management we don't mean control in the sense of strong authority and direction. This style of management fails with knowledge because no one can control another person's mind-where the knowledge is. Instead, managers must first set examples through leadership, management and personal behavior. Then they must strive to create and nurture a culture and an infrastructure that stimulate workers to create, use, and share their knowledge and that also supports their freedom to act effectively over a broad range of situations. When an organization lives in a turbulent, unpredictable, and challenging world, it must also be a learning organization, capable of handling change, uncertainty and complexity. That is, the culture and infrastructure must be such that individuals and groups of individuals can and will continuously questioning their beliefs in order to create and apply their new knowledge to achieve desired goals and objectives.

Knowledge Management is a conscious strategy of getting the right knowledge to the right people at the right time and helping people share and put information into action in ways that strive to improve organizational performance (American Productivity Centre, 1999). Therefore, Knowledge Management is nothing but cupping knowledge. It should be shared among the employees who are working at different levels in the organization in the most convenient way to get things done by others for enhancing and improving operations to gain competitive advantages and increase profits. Knowledge management can also help to evaluate the overall performance of the organization not at present but in the future.

Searching and retrieval facility, data ware housing and the proliferation of intranets has revolutionized that ability of organization to find, accumulate, organize and access information and knowledge. It is an organizational wide effort for capturing and synthesizing information from which knowledge can be created, stored and shared. The objective is to enable the human resource to work together more effectively and respond to customer needs quickly.

Knowledge Management is defined as "Management of Organizational knowledge for creating business value and generating competitive advantage. It consists of processing, sharing, using and storing knowledge".

"Knowledge Management is the explicit and systematic management of vital knowledge and its associated processes of creating, gathering, organizing, diffusion, use and exploitation. IT requires turning personal knowledge into corporate knowledge that can be widely shared throughout an organization and appropriately applied."

"KM involves blending a company's internal and external information and turning it into actionable knowledge via a technology platform". (Di Mattia and Oder).

3. NEED

The success of business in an increasingly competitive market place depends critically on the quality of knowledge, which those organizations apply to their key business processes. The factors, which make KM and in inevitable business process, are:

- Market places are increasingly competitive and the rate of innovation is rising.
- Reductions in staffing create a need to replace informal knowledge with formal methods.

- Competitive pressure reduces the size of workforce that holds valuable business knowledge.
- The amount of time available to experience and acquire knowledge has diminished.
- Early retirements and increasing mobility of the workforce lead to loss of knowledge.
- There is a need to manage increasing complexity as small operating companies are trans-national sourcing operations.
- Changes in strategic direction may result in the loss of knowledge in a specific area.
- Products and services are increasingly complex, endowing them with a significant information component.
- The need for life long learning is an inescapable reality.
- The market places increasingly competitive and the rate of innovation is rising, so that knowledge must evolve and we assimilated at an ever faster rate.
- Corporations are organizing their business to be focused on creating customer value. Staff functions are being reduced, as are management structures. There is need to replace the informal KM of the staff function with formal methods in customer aligned business processes.
- Competitive pressures are reducing the size of the work force, which holds this knowledge.
- Knowledge takes time to experience and acquire. Employees have less and less time for this.
- There are trends for employees to retire earlier and for increasing mobility, leading to loss of knowledge.
- There is a need to manage increasing complexity as small operating company's re-trans-national sourcing operations.

- A change in strategic direction may result in the loss of knowledge in a specific area. A subsequent reversal in policy may then lead to a renewed requirement for this knowledge, but the employees with that knowledge may no longer be there.

4. OBJECTIVES OF KM

The broad objectives of KM are:

- To leverage internal and external expertise to build and apply industry leading skills
- To develop and exploit intangible assets including brands, technology and know-how
- The primary objective of KM is to provide right knowledge at the right time to the right person. This would enable individuals to make appropriate and informed choice, based on relevant information pieced together through intelligent systems.

5. IMPORTANT FEATURES OF KM

The following are the important features of KM:

- KM should not be thought of all about people only but of technology also, and therefore human resources department and the technology dept should drive KM together
- KM is to implement the concept of sharing information and expertise, by which employees not only share their knowledge but also make it available to the entire organization
- Knowledge is a very different kind of asset to other assets such as property and equipment. And at the same time peoples are always reluctant to change. It is observed that for many workers and managers, knowledge has become the source of authority. Therefore they may not like to share knowledge. This

will be the stumbling block to introduce KM in any organization

- The KM is to change the culture from "Knowledge is power" to "Knowledge sharing is power"
- KM is the subject that accepts intellectual capital as the main management assets
- KM provides an environment and opportunities of learning while doing

7. COMPONENTS OF KM

KM basically involves the following three components:

1. People create share and use knowledge
2. Processes acquire, create, organize, share and transfer knowledge
3. Technology the enabler and facilitator to store and provide access to KM

Thus, KM can be visualized as a three legged stool, where the stool would cease to be functional even if one or more legs are not developed and shaped. While technology and processes are important to KM, it is people who determine its success.

8. REQUISITES FOR KNOWLEDGE MANAGEMENT

- Build a strong data structure
- Change in the organizational structure
- Create skilled workforce
- Tools and Techniques
- Develop a new atmosphere
- Bridge the gap between practice and preaching
- Average seminars/ workshops at regular intervals
- Top management support
- Good communication and information sharing

- Assessment of knowledge requirements for new jobs
- Better HRM policies for proper identification and reward of knowledge workers
- Adoption of effective KM solutions

KM initiatives would be centered on the three things of the Organization: They are:

Knowledge of the Organization : Knowledge of the Organization is available in people, files and networks. But the centre is the people. As per Prof Nonaka, the knowledge states are: a. Tacit to Tacit- A socialization process learning by observations and imitation, b. Tacit to Explicit-Externalization that refers to finding ways to structure and record knowledge for the purpose of sharing, c. Explicit to Explicit- Combination a form of synthesis of recorded knowledge to derive new knowledge, and d. Explicit to Tacit-Internalization that achieve s a coherent structure and insight. The socialization, externalization, combination and internalization (SECI) together give a subjective structure of knowledge management for any organization.

Technology : This necessarily means network support among others. In reference to weightless economy, an issue promoted by KM, the main rule is," The Law of Connexion", that states that; "the network economy is fed by the deep resonance of two stellar bangs: the collapsing microcosm of chips and the exploding telecoms of connexions. The era of computers is over. That of communication between computers is opening".

Culture Change : KM is based on sharing of knowledge. This culture is required to be brought in the organization for KM initiatives. By sharing knowledge all the three components of the organization, namely individual, team and organization become gainful. By the sharing of knowledge the best idea and best solutions are arrived at; and ultimately every component gains by it.

9. TOOLS OF KNOWLEDGE MANAGEMENT

Tools make it easier to implement KM processes and functions but they do not take the place of them. Tools help a knowledge manager deliver the right information at the right time, but don't tell him/her what to collect, how to collect it, or how to get people to use it. Tools can also be the catalyst to help transform how people work by giving them new ways to collaborate or access content. But they are not a substitute for the thinking, analysis or, management that must drive and direct the change. At present, there are numerous tools available to facilitate KM and most organizations have implemented several of these. Key types of knowledge-related tools that are currently available in the marketplace are given below:

Tools

E-Mail/ Messaging	*Content Management*
Conferencing/ Chat	Document Management
Workflow	CRM
Groupware	Data Mining
Collaboration	Data Warehousing
Web Publishing	Imaging and OCR
Portals	Knowledge Mapping
Indexing	Knowledge Auditing
Search and Retrieval	Expertise Networking
Category Builders	Training
Taxonomy Builders	Intelligent Agents
Push	Capturing/ Codifying
Publish and Subscribe	XML

10. IMPORTANCE OF KM TO ORGANIZATIONS

1. Enable E-Government-

a. Provide an IT-enabled information base to enable citizens and customers to access information and services they need.

b. Establish a network of knowledgeable govt. employees who can add value to citizen or customer's requests.

2. Increase Productivity

a. Reduce costs, risks, learning curves and start-up time.

b. Contribute to bottom line/ mission goals.

3. Share Best Practices/ Processes

a. Share best known practices across the enterprise.

b. Learn from failed efforts.

c. Provide platform for knowledge re-use and innovation.

d. Establish benchmark for internal and external performance-individuals and teams.

e. Acclimate new employees to "the ways we do things around here".

4. Provide Leadership and Decision Making

a. Provide the right information in a context that aids decision-making.

b. Integrate new information into decision processes by sharing and collaborating with players and stakeholders in decision processes.

c. Use information and knowledge to align organizational actions with missions and visions.

5. Increase Customer Satisfaction

a. Focus on knowledge of customer needs to drive the organizations' efforts.

b. Improve customer outcomes and experiences with services rendered.

6. Create Competitive Advantage/ Market Differentiation

a. To achieve knowledge superiority over adversaries or competitors.

b. As a business proposition, product or service.

c. Change the value proposition from delivering goods and services to delivering knowledge and expertise about those goods and services.

d. Focuses collective organizational intellect on customer needs

e. To meet business/ mission goals.

7. Foster Innovation

a. Provide an infrastructure for electronic and social networking to develop new products or services.

b. Foster and provide access to rich pools of ideas so others can capitalize on them.

8. Foster Collaboration-

a. Increase collaboration opportunities -enrich the exchange of tacit and explicit knowledge between people.

9. Encourage and Use learning

a. Facilitate and accelerate learning- create opportunities for individuals and groups to put new knowledge to use.

b. Leverage Organizational knowledge- brings the right information to the right people in an understandable context that addresses new challenges.

c. Value individual learning by rewarding it and leveraging it to the enterprise level.

10. Foster social capital

a. Increase the transfer of individual knowledge to the organization

b. Foster across organizational boundaries, time, and space.

c. Link people who have the requisite tacit and explicit knowledge with those who need it to do their jobs.

11. Attract and retain human capital-

a. People are our primary asset and are crucial to maintaining organizational expertise.

b. Capture and leverage what people know, know-how and know-what.

c. Promote career growth.

12. Create and Use Structural Capital-

a. Convert intellectual capital to structural capital

b. Focus strategic thinking on capitalizing on knowledge vs. focusing on the budget.

11. THE CHALLENGES OF KM IMPLEMENTATION

An organization, which has decided to implement KM, will have to take up various challenges. These are:

1. Employee Participation: Employees view information as power and as such avoid sharing it with others. Organizations usually ignore the people and cultural issues, and this result into major problems that occur in KM. KM is not only a change, but also a paradigm shift. To ensure employee participation, management should try and create an environment, where an individual knowledge is valued and rewarded, establishing a culture that recognizes tacit knowledge, and encourages employee to share it. One way companies can motivate the employees to participate in KM is, by creating an incentive program. However, there is a danger that employees will participate solely to earn incentives, without any regard for the quality, or relevance of the information they contribute.

2. Not All Information is Knowledge: It is necessary to lookout the information overload. Quantity rarely equals quality, and in case of KM, this is more so. Indeed, the purpose of KM program is to identify and disseminate relevant knowledge from a sea of information.

3. KM not Static: As with many physical assets, the value of knowledge can erode over time. Since knowledge can get stale fast, the content in a KM program should be constantly updated, amended and deleted. The relevance of knowledge at any given time changes, like the skills of employees. Therefore, there is no end to a KM program. Like product development, marketing and R & D, KM is a constantly evolving business practice.

4. Not Allowing Technology to Dictate KM: It is often confused that the KM is a technology-based concept. Companies that implement a centralized database system, electronic message board, web portal or any other collaborative tool, should do so to facilitate their own business goals, and not for a KM program. However, the KM is technology independent, but at the same time, it is often facilitated by IT. The systems developed for business purpose can be used for KM. While technology can support KM, it is not the starting point of a KM program. An Organization has to make KM decisions based on people, knowledge and business objectives. The technology will come last, only as a tool.

5. HRM Policies: The HRM policies give more weightage to seniority than merit in the promotion process, and also there is no separate placement policy for knowledge workers. These policies are hindrance in the way of effective knowledge Management.

12. IMPACT OF KM ON ORGANIZATIONAL DEVELOPMENT

According to Peter, "The successful companies, in the KM terms are the ones that have looked at the business processes rather than seeing the solution revolving rounds the company intranet". The main reasons for using KM techniques are to be competitive. Through Globalization, there are a lot more competitors coming into markets quickly.

Therefore, you need to do more in order to appear different. Another layer of knowledge is how to integrate things in the organizations so that this process makes the organization look different. KM is not dumping data on the intranet, but for sharing of knowledge and information.

Knowledge management is relevant, when the market is dynamic, uncertainty dominates, technologies proliferate, and competitors multiply, resulting in products and services becoming obsolete rapidly. Innovation in products and services is essential for survival. Hence, successful organizations are characterized by their ability to create new knowledge consistently, disseminate it quickly, and embody it in their new products and services. Successful management of organizational knowledge is essential for creating business value and generating competitive advantage. Flexible organizations with a focus to learn more new things and manage to adapt to new cultures having the knowledge as primary driver, have emerged as market leaders. Continuous strife in business have helped the leaders to acquire, retain and use knowledge to serve the customers better and blend them to be competitive by using technology and engaging knowledge employees.

We can categorize organizations into two categories, based on when, where and how they use KM to derive benefits for the organization from the expanding opportunities of the markets.

1. It is the organization, which realizes the need to cope with competitors and stand as a valid player in the competitive and open markets through the core knowledge to play in it.

2. The organization which realizes the potentials of the markets and positions itself to exploit them to its advantage through risk taking ability coupled with innovative knowledge of today obtained through

insight, which shall become the core knowledge of tomorrow.

Now, it's clear that one who adapts to market and applies the innovative knowledge of today with insight is the creator of core knowledge of tomorrow. Therefore, it is the KM that makes an organization as a trendsetter or leader or competitor or participator or straggler in the market and the environment. Hence, the sustainability of an organization depends on how well it is involved in KM and its lifecycle is altered by none other than KM. Every leader knows this to be true, yet few have continued systematic methods for KM processes. A new organizational form is emerging in the companies that run on knowledge and new positions like Chief Learning Officer has come in place. Management caters to the critical issues of organizational adaptation, survival and competence in face of increasingly discontinuous change. In an organization, an effective KM system helps employees to seek support in decision-making processes by obtaining answers from knowledge base. KM system is facilitating the present and future employees with various levels of access rights for individual to access the knowledge base, created and updated through individual or organizational know-how with the help of technology. KM system, basically aids employees through collection of information from different sources, i.e. internal and external, such as documents, databases, etc., and by capturing and storing it in knowledgebase through continuous updating process, for ongoing use.

KM is the systematic process of finding, selecting, organizing, distilling and presenting information in a way that improves an employee's comprehension in specific area of interest. It helps an organization to gain insight and understanding from its own experience. KM addresses business problems particular to a business-whether it is creating and delivering innovative products or services or managing and enhancing relationships with customers, partners and suppliers. KM initiative includes leader with a business vision, knowledge employee to share and appropriate technology to capture.

13. VALUE PROPOSITION OF KNOWLEDGE MANAGEMENT IN ORGANIZATIONS

i. Better Customer Knowledge: KM techniques focus on capturing knowledge about customers, understanding their needs and preferences, and integrating them with business processes enabling increased sales and revenue, as also customer satisfaction and retention.

ii. Better Knowledge about Products: Information and knowledge about the product behavior, and deficiencies can enable organization to bring about suitable modifications and enhancements, in time, to tailor them to customer needs.

iii. Better Knowledge of Processes: Knowledge gaps in the area of laid down processes and procedures many a times also hinder customer service. If not addressed adequately and quickly, resulting delays can translate into a loss of business. The KM framework provides a vibrant and throbbing arena for getting requisite information in least time, as also enable continuous improvements, leading to better decisions and better customer service.

iv. Better Knowledge of People- Tacit knowledge residing in people's heads, and gained through experience is often more valuable than that encapsulated in databases. On account of no formal methods of recording this tacit knowledge of people, it remains a personal domain. Organizations are often not aware of their own knowledge storehouses. KM enables the tracking and recording of the skills and experience of the employees, which needs to be continuously tapped for much larger business benefits. It also enables organization to know who are the experts in different fields.

v. Better Market Intelligence: External environments-regulatory, corporate and consumer- driven, is no longer as stable, as they were even a decade back. This creates a volatile business environment. Updated and continuous information of this environment provides an organization the most vital input for staying ahead in the highly competitive world. New products and services must come out of a centralized knowledge pool of a stable, reliable and intelligent knowledge base.

vi. Sharing of Best Practices: Knowledge management provides a business critical platform for continuous sharing of thoughts, ideas and innovations. Providing effective knowledge about past projects, initiatives, failures, successes, and efforts readily available and accessible, can make significant contribution towards better and correct decisions and avoiding costly mistakes. KM helps avoid unnecessary work duplication, expansive re-invention and repeated mistakes.

vii. Better Customer Service: By developing learning networks and learning from past situations, organizations can improve their customer efficiency and satisfaction, thereby accelerating business growth.

viii. Prevention of Knowledge Walkouts: When employees leave organizations for various reasons, there is substantial knowledge-loss in these organizations. The collaboration techniques of KM enable sharing of tacit knowledge residing in the head of employees, which can be put to use even after the employee has left. Thus, KM serves organizations from knowledge walkouts and also increases productivity.

The KM techniques enable the organizations to exploit the above value propositions to their full extent, thereby resulting in achieving the business goals and objectives. All things being equal, better knowledge and its efficient management would be the key differentiator for becoming the first among equals.

1. Matching Business Strategy with KM Strategy

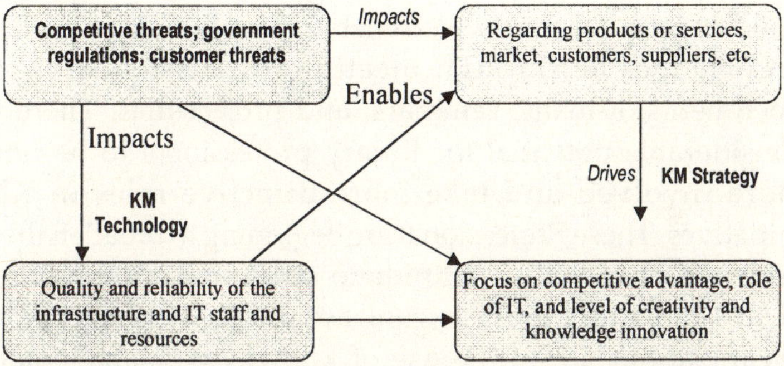

15. ROLE OF LIBRARIANS

Tools of Knowledge Management consists 70% of services and 30% of Technologies. Librarians provide these 70% services. This indicates the role of Librarians as Knowledge Manager. Where their functions are: -

- Providing services to the user community
- Sharing of information and understanding of user needs
- Analyzing documents, classifying and sorting them for easy retrieval
- Building the index etc.

From an organizational perspective, there is much merit in encouraging an adaptable learning environment and in focusing on identifying and gathering organizational intelligence in a strategic manner. There is also value to the organization in encouraging the effective transfer of expertise, know-how and knowledge. These ideas might be summarized as a "**Knowledge Awareness Strategy**". The application of knowledge strategies means the capturing of all types of knowledge and all types of information available including tacit and explicit knowledge residing in people's heads and consciousness, and information residing in production, research, marketing as well as many other information sources. Today, all organizations are trying to build an infrastructure which enables people to share explicit knowledge- be through meeting, discussion groups, documents, E-mails, seminars, and project files. There is considerable potential for library professional to become more involved and take more directive roles in KM initiatives. These Professional are beginning to broaden their horizons, change their attitude to obtain the opportunities of KM initiatives in the organizations. As more and more organizations adopt the use of knowledge management methods and practices, the need for trained and qualified knowledge management professionals will continue to grow.

Of course, the basic role of the library professional in an organization is unchanged. The organization will expect the library professional to acquire and organize information, make it available for use, disseminate it and, ultimately, dispose of information resources in all media and formats. A knowledge awareness perspective in the organization calls for the library professional to be more systematic in tracking existing organizational informational strengths and this will probably lead to developing new information resources relating to the available in-house expertise. Library professional can adopt a more strategic organizational view of their work by monitoring what is really happening in the organization through "Management by walking about". He/ She can spend a third of his/her time walking around the organization, talking to people about what they were doing, gathering information on what was going on in different departments. However, to engage them fully requires that the librarian or information manager find a new focus within the organization-ideally, if information profession has to play its role and make impact. In such organizations, they should be located in the chief executive's office. They should form part of a team devoted to acquiring external information of value to organizational strategy and establishing systems to ensure that the knowledge held in people's minds can be tapped when it is needed. Merely to leap into the "Knowledge Management" balloon without being in a position to deliver, will simply mean being first out of the balloon when ballast is jettisoned.

To succeed in a KM environment every library professional should:

1. Apply their own skill and experience confidently, in unfavorable and critical situations to tackle the problems.
2. Realize the goals and objectives of their organization carefully, its strategies, its challenges, its products and services, where knowledge and information can add value.
3. Update the existing skills and experience of the information professionals for capturing individual knowledge and information available in the organization and sharing it with others for getting better results than before.
4. Create knowledge culture within the organization to achieve the objectives successfully in competitive environment.

The information professionals' roles need redefinition to deal with both formal and informal knowledge within the organization. They apply their knowledge to create value for the organization and are responsible for managing the creation, capture, synthesis, sharing and application of the collective intelligence of the organization. They will manage the process to ensure that business needs are served, develop high-level knowledge management strategies, and create a knowledge management infrastructure. Turning information into solutions, information professionals piece information together and reflect on their experience, generate insight, and use this insight to solve problems.

For this the information professional needs to have a good overall understanding of the business and organization, and creativity in gathering information and creating synergy from the use of information. They also need to proactively anticipate and respond to changes in the environment, be lifelong learners, exhibit self-learning capabilities, and demonstrate self-control and problem-solving skills. Finally they must promote a culture of sharing information and knowledge, and be knowledgeable and competent in adapting applications of new technologies in their organization. Information professionals are already educated and trained to exhibit a number of important skills like IT skills, information skills, communication skills, leadership and management skills, analytical skills, and personal characteristics. With the addition of an appropriate mix of these skills, they are poised to take on the expanded role of knowledge work and play a key role in the emerging information and knowledge-intensive organization.

16. FUTURE OF KM

As uncertainty and complexity increase in the future and decisions become more challenging, individual, team and organizational learning, coupled with a strong knowledge management program, offers the best capability an organization can have to change, adapt, and influence its environment in a way that maximizes its performance over time. Within the organization, focused, flexible and friendly communities will help knowledge workers continually learn and change. By combining the strengths of organizational learning and knowledge management, smart organizations will create cultures, structures, and leadership styles that enable them to scan, perceive, anticipate, and take effective action on new, ambiguous, unexpected and complex threats and opportunities. Achieving such an ideal is as challenging as it is productive.

The emphasis of knowledge exchange is shifting. Although corporate information exchange used to be limited to just personal use or peer-to-peer sharing within departments, it is fast becoming a more free-flowing global process. In the near future, we will see KM practices becoming the foundation of the changing business landscape. Business leaders will shape the company culture to be more conducive to KM, and technology will help employees more easily re-use information in a world of escalating connectivity.

The capacity to turn knowing into knowledge and knowledge into productivity and innovation will be the hallmark of the successful enterprise in the Twenty-First Century. The industrial revolution is giving way to the knowledge revolution. The stage is set, the players are moving into place, and those who see the new vision are writing the script. In many ways this will be a quiet revolution- no gunfire, no loud machines, and no armies of workers marching into the cities. Managing an organization in the knowledge era will become synonymous with managing all forms of knowledge. The rules of the game will evolve- the principles of good management will become synonymous with the principles of KM.

The future world where knowledge shared becomes power and the entire organization behaves as an intelligent, self-selecting, self-adapting system continually integrating and processing incoming data and information to determines its actions, is clearly idealistic- but not beyond the possible. The ultimate challenge of the future is to liberate and amplify the knowledge and creativity of all organizational members. For in them alone lives the source and power of intelligence and wisdom, which will enable the rise of the Knowledge Organization.

17. CONCLUSION

KM is gradually taking hold in the business world as the key component to unlocking the enterprise's intellectual capital. Company recognizes, more than ever, the business is about value. In today's knowledge economy, it is not just basic transactions that determine corporate value. Intangible asset growth, such as successful test results for a software program or a new medication, creates market value. Supporting, promoting and valuing the intellectual and human capital that produce profitability are the primary business challenges of this decade. More and more companies are meeting the new challenges by learning how to fuel the knowledge engine that powers twenty-first century business with shared information, experience and know-how.

Today, knowledge is the business asset of any progressive organization. All things being equal, it is the smarter, intelligent and learning organizations that get ahead. The implementation of knowledge management helps the information flows in the organization and in implementing organization- learning practices. KM is not about just managing or organizing books or journals, searching the Internet for users or arranging for the circulation of materials. Each of these can of course, be an isolated part of KM. The focus and thrust of KM, however, is in putting the accumulated knowledge to use. Knowledge resides in people, and is manifested through their actions. Such Knowledge is tacit knowledge. Knowledge is also explicit, and is recorded as information. Readers can learn and effectively use explicit knowledge though library resources.

In today's competitive business environment, many organizations are struggling to meet or keep up with the demands put upon them by their customers, competitors, investors, and regulators. With the globalization of business, no organization is immune to this pressure. Organizations that excel at leveraging their know-how in a systematic way will create and sustain a competitive advantage that will exceed the current and future demands placed upon them.

KM will create sustainable competitive advantage for organizations if approached in the appropriate manner. KM is not a single program or series of programs or projects, but the synthesis of core business processes that should permeate every aspect of organization. Ultimately knowledge management is not about managing knowledge but nurturing people with knowledge. KM is not just a database or software, it is system that captures and collects organized, unorganized, documented and undocumented knowledge of the organization, and scientifically processes it for further retrieval, sharing and reuse to handle the management of the organization with the help of the networked system of the organization.

REFERENCE

1. Suliman Al-Hawamdeh, Knowledge Management: Cultivating knowledge professionals, Oxford: Chandos Publishing, 2003, pp. 20 & 173
2. Carl Davidson. Knowledge Management, New Delhi: Vision Books, 2003, pp. 11
3. A Thothathri Raman. Knowledge Management: A Resource Book, New Delhi: Excel Books, 2003, pp. 113 & 122
4. Microsoft. Unlocking Knowledge Assets: Solutions from Microsoft, New Delhi: PHI, 2002, pp. 8
5. E. Sudhir Warier. Knowledge Management, New Delhi: Vikas Publishing, 2003, pp. 58, 72
6. Holsapple, C.W. Hand Book on Knowledge Management, New Delhi: Springer, 2003, pp. 407
7. http://www.skyrme.com/insights/22km.htm

37

Knowledge Processing Need for a New Technology

Dr. K. N Soman

ABSTRACT

Information technology and knowledge technology can be parallelly used for the information / knowledge processing and generation of new knowledge/ information for the development of the society and nation .Knowmatics provides the methodological and theoretical tools for knowledge Technology to process and handle knowledge in diverse domains at different levels by knowledge workers and experts so as to develop knowledge industry to bring out knowledge based products , packages and services as tradable commodities , for the global market.

1. INTRODUCTION

Information now available through IT application, especially through internet is enormous and very difficult to determine what is needed. Human brain is now mostly engaged in mechanical tasks of knowledge processing. But if processing works such as filtering, extracting the contents and organizing the information in a well defined pattern and presenting are left to computers, human brain could concentrate on thinking and creating new knowledge.

2. OBJECTIVE

- To understand the advantage of knowledge over the information.
- To understand the disadvantages of the present application of IT in knowledge processing.
- To understand the concepts like knowmatics, knowledge technology, knowledge industry etc.

3. DEFINITIONS

Knowledge: Knowledge is fluid mix of framed experiences, values, contextual information and expert insight that provides a framework for new experiences and information. It originates and applied in the minds of knower

Information: Information is a set of processed data, organized and presented symbolically for communication.

Knowledge can only reside in the minds of people. When it is outside the minds of people, it is information. Knowmatics is a new scientific and engineering discipline to study the structure, properties, behaviour, representation and communication of knowledge so as to develop algorithms to process knowledge.

4. HIERARCHICAL REPRESENTATION OF KNOWLEDGE

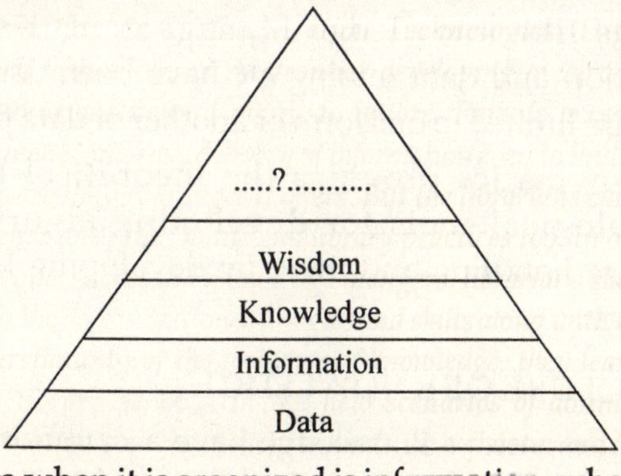

Data when it is organized is information, when filtered,

logically organized and structured and meaningful becomes knowledge. Wisdom is the still at a higher level.

5. MAIN CHARACTERISTICS OF KNOWLEDGE

- Context independent.
- Structured, organized, related and easily assimilable to human brain.
- Dynamic and multi dimensional
- Existing pattern relations
- More conceptualizing
- Experience and judgment is involved and decision-making is possible.
- Highly subjective and hard to codify

Since the information is lacking the above characteristics, the information technology also has the same drawbacks.

6. NEED FOR NEW TECHNOLOGY FOR KNOWLEDGE PROCESSING

All the advancements in information technology are confined to data or information processing are related to preservation and use of knowledge. No technology has been developed so far to process and organize knowledge. There are terms like knowledge Management, Knowledge organization and data mining etc have been used widely, but they are limited to one form or another of data processing.

Knowmatics provides the theoretical basis and methodological tools for developing algorithms for knowledge handling and there by developing knowledge technology.

7. STRUCTURE OF KNOWLEDGE

All domain of knowledge have a common structure very much similar to the thinking pattern of the human brain and the way in which brain processes information so as to make them the integral part of the knowledge base subjected to frequent revision and updating based on new evidences and experiences. Hence networks like structure passing through all the domains of knowledge. All the traditional knowledge in religion or spirituality, medical care and literature are well structured and presented in a way so that people can easily learn, remember, recollect, revise and use them. People find it difficult to learn or recollect a database, like a telephone directory or dictionary in total. By developing sophisticated computer programs it is possible to study the structure of all such works of knowledge and to give mathematical models for them so as to develop algorithms for knowledge processing. It must be emphasized that while data structure is static and one-dimensional, knowledge structure in multidimensional and dynamic in nature.

8. KNOWLEDGE TECHNOLOGY VS INFORMATION TECHNOLOGY

Information technology process data and information, which are static and uni-dimensional, it is unable to process the multi dimensional and dynamic knowledge in nature. Hence instead of IT, knowledge technology, i.e. value added information technology for enabling knowledge processing/ handling instead of information data processing / handling so as to deliver knowledge based products and services in diverse forms at different levels or standards globally. By the application of such knowledge technology could make the brain free from mechanical tasks of data/information processing.

The IT could be effectively need in processing of knowledge through filtering, extracting the contents and organizing information in a well defined pattern and presenting them in basically mechanical, time consuming and laborious as is in the case of mathematical calculations and tabulations.

9. CONCLUSION

Information technology and knowledge technology can be parallelly used for the information / knowledge processing and generation of new knowledge/ information for the development of the society and nation .Knowmatics provides the methodological and theoretical tools for knowledge Technology to process and handle knowledge in diverse domains at different levels by knowledge workers and experts so as to develop knowledge industry to bring out knowledge based products, packages and services as tradable commodities , for the global market.

REFERENCE

1. Soman, K. N. (2001). A Study of Scientific productivity and information use pattern of scientists in the context of new information technology with special reference to Universities in Kerala. Ph.D. Thesis. University of Calicut.
2. Rao, A. Sajeevan et al. Knowledge management: Emerging trends in professional education. University News, 42(35) August 2004, p55-58
3. Virdi, Jugsharan S. Knowledge society and the Universities. University News, 42(45), November 08-14, 2004, p13-14.
4. Singh, R. P. Universities as service institutions (Birth of high-tech societies). University News, 42(46), November 15-21, 2004, p153-163.

38

Awareness of Library Professionals on Knowledge Management

R. U. Ramasamy
K. Sivasekaran

ABSTRACT

Library and Information centers have been adapting modern techniques with IT applications in different service and functional areas. Librarians apply emerging concepts like Digital Library, Knowledge Management, Expert systems and so on. The application and practice of Knowledge Management in libraries elevate the present system and it leads to adopt this kind of modern concept for the effective functioning. Application of such modern practices become essential in digital era . This practice fulfills the requirements of the readers and visitors at a large. Knowledge Management leads to fruitful result which can be achieved for the betterment of both members and institution. It is a process, gathering information, storing and processing them and giving the outputs, called Retrieval of Information.

1. INTRODUCTION

Knowledge Management refers to strategies and

structures for maximizing the return on intellectual and information resources. Intellectual capital resides both in tacit form (Education, Experience and Expertise) and explicit form (Documents and Data), Knowledge Management depends on both cultural and technological processes of creation, collection, sharing and recombination.

Knowledge Management deals with managing Knowledge assets on the processes. The key process of Knowledge Management is closely associated with knowledge generation, storage and knowledge utilization. Knowledge assets are known as Markets, Products, Processes and technologies. Knowledge generation, which is otherwise known as knowledge creation, leads the organization to create new knowledge for sound functioning. It is an artificial intelligent pattern of exploration and creation of new ideas called knowledge solution.

2. CONCEPT OF KNOWLEDGE MANAGEMENT

At present, Knowledge management has become a most desired function for many public and private sector organizations in the world Knowledge comes in many shapes and sizes. It can be stored in databases, printed on paper, integrated into an organization's policies, procedures, and reports, or contained within an employee's memory. Generally, knowledge Management is a discipline that promotes an integrated approach to identifying,, managing and sharing all of an organization's information assets, regardless of how or where they are located. It is strategic in nature and involves the careful interaction of people, process and technology.

3. KNOWLEDGE MANAGEMENT TOOLS

Intranets/Extranets : It allows the users to access the organization's information at any geographical boundary.

Groupware : It provides a platform for

intercommunication between the employees in an organization.

Electronic Document Management : This technology meant for managing the knowledge contends documents electronically mainly online in the knowledge management system.

Information Retrieval Tools : Information retrieval offers searching the required knowledge through free text search and search with advanced algorithms so that all the related knowledge can be found out.

Data Analysis Data Warehousing : These are commonly used methods of data analysis. Data analysis are pattern recognition, classification and forecasting.

Data Warehousing : Data warehousing and data mining are the technology where the structured knowledge can be stored.

Metadata : It refers to information added to a document, which makes easy to access, otherwise called as "data about data"

Help Desk Technologies : This is primarily concerned with routing requests for help from information gathers to the right technical resolution person in an organization.

4. GOALS OF KNOWLEDGE MANAGEMENT

The following are the goals within the context of knowledge management:

- To make sure of an effective development of new knowledge and improvement of existing knowledge with a view to the strategy;
- Ensure an effective securing of knowledge, make easily accessible to the organization;
- To ascertain a specific distribution of new knowledge to other departments and transfer of knowledge to new employees through knowledge transfer;

- Ensure the efficient combination of the best knowledge available within an organization;
- Make the content of knowledge bearers up dated and make them ready to the changing circumstances;
- Make the location of knowledge bearers optimal in the context of service process and apply knowledge;
- Improve the form of knowledge bearers in relation to the users;
- Adapt availability of knowledge to the time where knowledge is needed.

5. KNOWLEDGE MANAGEMENT AND DIGITAL LIBRARIES

Digital revolution has transformed the intellectual function of traditional libraries. Digital libraries are providing the base for a set of distributed activities. It is also providing a one-stop solution for speedy delivery in a reliable fashion. Libraries are being digitized and patrons demand is growing the concept of content management has been adapted to the library world.

6. LIBRARIAN: KNOWLEDGE COORDINATOR

The role of the chief librarian is an academic library is that of a designer, teacher, and steward who can build shared version and challenge prevailing mental models. The librarian needs to be responsible for knowledge coordination, he or she needs to have an understanding of developing the human and cultural infrastructure within a library, which will facilitate information sharing, specifically the conversion of tacit knowledge of librarians into explicit knowledge that may be shared across the library.

7. LIBRARIAN: KNOWLEDGE CREATOR

As far as Library is concerned, knowledge creation implies participating more in user's reading and studying by identifying users' information needs and developing appropriate service and products to meet the needs. While a user is seeking knowledge, explicit knowledge stored in documents either in print or electronic format is needed to be implanted in the user's head and to be analyzed and synthesized with the user's tacit knowledge and / or his previous experience, etc That is the process of internalization o knowledge. In the meantime, the user can generate new ideas, concepts and methods.

8. RESEARCH METHODOLOGY

The present study focuses on the level of Awareness on Knowledge Management among the library professionals in the study area. This chapter provides the steps involved for the smooth conduct of the research. Descriptive type of research is applied. It includes both primary and secondary data sources. Questionnaire method has been adopted to collect the required primary data. Secondary data have also been collected through published and unpublished resources. Fifty (50) samples were chosen for the present study. The library professionals were requested to fill up the questionnaire. The collected primary data were fed into system by using the Statistical Package for Social Sciences (SPSS) to analyze data and to the generate tables. The study covers the professionals who are working in different types of College Libraries in Madurai District.

1. Engineering College Library
2. Polytechnic College Library
3. Arts & Science College Library

Age wise Classification

S.No	*Age*	*No. of Respondents*	*Percentage*
1.	20 - 30	14	28
2.	31 - 40	15	30
3.	41 - 50	16	32
4.	51 & above	5	10
Total	*50*	*100*	

It is found that 32% of the professionals belong to the age group of 41–50 and 30% of them are in the age group of 31–40.

Classification by Experience

S.No.	*Experience in Years*	*No. of Respondents*	*Percentage*
1.	1 - 5	20	40
2.	6 - 10	10	20
3.	11 - 15	7	14
4.	15 & above	13	26
Total	50	100	

It is identified from the above table that 40% of the respondents are having only 1–5 years of working experience.

Classification by Designation

S.No.	*Designation*	*No.of Respondents*	*Percentage*
1	Librarian	14	28
2	Asst. Librarian	23	46
3	Lib. Asst.	8	16
4	Others	5	10
Total		*50*	*100*

From the above table, it is important to note that 46 % of the respondents belong to the category of Assistant Librarian.

Classification by Qualification

S.No.	*Qualifications*	*No. of Respondents*	*Percentage*
1.	B.L.I.Sc.,	14	28
2.	M.L.I.Sc.,	16	32
3.	Ph.D.,	1	2
4.	PG & M.L.I.Sc.,	15	30
5.	M.L.I.Sc., & M.Phil.,	4	8
Total		*50*	*100*

It is observed from the above table that 30% of the respondents are possessing Postgraduates degrees along with Master degree in Library and Information Science and 32% respondents possess Master degree in Library and Information Science with their basic qualification.

Classification by Type of Library

S.No.	*Type of Library*	*No. of Respondents*	*Percentage*
1.	Arts & Science College	26	52
2.	Engineering College	20	40
3.	Polytechnic College	4	8
Total	*50*	*100*	

It is noteworthy to state that majority of the respondents (52%) are working in the Libraries of Arts and Science colleges and 40 % of the respondents are from Libraries of Engineering Colleges.

Awareness on Digital Collections

S.No.	*Resources*	*No. of Respondents*	*Percentage*
1.	Multimedia	50	100
2.	Internet		
3.	DVD		

The entire populations of the respondents are well aware about Multimedia, Internet and DVD resources. It reveals that the respondents are having basic ideas on Digital Collections.

Awareness on Digital Collections

S.No.	*Resources*	*No. of Respondents*	*Percentage*
1.	E-Books	22	44
2.	E-Journal	18	36
3.	E-Publishing	10	20
Total		*50*	*100*

Maximum number of respondents (44%) are knowledge on E-Books and 36% are knowledge on E-Journals and 20% of the respondents are knowledge on E-Publishing.

Availability of Collections

S.No.	*Collections*	*No. of Respondents*	*Percentage*
1.	Text & Ref. Books	50	100
2.	CD-ROM		
3.	Floppy		
4.	Video & Audio Cassettes		
	Total	50	100

The above table states that the entire population of the respondents are said that they have various kinds of collections such as Text and Reference books, CD-ROM sources, Floppy diskettes and Video & Audio cassettes.

Opinion on Automation

S No.	*Opinion*	*No. of Respondents*	*Percentage*
1.	Yes	33	66
2.	No	17	34
	Total	50	100

From the above table, it is found that majority of the respondents (66 %) has favourable opinion on Automation.

Awareness on Knowledge Management

S.No.	*Opinion*	*No. of Respondents*	*Percentage*
1	Yes	30	60
2	No	20	40
	Total	50	100

It is observed from the above table that 60 % of the respondents are aware of the concept of Knowledge Management and 40 % of the respondents are not.

Opinion on Application of Knowledge Management

S.No	*Opinion*	*No. of Respondents*	*Percentage*
1	Yes	36	72
2	No	14	28
Total	50	100	

The above table shows that 72% of respondents are eager to apply the concept "Knowledge Management" and 28% of the respondents are not willing.

Participation in Seminars / Workshop

S.No.	*Opinion*	*No. of Respondents*	*Percentage*
1.	Yes	7	14
2.	No	43	86
	Total	50	100

It is interesting to note that majority of the respondents (86%) were given opportunity to attend State / National level seminar on Knowledge Management through their Institutions.

Organizing Seminar on Knowledge Management

S.No.	*Opinion*	*No.of Respondents*	*Percentage*
1.	Yes	42	84
2.	No	8	16
	Total	*50*	*100*

It is inferred from the above table that majority of the respondents (84 %) have an Idea to organize Seminar / Workshop on Knowledge Management and 16 % of the respondents are not having such opinions.

Opinion on Participation of Seminar / Workshop

S.No.	*Opinion*	*No. of Respondents*	*Percentage*
1.	Yes	46	92
2.	No	4	8
	Total	50	100

The above table shows most (92%) of the respondents have attended Seminar / Workshop on Knowledge Management during their career.

9. FINDINGS

1. 32 % of the respondents are in the age group of 41 - 50 years and 30 % of them are in 31 - 40 years.
2. It is identified that 40 % of the professionals have obtained experience in between 1- 5 years.
3. Most of the respondents belong to the category of Assistant Librarian.
4. It is noteworthy to mention that a respondent has Ph.D., and 8 % of them qualified for M.L.I.Sc., with M.Phil.
5. 26 % of the respondents belong to Arts & Science Colleges.
6. It is time to high light that most of the professionals are well aware of digital creations like E - Books, E - Journals.
7. It is noteworthy to state that the entire populations of the respondents are having CD - ROM, Floppy and Audio - Video collections in their library.
8. It is important to mention that 66 % of them have opinioned favorable for the Automation for resources.
9. It is noteworthy to state that 60 % of them are aware of the concept "Knowledge Management".
10. 72 % of the professionals felt that knowledge

management can be applied in libraries.

11. Most of the respondents (64 %) agreed that their library system would get elevated through the application of Knowledge Management.
12. It is time to state that most of them are willing to attend seminar and workshop on "Knowledge Management" to enrich their knowledge.
13. It is interesting to note that 84 % of the professionals are willing to organize Seminar/ Workshop on "Knowledge Management".
14. Most of the respondents have attended to make them updated with emerging concepts.
15. It is noteworthy to state that by the application of Knowledge Management, readership of the library will be enhanced to an extent.

10. RECOMMENDATIONS

1. Librarians should be encouraged to update them in modern concepts so as to make the readers satisfied.
2. Periodical training should be offered to the professionals at different levels.
3. The management of the Institution should come forward to develop Digital collections to meet information requirement of the readers.

11. CONCLUSION

Knowledge Management connects people with people, as well as people with information. It is a combination of Information Management, Technologies and Human resources. In the recent times, it has become a powerful tool for promoting innovation and realizing re-engineering. Librarians have excellent skills in organizing and codifying information sources and making these accessible to others. This represents the top layer of the knowledge map (information) rather than tacit and explicit knowledge). Librarians have to change their transactional mindset to become a part of the organizational change. Knowledge Management would play a key role in the future of libraries.

39

Practical Problems in the Process of Digitization : A Case Study of ETD@IIT Kanpur

Noufal. P. P

ABSTRACT

Establishing an ETD system with the mass digitized collection is a really challenging and innovative task. As a part of Digitization Initiatives started in 2005 at P. K Kelkar Library, Indian Institute of Technology Kanpur, we have digitized our entire theses collection from 1964 onwards and set up a marvelous and outstanding ETD system powered by DSpace, an OAI -PMH compliant software, with our own unique and flourishing features including the options for future transactions and related activities. This paper made an attempt to highlight and expose our practical experiences of digitization of theses of 9 lack pages and describes the formulated strategies and adopted parameters for its quality checking and the silent features of our well fledged ETD system.

1. INTRODUCTION

In recent years, developing of IR (Institutional Repositories) at academic and research institutions is a promising trend and multifaceted assignment among library fraternities. IR as a Knowledge hub of academic thought content of any institution, it has a major role for enriching its teaching activities and enhancing research and development works.

IIT K is one of the preeminent Engineering and Technology Institute in India. It is well known and reputed for its activities and research in various disciplines. P K Kelkar Library serves its community as a dynamic learning laboratory with its excellent collection of print and online resources. Library is fully automated and well utilized the explorations of Modern ICT Tools and developments.

2. DIGITIZATION INITIATIVES

Keeping in mind the recent trends, technological growth and multi dimension of research and learning, our Library has initiated its digitization program in 2005 under the leadership of Librarian as a Principal Investigator with a team consisting of an Assistant librarian, as Co Project Investigator and Two Sr. Library and information assistants as quality and Metadata analysts and two more project associates. After detailed study of the system and analyzing the scope, we have designed the road map of our digitization program. Its first phase was the establishment of a full fledged ETD system with digitized theses.

2.1. Digitization of Theses

Considering the time for establishing a digitization facility at our own premise, we utilized the scanning facility of IIITA, Mega centre of UDL (Universal Digital Library) Project. Digitization is started on 29 July 2005 and after thorough quality checking and rectification, it wind up as late as April, 2006

2.2. Recommended Specification for Digitization

TIFF for archival and **PDF** for presentation purpose.

Resolution of Image: 600 dpi TIFF and PTIFF (Processed).

Compression: CCITT 4 Fax

Final Output: PDF Image

Scanner: Minolta PS7000

Software for scanning: AbbyFine Reader 7.0

Software for Conversion: Adobe Acrobat Professional

2.3. Pre and Post Scanning Process

After a comprehensive study, we have done the following pre and post scanning process to assure smooth functioning of the process and to get well reliable data without any damage and loss.

The *pre-scanning* process includes:

a. Item handling

b. Transporting to Scanning Centre

c. Record Keeping

Item Handling: Selection of the document from the theses collection, duplication verification, labeling and bundling are major tasks included in this stage.

Transporting to Scanning Centre: The first Lot of our theses was transported to IIITA on 29 July 2005 and it continued until 8th lot, sent on 14 October 2005.

Record Keeping: Detailed records have been prepared for the item transported with relevant bibliographical details extracted from our own existing theses database.

The *post-scanning* process includes:

a. Quality checking

b. Transferring data

c. Transporting back theses to IITK

Quality Checking: Digitization without quality is a meaning less exercises. While the progress of digitization, we observed various shortcomings and defects in the digitized data. (Some snapshots are given in Appendix.1.) we understood that Quality Checking is an essential and obligatory process to get the most consistent and reliable data. After the systematic observation of scanning process and their work flow we understood that these defects are happened due to various causes like software errors, hardware defects and human errors.

In the case of the software errors, mainly occurred by automatic cropper which is a tool for automatic cropping which is a process to eliminate unwanted junks and discrepancies from scanned documents so as to get clean and legible output. But its result was not up to the mark. We suggested the best way is the manual cropping where ever this tool created problems. Even though it is a time consuming process and tedious job, the output was excellent. The used scanner has some limitations regarding the paper size. The maximum size to be scanned in the spread mode is A3 size. In rare cases, we had some theses with the graphs, charts and tables, more than A3 size.

Most of all, lion portion of the time and effort of our quality analysts was consumed by the problems by human errors such as missing, duplicate and misplaced pages, data conversion scan fixing and file naming. After the comprehensive study and systematic consultations, we formulated a well defined strategy and predefined parameters for rectifying problems by keeping in mind the following elements,

- Completeness and Contrast
- Sharpness, skew and resolution
- Bit depth level of compression
- Data conversion.
- File naming

Considering all the ground realities and keeping defined parameters, our quality assurance team has taken seriously this challenging and painstaking assignment. We have checked approximately 9 lack pages and prepared detailed reports of noticed problems and appropriate methods for rectification. Rectified data has again checked for assuring its completeness. In the worst cases, we recommended rescanning for some items. Finally we completed the quality checking and rectified the problematic items as late as April. 2006.

Transferring data: Having done the quality checking and rectification, we copied data to three USB discs each of the capacity of 300 GB.

Transporting Back theses to IITK: After copying to USB, we have taken back all theses from IIITA to IITK.

3. SETTING UP OF ETD SYSTEM @IITK

Proper planning and right expertise is essential for establishing an ETD system. The various phases involved in setting up of our ETD system are:

- IT Infrastructure: Hardware /Software
- Configuration and customization
- Selection of Metadata Standard
- Designing standard workflow pattern
- Content Management
- Metadata extraction and injection
- Uploading: Mode of Submissions

IT Infrastructure : Library is equipped with all modern ICT gad guts. Internet access is provided 24 hours a day, 365 days an year through VSNL 34 Mbps and ERNET 2 MB dedicated Internet link.

Software selection : After Exhaustive analysis of strengths and weakness of most popular content management/DL systems like DSpace, Eprint, ETD-db,GSDL, Fedora, VTLS Vital , Ex Libris DigiTool, ProQuest / BePress Digital Commons. We analyzed that DSpace was the appropriate one for ETD due to its following features:

flexibility, scalability and granularity, adherence to standard, multi-format support, customizable interface, OAI-PMH compliant, support with fully qualified DCMI, remote submission, authorization and reviewing, community/sub-community based collection architecture, import and export features, Persistent Identifiers Handle System, Open URL Support, Lucene search engine and generation of statistical reports.

Hardware Specification : HP Proliant DL 385 / Dual Processor Capable / AMD 8000 Series chipset / Op 2.4 GHz with 1024KB L2 Cache / 4 GB RAM, 2x 73GB Ultra320 10k Hp Universal, 3x 300 GB Ultra320 10k Hp Universal, DVD+RW Drive, Hot plug Redundant power supply, 17" TFT

Configuration and Customization

First Phase : Test Bed installation: 19 July 2005

DSpace (Version: 1.2.2)

Plat form: Linux

Second Phase

ETD Server configuration:

DSpace (Version.1.4)

Platform: Linux

Chosen Metadata : We are using Qualified Dublin Core due to its usability, flexibility; repeatable elements and qualifying nature are widely appreciable.

Content Management : Proper content management is required for making your system more meaningful and informative before uploading to the system. Details are given below in the table.

- Embedded Watermarking
- Metadata extraction and injection
- Scanning & Insertion of Signed Certificate page

Process	*Tool used*	*Purpose*
Embedded watermarking	iText Library. http://www.lowagie.com/iText/	Copyright infringements
MetadataExtraction/ Injection	In house developed Perl Script/Java script	Extracting from existing theses database/save time and effort
Certificate pageInsertion	Adobe acrobat Professional	Authenticity for digitally born theses from 2005 onwards

Uploading: Mode of Submissions : After getting done above mentioned various content management process, we followed three mode of submission to the ETD system.

1. **Bunch processing:** Digitized theses are uploaded as bunch process by using customized workflow and export/import utility of DSpace.
2. **CD Mode:** As a current practice, scholars are

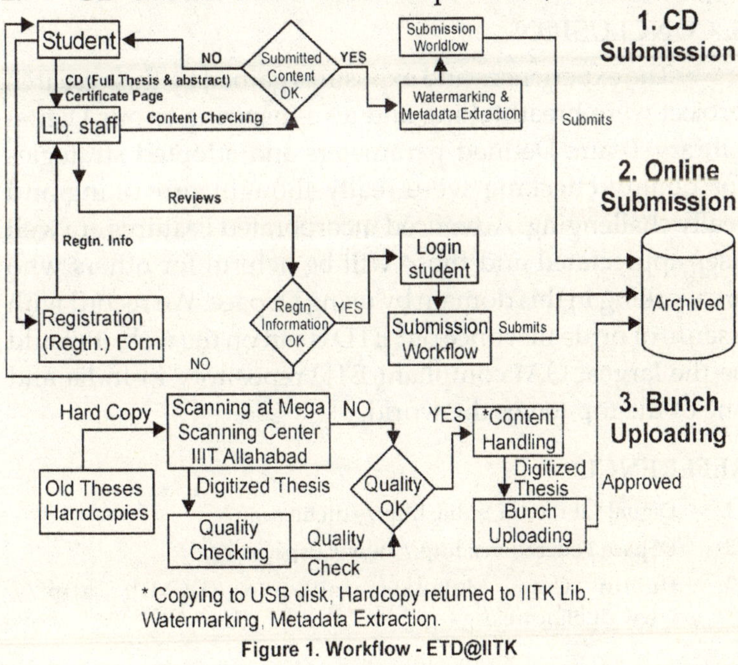

Figure 1. Workflow - ETD@IITK

submitting CD containing their e-theses to the library; our team is manually uploading to the DSpace after the completion of essential content processing like quality assurance, file naming and related content management process.

3. **Online submission: ETD** system is full fledged with the option and modified work flow for online submission for coming years.

3. INCORPORATED FEATURES

After continuous evaluation and exposures, we came to know that DSpace is lacking some features in its design and architecture, mainly search, browse and work flow options. We have deeply customized the system for enhancing its default features with some value added features. Details are given in the Table (II) and snap shots are given in Appendix. I.

4. CONCLUSION

The experiences and exposures gained by this research project were breathtaking and awe-inspiring to our Digital Library Team. Defined parameters and adopted strategies for quality checking were really thought provoking and really challenging. Advanced incorporated Features are well user appreciated and those will be helpful for others who are working in this domain by using DSpace. We record with a sense of pride that once our ETD is put on the web, it would be the largest OAI compliant ETD repository in India and one of the top ten in the world.

REFERENCE

1. Digital Library of India: http://dli.iiit.ac.in/
2. DSpace Federations: http://www.dspace.org/
3. Dublin Core Metadata Initiative (DCMI): http://www.dublincore.org/

No	*Default features by DSpace*	*Incorporated Features by us*	*Purpose*
1	<u>Search options</u> Search all DSpace, Bounded Search Simple search Advanced search.	<u>Search options</u> Cross collection search	More user friendly in interdisciplinary/multidisciplinary emerging trend
2	<u>Browse Options</u> Communities / Collections Authors, Titles Issue Date , New Collection and Recent Submission Subjects	<u>Browse Options</u> SupervisorCitations.	To browse all theses guided by a supervisorImpact factor on IITK theses
3	<u>Item strength</u> Communities / Collections	<u>Item strength</u> Supervisor, Author, Subject and Citations	Total no of theses guided by supervisor, of work created by author, of subjects related to item and of Cited theses
4	<u>Linking</u> NIL	<u>Linking</u> Subject, KeywordsCitations	Easy navigation and user friendly
5	<u>Registration</u> First Name.Last Name Contact No	<u>Registration</u> Roll No.Degree Department	To assign a scholar to a particular E-Group and for user to submit his/her item to collection without any problem
5	<u>Feedback</u> E Mail address General Comments	<u>Feedback</u> Required personal informationDescription parameters	Understanding ScholarTo solicit ratings, Assessment of ETD

4. Gail, McMillan. (2003). Electronic Theses and Dissertations. *Encyclopedia of Library and Information science,* (pp1034-1040)New York: Marcel Dekker.

5. iText Library: http://www.lowagie.com/iText/.

6. Mishra, R., Vijaianand S. K., Noufal P. P., Rajesh Kumar and Shukla, Gaurav., (2006). Digitisation Initiatives to Destress Library Collection: A case study of ETD at P. K. Kelkar Library, IIT Kanpur. International Conference on Digital Libraries, New Delhi, Dec. 5-8.

7. Mishra, R., Vijaianand S. K., Noufal P. P. and Shukla, Gaurav., (2006). Development of ETD at IITK Library using DSpace: Practical Exposures and Experiences. International Conference on Semantic Web and Digital Libraries, Bangalore, 2007.

8. Open Archives Initiatives: http://www.openarchives.org/

9. PDFbox: http://www.pdfbox.org/

10. Registry of Open Access Repositories (ROAR): http://archives.eprints.org/index.php

40

LIS Education: Need for A Change

Sreekala P K
Sangeetha T G
Dr. M D Baby

ABSTRACT

This paper emphasizes the role of manpower in the modern libraries and the significant impact of library innovation on staff. The paper has examined and analyzed the present Library & Information Science education and tried to find out how far the library science students are getting trained in the latest developments in ICT. The paper highlights the importance and relevance of in-service training for the library professionals during their course

1. INTRODUCTION

Libraries are undergoing profound changes as a result of the application of latest information technologies and the increasing capabilities of users to access, retrieve and process information. Now the use of large variety of ICT applications in libraries and information centers has resulted a drastic change in the face mark of libraries. M The use of Internet resources and electronic communication are playing an increasing role in education and research. These types of developments are demanding advanced type of services from the part of library professionals. The new concept of library brings changes in the task of the library, the relation with the end users in the nature of jobs, staff requirements and educational requirements of staff. Therefore development of a competency-based curriculum is inevitable in the present scenario.

2. PRESENT STATUS OF LIS EDUCATION

Kerala state is in the forefront in the field of education and employment when compared to other states in India. There are 7 universities in Kerala, which offers variety of courses. In these three universities are offering Bachelor of Library and Information Science (B.L.I.Sc) and Masters in Library and Information Science (M.L.I.Sc) courses. The Kerala University and Calicut University also offer the M.Phil and Ph.D programmes. Kerala University started the library and information science education for the first time in our state in the year 1961 and Calicut University in the year 1978. Mahatma Gandhi University started the course in the late nineties. In addition to formal teaching courses, Calicut University has introduced correspondence course for BLISc and Mahatma Gandhi University is offering BLISC in distance education. Two colleges affiliated to Calicut University and six colleges affiliated to M G University are offering B.L.I.Sc and M.L.I.Sc. programs in regular and self-financing stream respectively.

Kerala University and Calicut University has started integrated M.L.I.Sc program instead of 1+1 stream of B.L.I.Sc and M.L.I.Sc. The duration of the course is two years with 4 semesters. M G University is still offering one year BLISc and one year MLISc under self-financing scheme.

The perceptible thing is that even though these universities are offering the above mentioned courses for more than thirty years none of them have introduced a revision for a competency based curriculum in LIS education. Many times the program had undergone revision, but the modification confine to nomenclature and bifurcation of existing papers. Professor Seetharama comments that "it is ironical that while department of library science have changed their names as "Departments of Library and Information Science", they have done precious little in reorganizing their curriculum. As a matter of fact these new named departments continue to teach what they have been teaching all these many years". [1]

The conventional papers offered in the course for the past years is not adequate to accommodate the recent developments emerged in the field of knowledge management and so the students are not equipped properly to cope with the present ICT enabled working conditions of library and information centers. The situation is graver in the case of courses conducted in the Distance education mode. Almost all the universities have removed the internship or work experience programs from their syllabi by which the students of BLISc course denied to see and practice in the actual situation in libraries. This makes the stakeholders consume time to develop their working ability. Therefore at least in this juncture initiative taken by the two well-known universities in Kerala. (Kerala University & Calicut university) to start integrated program is worth appreciating. The curriculum for these programs has been revamped and restructured pruning many of the conventional courses and introducing new courses with emphasis on IT components. Still the curriculum is lacking some of the ingredients necessary for molding the students to compete with the developments.

The development in the field of library and information science is apparent. The teaching methodology of LIS education also is an important issue, which requires attention of academicians and professionals. "Chalk and talk are the only means of communication in almost all the library schools. Educational technology is yet to enter into our library schools."[2]

Every profession is a blending of theory and practice. Practical training to the students of library science is as important as the formal education in the subject. But the library science profession in India lacks practical training which forms a gap between theory and practice of the content of the course. The special nature of the library science course warrants the necessity of practical training. The importance of practical training or internship for library science students has been highlighted in the following words of Satish and Reddy, "Subject taught in the class room will be made most relevant to the working situations; enables the students to develop the necessary skills required to operate various library activities; confidence to handle things individually is developed; enables the students to adopt himself to varied working situations and conditions; practical training while learning provides student better understanding of the subject, than any best tutor can provide; student need not put sorry face in the selection/interview process, if any questions relating to library services are asked; working under able librarians and documentation officers boosts the morale of the students; ensures thorough theoretical knowledge with sound practical skills; new technique and current research are first applied in the libraries, normally it takes long time for its inclusion in the library science curriculum."[3]

To keep pace with these new techniques and current research applications in actual working conditions for students it is high time to change our teaching methodology. It should give due importance to employment potential in the changing scenario. More ICTs have to be employed in class rooms and along with the new steps taken in the integrated curriculum, teaching methodology must give attention in providing required infrastructure facilities to practically educate for the high level professional capabilities. Despite our conventional teaching, a methodology with simulated packages is essential.

3. LIBRARY AND INFORMATION SCIENCE AT RAJAGIRI

The B.L.I.Sc program is being started at Rajagiri College of Social Sciences in the wake of great demand in the present day business and education industries, for Knowledge Managers. The school envisions delivering world - class professionals in the field of Knowledge Management for the ever-increasing market for such managers.

The B.L.I.Sc program offered at Rajagiri College of Social Sciences affiliated to the Mahatma Gandhi University equips the learners with the ability to function dynamically and acquire the requisite knowledge and skills to manage libraries and information systems. The main objectives of the course are;

- To train and equip students in Knowledge Management.
- To develop skills in ICT enabled library management.
- Infuse in the learners the ability to function dynamically.

The course is a two - semester program with focus on experiential learning. Each semester shall comprise a minimum of 16 Instructional weeks; continuous internal evaluation and University Examination at the end of each semester shall be conducted.

Following strictly the norms and conditions of the university the college focus on the following course highlights.

- Study visits (in and outside Kerala)
- Weekly training program in different types of libraries

(Friday and Saturday)

- Two months hands-on-training (in & outside Kerala)
- Guest Faculty program
- Enrichment programs - Yoga, Social sensitization program (Rural camp), Communicative English, Psychology Lab
- IT training program (Computer Science Department of the college conducts the training)
- Initiation program for freshers (10 days orientation in well established libraries)
- Students' mentoring program
- Documentation and other SDI services to the Rajagiri community.
- Placement Training Program

These value added programs mold the students as professional librarians by the completion of the course and the feed back we received from the employers are very encouraging. The Weekly training program in different types of libraries (Friday and Saturday). Two months hands-on-training program gives the students an opportunity to see and experience the actual working conditions.

4. CONCLUSION

Human resources are the most important resources in a library. The present day library needs staff with a proper mixture of skills in:

- Knowledge management
- Information Technology
- Subject knowledge
- and above all communication.

Hence our library schools must provide a training, which will enhance the above skills to the students.

REFERENCE

1. Seetharama, S "Knowledge, skill and role of future information professional implications of information technology in S K Kapoor, ed., Education for special library and information work (Calcutta: IASLIC 1987), p. 87.
2. Kumar, P S G "Some issues in education for librarianship in India" in S K Kapoor, ed., Education for special library and information work (Calcutta: IASLIC 1987), p. 13
3. Satish, N and Yadgin J Reddy "Internship in Library Science curriculum: a neglected aspect in S K Kapoor, ed., Education for special library and information work (Calcutta: IASLIC 1987), p. 23.
4. Baby, M D *"Manpower requirements of library and information science personnel in special libraries and library and information science education with special reference to Kerala"*. Thesis, Calicut University, 1993.

41

Knowledge Management in Libraries and Information Centres in India

G. Dhanasegaran

ABSTRACT

Defines Knowledge, its types and the transformation from data to information and to Knowledge – Provides a conceptual view of Knowledge management - Explain the Steps and Processes in Knowledge Management - Discusses the ***applications of Knowledge Management*** *- Speaks about the Categories of Knowledge Management – Explains the Human aspects of Knowledge Management - Talks about the knowledge transfer in the digital era – Discusses How the Libraries and Information Centres serve as Gateway to Knowledge - Elucidates the role of Knowledge Management in Libraries and Information Centres in India.*

1. INTRODUCTION

The unprecedented growth of information and knowledge has impacted all organisations, including libraries. This has made knowledge management important. The conventional functions of libraries are to collect, process, disseminate, store and retrieve information to provide better service to the clientele. The environment in which libraries operate and the users who seek information is changing. The role of Libraries is changing to provide the competitive advantage for the users. The success of a Library depends on their ability to utilise information and knowledge of its staff to better serve the needs of the user community. This requires the librarians to reappraise their functions, expand their roles and responsibilities to effectively contribute and meet the needs of wide spectrum of user community. Knowledge management is a viable means in which libraries could improve their services in the present knowledge era..

2. DATA, INFORMATION AND KNOWLEDGE

Knowledge management is a concept that has emerged explosively in the business community and has been the subject of much discussion over the past decade by various researchers and authors. Data becomes information when organised, patterned, grouped, and or categorised; thus increasing depth of meaning to the receiver. Through learning and adoption, information can be changed into knowledge. Knowledge can be divided into two categories namely

- Tacit knowledge - is the "Know how" acquired by persons which is intutive
- Explicit knowledge - is systematically documented records in any kind of format which guides the users to gain the knowledge and to expand the knowledge base further.

3. CONCEPT OF KNOWLEDGE MANAGEMENT

Knowledge management is the classification, dissemination and categorization of information and people throughout an organization.

Knowledge management is the explicit and systematic management of vital knowledge and its associated processes of creating, gathering, organising, diffusion, use and exploitation. It requires turning personal knowledge into corporate knowledge that can be widely shared throughout an organisation and appropriately applied.1

Knowledge management is a discipline of dentifying, capturing, retrieving, sharing and evaluation an enterprise's information assets.

Knowledge management is a conscious strategy of getting knowledge to the right people at the right time.

4. STEPS AND PROCESS OF KNOWLEDGE MANAGEMENT

Oosterlink and Leuven2 argued that " Universities are no longer living in splendid isolation. They have their own place in society, and they have a responsibility to society, which expects something in return for privileges it has granted. In other words, universities do not exist as single entities. They are part of society through engaging in teaching, research and community service. Hence it is essential from the librarians point of view to consider knowledge management as a tool enabling better services to the user community.

Knowledge Management can be considered as a four by four matrix of steps and processes:

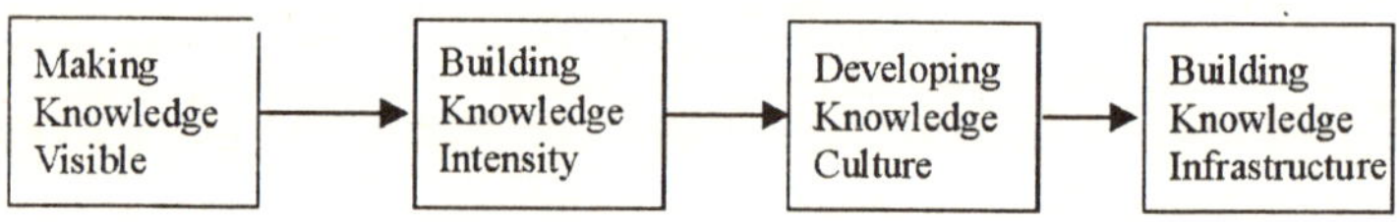

5. KNOWLEDGE MANAGEMENT APPLICATIONS

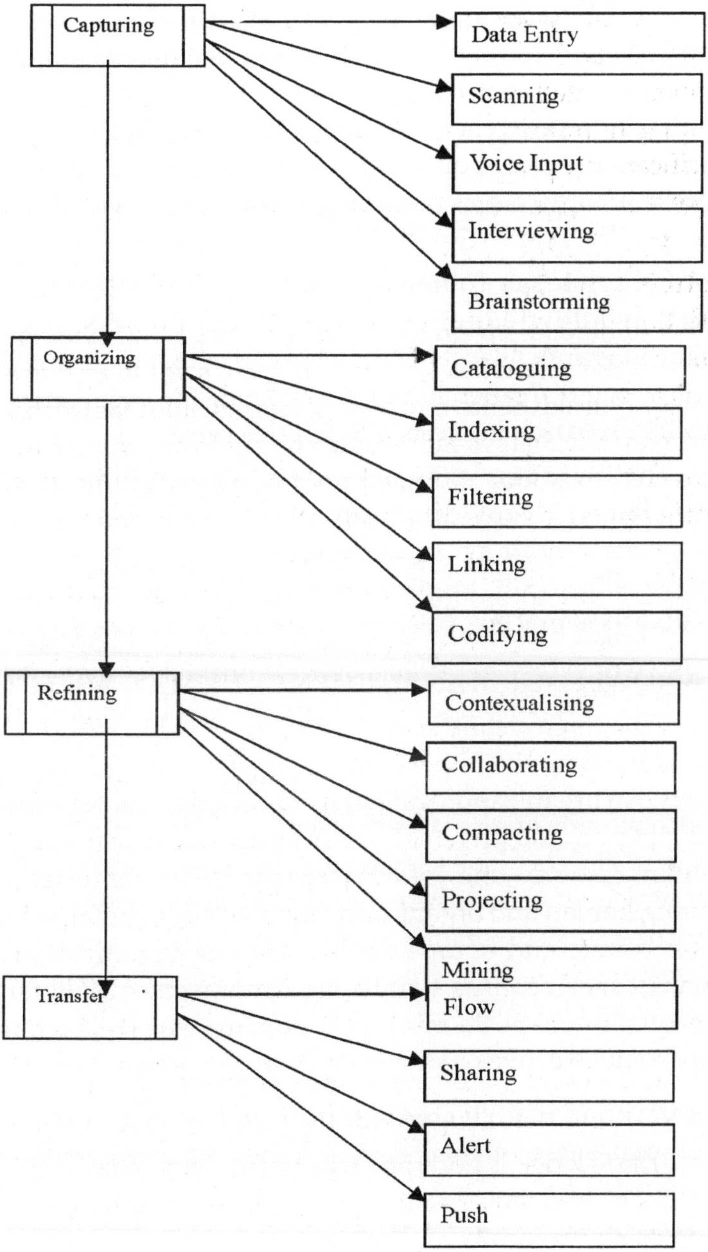

6. CATEGORIES OF KNOWLEDGE MANAGEMENT

Knowledge databases and repositories (explicit knowledge) : storing information and documents that can be shared and re-used, for example, client presentations, competitor intelligence, customer data, marketing materials, meeting minutes, policy documents, price lists, product specifications, project proposals, research reports, training packs = The Library Routines including reference service

Knowledge routemaps and directories (tacit and explicit knowledge) : pointing to people, document collections and datasets that can be consulted, for example, 'yellow pages'/'expert locators' containing CVs, competency profiles, research interests = Referral Services

Knowledge networks and discussions (tacit knowledge) : providing opportunities for face-to-face contacts and electronic interaction, for example, establishing chat facilities/'talk rooms', fostering learning groups and holding 'best practice' sessions - Current Awareness Services

7. KNOWLEDGE MANAGEMENT - HUMAN ASPECT

The main theme in managing knowledge effectively is understating the importance of people as organizational assets. An organization guided by knowledge management principles should preferably be a human intensive industry. Human resource and information professionals focus on mining human and organizational knowledge contained in brain power and competence as well as organizational databases and routines. An all round improvement of library staff quality and positioning of the human value will become important objective of knowledge management in libraries.

8. KNOWLEDGE TRANSFER IN THE DIGITAL ERA

Knowledge is not a one way traffic . It is often one-to-one, or one-to-many or many-to- many through technological gadgets electronically. Technology is an important part in knowledge management. Technology -including an intranet, groupware and extranet-plays a major role in knowledge transfer and knowledge sharing. E-Business and E-Commerce are the most popular areas where knowledge transfer has gained its popularity.

9. GATEWAY TO KNOWLEDGE

The gateway is a bridge that provides digital means to enable access to information and knowledge sources that are needed. The gateway provides services that enable the end users and researchers to locate and to get access to resources. The gateway is a place for individual and group study and a centre for interactive learning using digital resources and networks. The goals of the gateway are convenience, efficiency, timeliness and unification of services and programmes. No doubt Libraries and Information Centres serve as the gateway to knowledge and the Librarians are becoming ***Cyberarians***.

10. ROLE OF KNOWLEDGE MANAGEMENT IN LIBRARIES AND INFORMATION CENTRES

Libraries are the institutions for knowledge management. They deal with both the categories of knowledge, tacit knowledge for the library personnel and explicit knowledge for the end user. Library personnel must have a clear view of the "Know how" of information sources, management, retrieval and dissemination as well as global access to information. This tacit knowledge helps the end-users to gain explicit knowledge. They must be guided to the gateway of knowledge. The objective of knowledge management in libraries is to promote knowledge innovation, relationship in and between libraries and between library and user.

11. KNOWLEDGE MANAGEMENT IN LIBRARIES AND INFORMATION CENTRES IN INDIA

Knowledge management initiatives are taken by organizations and practitioners world wide. The initiatives are in the external structure , the internal structure and the competence of the people. The knowledge management initiatives has started in different sectors of the economy. They are categorized as

1. Initiatives at the corporate level
2. Initiatives at the R & D level
3. Financial institution level initiatives
4. Initiatives at the NGO level
5. Initiatives at the Academic Institutions level

12. INITIATIVES AT THE CORPORATE LEVEL

1. Infosys knowledge shop - Today their body of knowledge covers not only issues relating to soft ware development and tools but also fields like travel tips, loans, online library catalogue, HR as well as administration issues at the knowledge shop
2. Tata consultancy service (TCS) - TCS's knowledge management solutions was conceptualized in 1995. It has developed its knowledge management solution from its intranet. TCS has built knowledge management systems using a Lotus Domino Server.
3. Oil and natural Gas corporation (ONGC) - Has set up a taskforce to implement knowledge management system and practice..

13. R & D LEVEL INSTITUTIONS

1. National Aerospace Laboratories(NAL) - Has already taken steps to create the basic infrastructure required for knowledge management systems.
2. Indira Gandhi centre for Atomic Research, Kalpakam

(IGCAR) - Covers a wide range of computer facilities including a campus wide network. Knowledge management applications of the center cover hospital management and Library management Services and training.

14. FINANCIAL INSTITUTION LEVEL INITIATIVES

1. ICICI knowledge park - ICICI has been developing a "Knowledge network" that would enable collaboration between research and industry. The park has taken up a unique project called "Knowledge network"
2. Export -Import park if India - They have established a knowledge management system which has helped them in solving loan related problems.

15. INITIATIVES AT THE NGO LEVEL:

1. Tata Energy and Resource Institution (TERI) - has developed a comprehensive knowledge management system organizing its research outcomes.
2. CMIE (Centre for Monitoring Indian Economy), Chennai has developed many products that can be used as knowledge management tools. Eg. Prowess, Business Becon, etc

16. INITIATIVES AT THE ACADEMIC INSTITUTION LEVEL

1. IIT Bombay (IITB) - has established Knowledge Management system encompassing the entire Library Catalogue of Thesis / Dissertation of IITB.

17. CONCLUSION

It can be clearly seen that the environment in which modern libraries operate is changing. It is both faced with challenges and opportunities. Libraries, despite of their type, need to respond to these challenges in order to serve the needs of the entire user community in a pinpointed way.

One way of doing that is engaging in knowledge management activities, that is, creating, capturing, sharing and utilising knowledge to achieve the library goals. Knowledge management is a viable means in which libraries could improve their services and become more responsive to the needs of users. People gain more knowledge from their experiences and their peers' expertise. Libraries need to recognise the knowledge, its staff and create a knowledge environment in which their knowledge can be valued and shared. So Librarians! Let us all awake! Surely Knowledge Management domain is ours!

REFERENCES

1. Awad, Elias M and Ghaziri, Hassan M. Knowledge Management.-Delhi: Pearson Education, 2004. Pp. 1-456.
2. http://www.skyrme.com/insights/22km.htm
3. Mahapoatra, P.K and Chakrabarthi, B. Knowledge Management in Libraries.-NewDelhi: Ess Ess, 2002. PP.1-288.
4. Murthy,T.A.V...[etal.] ed. Road Map to New Generation of Libraries using Emerging Technologies.-Ahmedabad: INFLIBNET Centre, 2004. PP.586-613.
5. Oosterlink, A. and Leuven, K. U. (2002). *Knowledge management in post-secondary education: universities.* http://www.oecd.org/pdf/M00027000/M00027356.pdf
6. The ICFAI Journal of Knowledge Managemnet Vol. 1. No.1. Dec.2003.PP.1-90.

42

Human Resource Management The Core of Knowledge Management in Libraries

S. V. Gumaste
S. Y. Amdani
Dipak Krushnarao Bhalekar

ABSTRACT

"A developed country is one which is able to utilize its core strength to the best possible extent. A country remains underdeveloped if its core strengths are not utilized up to the proper extent ". India is known in the world for its enormous technical manpower. Yet there is a scope and need to adapt improved technical education to the changing technological scenario and also to make it competitive in terms of quality. The thrust provided to technical education in the recent years, both for expansion and towards improving quality, will generate a technical workforce that will make India compete well in the technology- driven world. The role of knowledge management in libraries will become more and more important along with the development of knowledge economy. It is a new management mode, boasts the following superiority and characteristics incomparable with conventional management.

1. INTRODUCTION

Information Technology is a tool for Knowledge Management in Libraries. The effects of information technology are revolutionizing almost every sector of society, education and training is not the exception. Numbers of major steps have been taken in the recent years in these regards. Indian Government is utilizing its maximum efficiency to make available the every sort of information for this. They include the ambitious "Sarva Shiksha Abhiyan" and the 86th constitutional amendment to make education a fundamental right. Similarly, highly effective measures have also been taken relating to reforms and expansion in the area of technical education.

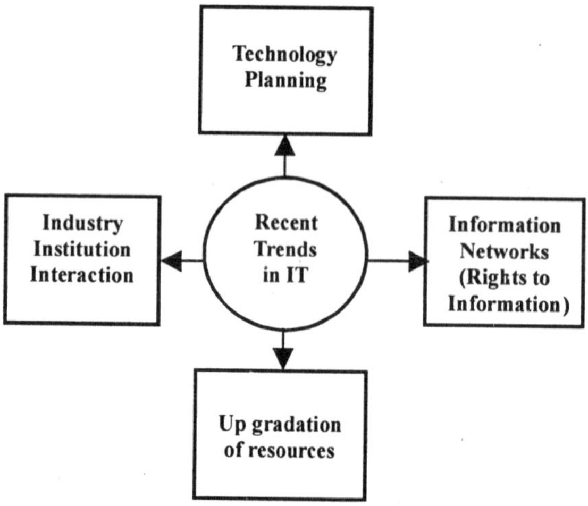

2. TECHNOLOGY PLANNING

Technology planning is unending. A technology plan cannot be a developed it is always developing.

After human being's existence on the earth, we can summaries the era and their duration.

– Stone Era (Approx 50 Lacs of years)

– Metal Era (Approx 5000 Years)

- Industrial Era (Approx 500 Years)
- Electric Era (Approx 200 Years)
- Electronic Era (Approx 50 Years)
- Computer Era (Approx 30 Years)
- Knowledge Era (Currently running!)

The project is implemented, as technology changes, as the institution grows, the plan must change. To realize more of the potential benefits of technology in education, an institution must invest considerable time and effort in technology planning. A long-range technology plan is essential to make more effective use of technology and to implement technology cost effectively. A technology plan is the single most important ingredient to effectively using technology the organization. The technology planning process helps to minimize technology-related crises.

3. INDUSTRY INSTITUTION INTERACTION:

Interaction between Industry and institution is the need of hour. Everyday the need of industry is changing, small-scale industry often depends on support in the areas of design, process improvement and machinery performance etc. Gap between industry and aspiration of academic community is very large, there is mismatch in perceptions of the two on the issue related to the technology developments. Today the academic community is not that much geared to face this challenge. Teacher is the only media who can solve this problem up to satisfactory level. Modernization must focus on producing engineers as leaders in industry and leaders in technology of world class standard, and not mere followers of technologies generated elsewhere in the world. The world has changed so technical education in India must change. Getting good marks in examination is good but not enough.

4. RIGHTS TO INFORMATION

Education For All or Right to the Information is now very much popular. With the help of information networks, it is possible to transmit different types of service to different audiences via a single channel. This also makes possible the improved provision of education and other services to small target groups and special audiences. Through increased cooperation and by exploiting the potential of technology, regional equality can be enhanced and the opportunities for individuals to acquire information can be improved. More effective use of resources will be possible

Internet connectivity : The Internet and its related developments today characterize the information and communication technologies The television, computing, home entertainment and telecom industries are obsessed with the talk of technology convergence, essentially voice, data and video over the single network. While the webs destiny is moving towards the television, Net access and cable connectivity are the two key constituents of this revolution. All universities must be linked through a common website.

5. UP GRADATION OF THE ENGINEERING CURRICULUM

Education has a significant role to play in economic growth of any country, especially the engineering and technological growth. Technical education is backbone of any industrialized economy. The increased awareness about new technology in business has also created interest about new technology and its possible application in education, particularly in higher education like Technical Education. Educational institutions have significant opportunities for applying new technology practices to support different activities that are carried out in the process of delivery of education. The technical manpower created by institutions, offering technical education needs to be amply equipped, to face the challenges cropped up with the advent of liberalization and globalization. The syllabus should be designed to lay more stress on analytical process aimed at total solutions and thinking process, rather than mere emphasis on memory.

The last decade is a witness of remarkable growth in the field of information technology. The technical institutions are left with no options but to rethink and reframe their curriculum incorporating latest technology changes and better style of curriculum implementation with due IT considerations. Even All-India Council for Technical Education (AICTE) has made accreditation of technical colleges mandatory so that all technical institutions maintain a proper standard of education.

Staff development: Providing training to teachers is critical and ongoing. Set aside time and money for formal training classes as well as opportunities for teachers to discuss discoveries or problems with their colleagues. Training should account for at least one third of the budget allocated for the educational technology program or initiative.

Currently, the level of information technology equipment available differs from school to school, and some of it is obsolete. Especially in non-technical institutions the situation is worst. Even where adequate equipment exists, it is often not fully utilized. Teachers have differing abilities in using information technology. The level of utilization of telecommunication services and information networks is still low in schools, mainly due to the slow development in equipment resources. Cooperation between educational institutions in using teaching resources has been rare. All these factors have slowed down the development of an organizational culture that utilizes information technology.

6. KNOWLEDGE MANAGEMENT IN LIBRARIES

The most important resource in the knowledge economy system is the talents who grasp knowledge. The talent competition has become the focus of market competition in the knowledge economy era. In the knowledge economy era, the libraries will attach importance to vocational training and lifelong education of library staffs to raise their scientific knowledge level and ability of acquiring and innovating knowledge. They also will and fully respect the human value, guide and bring into play wisdom potentialities of library staffs, take developing knowledge resources in the brains of library staffs as an important way for rising work efficiency. An all-round improvement of library staff's quality and positioning of the human value will become important objectives of knowledge management in libraries.

"The Objective of Knowledge Management in Libraries is to Promote Knowledge Innovation." Knowledge innovation is the core of the knowledge economy society. As bases for collection, processing, storage and distribution of knowledge and information, libraries represent an indispensable link in the scientific system chain, an important link in the knowledge innovation. Secondly, libraries take part in scientific research process directly. The library work is a component of knowledge innovation. Thirdly, libraries must pay attention to diffusion and conversion of knowledge. They act as bridges for turning the results of knowledge innovation into realistic productive forces. Knowledge management in libraries is to promote relationship in and between libraries, between library and user, to strengthen knowledge internetworking and to quicken knowledge flow. In the knowledge economy era, libraries will carry out researches on development and application of information resources, construction of virtual libraries, protection of intellectual property rights in the electronic era etc., thus founding the base for knowledge innovation.

Knowledge acquisition is the starting point of knowledge management in libraries. The application of information technologies enlarges the scope of knowledge acquisition, raises knowledge acquisition speed and reduces knowledge acquisition cost. It is impossible to accomplish such important tasks by using man's brains only in the modern society in which the knowledge changes with each passing day. It will be possible to link closely knowledge sources and knowledge workers by computer networks, thus constructing knowledge networks in libraries based on realization of single-point information.

The knowledge acquired must be accumulated and converged into knowledge warehouses of libraries. The priority of information technologies in the field of knowledge storage not only finds expression in quantity, but also in retrieval, sorting and security of the knowledge. Information technology is also indispensable in the application and exchange of knowledge and other fields. It functions as a source and tool for knowledge innovation.

7. ROLE OF LIBRARIANS IN KNOWLEDGE MANAGEMENT

Role of librarians in KM is not a new role but a continuation of many of the roles that the librarians have played already with the help of information technologies. Reardon (1998) has stated "There is a need for significant changes in thinking, attitudes, education and training before we can confidently face the knowledge management future that awaits in many important areas of the information and library professions"

The Librarians should have following type of knowledge:

- Knowledge about library's information sources or assets, products and services.
- Knowledge about where these sources stored are and what is its use.
- Knowledge about users including teaching staff and researcher and who is using these information sources.
- What are the current usage of these sources and how to increase its uses?
- Knowledge about the library's own competencies and capabilities.
- Knowledge about the emerging library trends and technologies.

The following are the personality attributes for Knowledge Manager (TPFL, 1999):

* Creativity.
* Ability to learn and adapt
* Will and ability to create, share, harness and utilize knowledge
* Understanding of knowledge creation processes
* Understanding fo the impact of knowledge
* Information literacy skills - creating, finding, sharing and using:
* Understanding of the knowledge process;
* Understanding of the principles of the "organization of knowledge" is key.

Anyone working in the field of knowledge and information management will require a range of skills, some of which can be grouped in the following categories which are related to knowledge and information management (Webb. 1998):

* Knowledge of sources : print/electronic, internal/external, whom to ask, how to look, evaluation.

* Subject knowledge and understanding.
* Information and records management: indexing methods, database development, thesaurus construction, retrieval/delivery methods, electronics storage, retention policy, structuring records, legislation, standards and controls.
* Internal and external networks.
* Users/patterns of usage: needs analysis, satisfaction measures.
* Current awareness services: monitoring/updating. Abstracting, new services.
* User advice and training.
* Contribution to knowledge and information strategy.

Academic libraries face unprecedented challenges in the 21st century. Libraries are human organizations, so they are subject to the same sort of influences that many other organizations must deal with the changing environment of academic life demands new competencies in academic librarians as a result, the knowledge and expertise of academic librarians needs to be seen as the library's greatest asset.

The rapid growth of information and communication technologies (ICTs) are said to be changing the way academic libraries operate today. Academic library collections are no longer collections comprised almost entirely of printed materials but collections comprised almost of materials in multiple formats and media (Budd, 1998). Information technologies such as computers, multimedia and CD-ROMs are bringing unprecedented abilities to academic libraries in providing services and resources to the university community. Over the past few years, the Web has had a tremendous effect on the growth of information and the speed of transmission. The problem with the Web is that, there is no real organization of information like in the case of libraries. New means to deliver information over the Web places a challenge to academic librarians in terms of helping students make sense of information found on websites.

Another challenge facing academic libraries in the networked online environment is to exploit all forms of digital and telecommunication technologies and find new ways and means to provide feasible forms of collections; services and access to library materials (Foo *et al.*, 2002). These technologies however, require greater responsibility to academic librarians. The challenge for academic librarians is to manage services, which offer users a carefully selected mix of multiple formats and media. Academic libraries should rethink their role in the whole university community. There is a need to support the needs of the users since the teaching and learning patterns in universities have changed. As information and research resources become more varied, this places a challenge to academic libraries. Hazen (2000) argued that the changes in the nature of information, in research strategies and in the structure of higher education are affecting academic libraries. These changes define much of the shifting context within which academic libraries must operate. The changes brought by electronic 11 media necessitate transformation in the way librarians think about their jobs, the users of information and communication process of which they are part (Budd 1998, p.270). Academic librarians must strive to remain competent navigators of each medium on order to assist the library users.

As universities' market demands are changing in terms of improving students learning outcomes. this has a direct impact on academic libraries and their delivery of services. Due to societal and technological developments, traditional teaching changes increasingly in creating learning environments. Students participate in flexible learning processes via more 'indirect' contacts with teachers and facilities, including scientific information (Van Bentum &

Braaksma, 1999). In addition, the teaching and learning patterns have developed towards greater modularization and place an emphasis on self-directed, independent study and student-centered learning (Farley, Broady-Preston & Hayward 1998, p.154). This places greater demands on the library, which is increasingly being used for group work, and librarians face increased pressure on the enquiry service and a greater need for user support and education. Academic libraries have to provide information services for users acting in the changing academic environment. Academic librarians need to liaise with library users, faculties and schools to support the effective teaching, learning and research in universities. As Parker and Jackson (1998) explained, liaison is particularly important in a world of resource-based learning where students are encouraged to carry out more independent work and make wider use of a range of learning resources (including electronic information resources). The challenges require academic libraries to offer user-friendly ICT oriented facilities (like remote access to information and services), analyze the changing user needs and give support to users in new academic environments.

8. CONCLUSION

The effective use of new technologies and innovations as well as continuous learning will be key factors. India cannot hope to aspire to become a great IT nation without adequate level of R&D work. Towards this, our National R&D institutions would be given encouragement to invest in R&D and bring about world-class technologies. And hence, Human Resource Management is the Core of Knowledge Management in Libraries.

REFERENCES

1. Corrall, Sheila (1998/1999): "Are we in the knowledge management business?, *Ariadne, (18) November 1998, pp. 16-18*
2. http://www.ariadne.ac.uk/issue18/knowledge-mgt

3. Executive Advisory Group to CILIP(2002): CILIP in the knowledge economy: a leadership strategy: The report of the competitiveness and the knowledge based economy.
4. http://www.cilip.org.uk/professionalguidance/knowledgeeconomy
5. Earl, Michael (2004): "Tantalised by the promise of wisdom", *Financial Times*, 25 August.
6. http://news.ft.com/cms/s/284c2fec-f6b7-11d8-a879-00000e2511c8.html

43

Applicability of Knowledge Management in Libraries in Digital Era

Suja.K
Shaini Gopinath

ABSTRACT

Library and information centers are now being digitalized in terms of collection, organization, assimilation and dissemination of information due to the changing needs and advent of information technology. In digital era digital libraries extend the services of a traditional library to assess materials outside the physical confines of the library. Due to electronic information explosion the users find difficulties to evaluate the valuable information in electronic media. So there is need to organize the materials for the purpose of effective retrieval and manage the collection. Nowadays Knowledge Management has been a phenomenal growth in interest and activity, as seen in many new publications, conferences, IT products, and job advertisement. Various professional groups, notably HR professionals, IT specialists, and librarians, are staking their claims, seeing Knowledge Management as an opportunity to move center stage. Librarianship is described, as the organization of recorded knowledge, so perhaps this is high time for library professionals to concentrate more on Knowledge

Management The Knowledge Management system in the digital era is mandatory. This paper tries to give an overall perspective of different aspects of Knowledge Management and its applicability in libraries in the context of digital environment.

1. INTRODUCTION

Knowledge Management is an emerging field, much hyped since 1990's. A primary characteristic of knowledge management is the representation of a range of business and academic disciplines including: human resource management, information management, information technology, sociology, organizational learning and strategic planning. As a consequence there is an extensive and diffuse literature on knowledge management reflecting differing perspectives and competing claims for ownership of the area.However due to complicated nature of knowledge and its consequent management, and it is often difficult to demonstrate the value of knowledge, and our understanding of what knowledge is, has come under new scrutiny in recent years. A new crop of knowledge management programmes is being created which were produced in knowledge management explosion.

Since knowledge has become the driving force for development, the attention of the society to information and knowledge are increasing step by step. This has provided for a good environment for library development. Moreover as information and knowledge has become an important productive for the modern economic system, the society will inevitably require intensified management of information and knowledge.

Definitions

Knowledge management enables the creation, communication and application of Knowledge of all kinds to achieve goals.

Knowledge Management is a conscious strategy of getting knowledge to the right people at the time.

Knowledge Management provides access to experience, knowledge, and expertise that create new capabilities, enable superior performance, encourage innovation, and leverages existing information and knowledge assets of the organization, facilitates information and knowledge dissemination across boundaries and integrates the information and knowledge into day to day business process.

According to Srinivasan " Knowledge Management refers to a collection of processes, technologies and principles that serves to promote a learning environment supportive of the search community goal".

According to Seonghee " knowledge management involves the identification and analysis of available and required knowledge and subsequent planning and control of actions to develop knowledge assets so as to fulfill organizational objectives.

In simple terms Knowledge Management means, management of Knowledge. It can be defined as "the art of creating value of an organization's intangible assets".

2. COMPONENTS OF KNOWLEDGE MANAGEMENT:

Following are the components of Knowledge Management: -

1. People management - recognition of skills of people
2. Process management - links into the identification and deployment of practices may be associated with Business Process Re-engineering.
3. Information Management

3. CLASSIFICATION OF KNOWLEDGE MANAGEMENT

Knowledge Management can be divided into two categories Tacit Knowledge and Explicit Knowledge.

Knowledge Management
↓
Tacit Knowledge — Explicit Knowledge

Tacit Knowledge

Tacit knowledge is the " know how" acquires by persons. It is presented in intuitions, emotions, values and beliefs. All information that goes unrecorded like the values inside and the judgment is stored with the individual falls in the category of tacit knowledge. Tacit knowledge is subjective, cognitive and experimental in nature. Tacit knowledge may exist in any of the two forms:

Embodied Knowledge : The knowledge, which cannot be detached from its knower, is known as embodied knowledge. It is difficult to articulate.

Embedded Knowledge : The Tacit knowledge, which resides in the things created by individual may be known as embedded knowledge. It may reside in the product as well as in process.

Explicit knowledge : Explicit knowledge is systematically documented records in any kind of format, which guides the users to gain the knowledge and to expand the base further. It is articulated knowledge. The word we speak, the book we read, the reports we write, and the data we compile are explicit knowledge. Explicit knowledge is objective, rational and technical. It is a rule-based knowledge. Explicit knowledge enables the organisation to enjoy a certain level of operational efficiency and control. It also promotes consistent organizational responses. Explicit knowledge is used in the design of routines and standard operational procedures.

Knowledge Management is thus explained as a process, by which individual learning and experiences can be accessed, shared and utilized in order to enhance individual knowledge and thus has organizational value.

4. OBJECTIVES OF KNOWLEDGE MANAGEMENT:

The objectives of the Knowledge Management include the following

– To create knowledge repositories, which store both knowledge and information, often in documentary form.

– To improve knowledge access, or to provide access to knowledge or to facilitate its transfer among individuals.

– To enhance the knowledge environment so that the environment is conductive to more effective knowledge creation, transfer and use.

– To manage knowledge as an asset to recognize the value of knowledge to an organization.

5. KEY AREAS IN KNOWLEDGE MANAGEMENT:

Knowledge is considered to be a semi tangible asset, which can be exploited, nurtured and managed. The literature on the subject of Knowledge Management covered three main areas.

Method approach : The use of systems, methodologies and associated technology -based processes that successfully capture, collate and manage knowledge.

Expert approach : The culture, organizational styles and protocols that enable successful access, dissemination and sharing of knowledge.

Research approach : The application of advanced computer modeling and artificial intelligence technologies to knowledge management.

Principles : On the basis of the commendable attempt, Thomas H Davenport has formulated ten principles of Knowledge Management as listed below:

- Knowledge Management is expensive
- Effective management of knowledge requires hybrid solutions of people and technology
- Knowledge Management is highly political.
- Knowledge Management requires knowledge managers
- Knowledge Management benefits more from maps than model, more from markets than from hierarchies.
- Sharing and using knowledge are often unnatural acts.
- Knowledge Management means improving work process.
- Knowledge access is only the beginning
- Knowledge Management never ends.
- Knowledge Management requires a knowledge contract.

6. KNOWLEDGE MANAGEMENT STRATEGY:

Karl Eric has listed six knowledge management strategies, which are as follows:

- Transferring information and best practice via IT system.
- Capturing knowledge about customers/uses.
- Use of research and development activities into several applications.
- Creating more value from existing intellectual assets.
- Creating strategy focused in individuals' innovations and knowledge creation.
- Commitment to a knowledge focused strategy

Infrastructure : In the Knowledge Management process three basic infrastructure concerns are required to be given stress.

- Cultural infrastructure
- Operational infrastructure
- Technical infrastructure

7. KNOWLEDGE MANAGEMENT- STEPS AND PROCESSES

Knowledge Management can be considered as a four matrix of steps and processes:

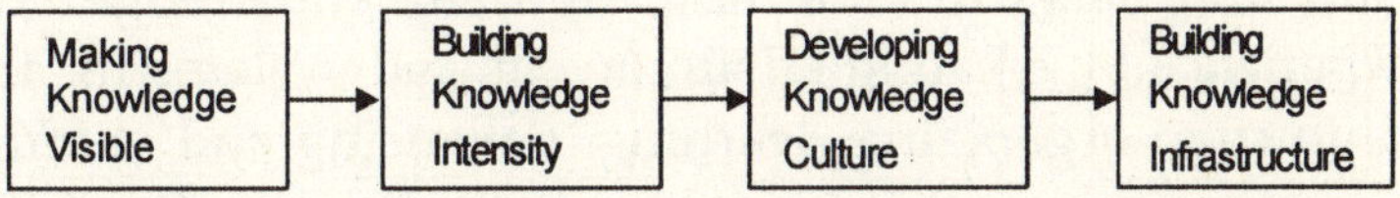

8. ROLE OF KNOWLEDGE MANAGEMENT IN LIBRARIES

Libraries are the institutions for knowledge management. They deal with both the categories of knowledge, tacit knowledge for the library personnel and explicit knowledge for the library user. Library personnel must have a clear view of the 'know how' of information sources, management, retrieval and dissemination as well as global access to information. This tacit knowledge helps the end-users to gain explicit knowledge. The objective of knowledge management in libraries is to promote knowledge innovation, relationship in and between libraries and between library and user.

Knowledge Management is about enhancing the use of organizational knowledge through sound practices of knowledge management and organizational learning. Thus, knowledge management is a combination of information management, communication, and human resources. How to manage knowledge will become an important subject facing libraries in near future. Knowledge Management in libraries should be focused on effective research and development of knowledge, creation of knowledge base, exchange and sharing of knowledge between library staffs (including its users), training of library staff, speeding up explicit processing of the implicit knowledge and realizing of its sharing (Shanhog, 2000). With the help of the knowledge management processes, libraries convert, data and information stored in various sources into knowledge and deliver only relevant knowledge to users.

Knowledge Management is about encouraging library staff and users to communicate their knowledge and experience by creating environments and systems for the capturing, organizing, learning, enhancing and sharing knowledge throughout the library for the benefit of the organization and its users. The libraries are moving from collection management to knowledge management and digital technologies offering new information services and products.

9. ROLE OF LIBRARIANS IN KNOWLEDGE MANAGEMENT:

Knowledge management has created new ground in the field of library and information science. It has also created new roles and responsibilities for LIS professionals.

Role of librarians in Knowledge Management is not a new role but continuation of many of the roles that the librarians have played already with the help of information technologies. Reardon (1998) has stated " there is a need for significant changes in thinking, attitudes, education and training before we can confidently face the knowledge management future that awaits in many important areas of the information and library professionals".

The librarian should have following type of knowledge:

- Knowledge about library's information sources for assets, products and services;
- Knowledge about where these sources stored are and what is its use.
- Knowledge about users including teaching staff and researcher and, who is using these sources and how to increase its uses.
- What are the current usage of these sources and how to increase its use
- Knowledge about the library's own competencies and capabilities.
- Knowledge about the emerging library trends and technologies.

The personality attributes for a knowledge manager has been described as (TPFL, 1999):

- Creativity
- Ability to learn and adapt
- Will
- And ability to create, share, harness and utilize knowledge
- Understanding of knowledge creation process
- Understanding of the impact of knowledge
- Information literacy skills-creating, finding, sharing and using
- Understanding of the knowledge process
- Understanding of the principles of "organization of knowledge" is key.

The traditional roles of librarian are modified to take advantage of the new technologies and tools to meet the requirement of the people. The responsibilities of the Knowledge Manager, as follows:

Collection Development : The Knowledge Manager can participate in a significant way in the selection and evaluation of the services by bringing a though understanding of the research interest and projects of the individual department by digital technologies through Internet.

Resource organization : The Knowledge manager is involved in resource organization at two levels. The fist one is the organization of specific resources. At department level reflecting domain Knowledge and creation of hyper lined document for the collection which functions as gateway to the related electronic resources.

Bibliographic Instruction : The knowledge manager should teach the user community how to use digital library to locate its potential information.

Reference Service : The digital reference is the provision of reference service over the Internet. A term that we have considered more recently, digital reference services, captures best the notion that the modern day library, to a great degree, is a web-based learning environment. To expand the boundaries of current reference service, from the library's point of view, is a natural outcome of both our commitment to digital resources and remote access.

Librarian as Knowledge Coordinator : The librarian needs to be responsible for the Knowledge coordinator so he needs to have an understanding of developing the human and cultural infrastructure within library, which will facilitate information sharing specifically conversion of tacit knowledge of librarian into explicit knowledge, which can be shared by the entire library.

Librarian as Knowledge creator : The Knowledge manager here acts as a catalyst between the knowledge and the user. The explicit knowledge retrieved by the user through the print or electronic media, applying their tacit knowledge may generate new concepts, ideas that may be new contribution to knowledge. This process is called as internalization and externalization of knowledge.

Librarian as Knowledge Architect : Librarian can act as both Knowledge Manager and Knowledge Architect. The Knowledge Architect can design and organize Knowledge infrastructure including training Knowledge base, libraries and database and data warehousing.

10. APPLICATION OF KNOWLEDGE MANAGEMENT IN DIGITAL ERA

The emergence of digital technology in the modern20th century has affected humankind's inventory of recorded information dramatically. The digital revolution has altered all walks of life and libraries are not exception to this. The role of knowledge management in digital libraries era will become more and more important along with the development of knowledge economy. It is a new management mode, boasts the following superiority and characteristics incomparable with conventional management:

- The objective of knowledge management in digital libraries is to promote knowledge innovation.
- IT is a tool for knowledge management in digital libraries.
- Human resource management is the core of knowledge management in digital era.

Objectives of Knowledge Management in Digital Libraries

- To have universal accessibility
- To access more information than possible physically acquire and maintain.
- To have access and maintain the expensive and rare information.

- Convenience, once books are converted to digital form, patrons can retrieve them in seconds rather than in minutes. Several users can share the documents at several places.

11. NEED FOR KNOWLEDGE MANAGEMENT IN DIGITAL LIBRARIES

Knowledge centers are slowly and steadily marching towards Digital Library services due to the changing needs and advent of information technology. The need is to make good choice and good decision about information in globally competitive information saturated environment. The key for all these is knowledge management. The knowledge in libraries resides in databases, knowledge bases, text bases and web bases. The efficiency of libraries may be measured not only on the provision of needed information to their users but also on the knowledge about related resources, skill and technology involved in it. The services of libraries are designed to encourage the use of information and thus increase the amount of academic knowledge used in higher education. In an organizational context data represents facts or values and relations between data and other relations have the capacity to represent information. Pattern of relations of data and information and the other patterns have the capacity to represent knowledge. The value of Knowledge Management relates directly to the effectiveness with which the managed knowledge enables the members of the organization to deal with today's situations and effectively envision and create their future.

CONCLUSION

The Knowledge Management concept is very much crucial in the successful running of any organization. Because it is only through Knowledge Management the capacity and ability of an organization are enhanced .In this digital era IT, also plays a crucial role in Knowledge Management in the process of identifying, capturing, organizing, sharing, transferring applying as well as creating of new Knowledge. Coming down to the field of libraries Knowledge Management has to play an indispensable and crucial role. To keep pace with the changing environment libraries should gear up its activities by giving their professionals training and education on Information and Communication Technologies, developing E-based resources and equipping with new ICT infrastructure .The future of the profession of librarianship thus seems clear if very complex and contingent. The profession will no doubt continue its generalist strategy and federated structure. Individuals will continue to flow in and out of the profession at many levels and career stages. To the profession as a whole, the central challenges lie in embracing the various information technologies of the future and the groups that service them. This embrace will end up redefining the profession. But that is necessary to survival.

44

Desktop to Web-top Emerging Trends in the Web

Jamsheer N.P

ABSTRACT

Library users are more Web savvy than ever and have high expectations for information providers. In order to satisfy the increasing number of web savvy library users, libraries should adapt the new trends and technologies in the web. In the growing era of Ajax (Asynchronous JavaScript and XML) and the web becoming more of a platform, many startups are emerging to explore the possibilities and attempt to comprehend this change in the web as a whole. This paper attempt to explore the possibilities of Web based applications, AJAX and its potential in libraries.

1. INTRODUCTION

For years, software makers and Web boosters have been forecasting that the Internet would break Microsoft Corp.'s stranglehold over business software. Instead of buying a copy of, say, Microsoft Word and installing it on your computer, you would travel to a Web site, type and edit your document there and store it online. The fee would be tiny compared with the cost of buying Microsoft's software, and you wouldn't have to pay anyone to troubleshoot the program or update it.

2. DESKTOP APPLICATION

Desktop applications refer to the software installed in a computer and used locally like the Microsoft Word or Excel software. In short, desktop applications are Web applications that physically run on your computer's desktop.

3. WEB DESKTOP OR WEBTOP

A web desktop or webtop is a network application system for integrating web applications into a web based work space. It is a *virtual desktop* on the web, running in a *web browser* as software. Web-based Applications are applications programmed to only be accessed through the internet. These applications are often based of programming languages which can conveniently output information through your browser window. Also, web-based applications often can be accessed from any computer with a web browser – making far more convenient

Desktop applications used to be highly rich and responsive unlike the web applications. The simplicity that provides the rapid proliferation of the web also creates a gap between the experiences websites can provide and the experiences a user can get from a desktop application.

3.1. Popular Web based Applications and Desktops

- Google Products
- Microsoft Live
- Netvibes
- Protopage
- AJAX write
- YouOS
- DesktopTwo
- eyeOS
- Xcerion.

4. DIFFERENCE BETWEEN DESKTOP APPLICATIONS AND WEB APPLICATIONS

The following are the difference Desktop applications and web applications:

File Size : Desktop Applications are larger, web-based are smaller because of the fact internet data through-put is slower than accessing from your hard drive.

Programming Language : If your using a Desktop Application, it will probably be written in a language such as Java/C/C++, while many web-based applications are based in Perl, PHP, Javascript, and XML.

– Web applications can be accessed from anywhere whereas desktop applications are tied to a local computer .

5. THE CLOSING GAP

The gap between Desktop applications and web applications is closing thanks to the new experiments like AJAX. Google has popularized AJAX technology. Its online products like the google suggest, Google earth, Spreadsheets and Docs are highly rich and as responsive as desktop applications. Everything happens almost instantly, with no waiting for pages to load.

6. AJAX: THE TECHNOLOGY BEHIND WEB DESKTOPS

Ajax is only a name given to a set of tools that previously existed. Ajax shorthand for Asynchronous JavaScript and XML is a web development technique for creating interactive web applications. The intent is to make web pages feel more responsive by exchanging small amounts of data with the server behind the scenes, so that the entire web page does not have to be reloaded each time the user requests a change. This is meant to increase the web page's interactivity, speed, and usability. There's no loss of data or waiting for pages to reload for an answer.

Ajax mainly used to build a fast, dynamic website; and to save resources. For improving sharing of resources, it is better to use the power of all the client computers rather than just a unique server and the network. Ajax allows performing processing on client computer (in JavaScript) with data taken from the server. The processing of web page formerly was only server-side, using web services or PHP scripts, before the whole page was sent within the network. But Ajax can selectively modify a part of a page displayed by the browser, and update it without the need to reload the whole document with all images, menus, etc. For example, fields of forms, choices of user, may be processed and the result displayed immediately into the same page..

Another argument for AJAX is the ability to save bandwidth usage. For sites that experience a highly variable load, AJAX can mean fewer servers, lower bandwidth bills, and less risk of failure. This is a huge, public win for AJAX as a bandwidth optimization strategy.

Components

Standards-based presentation using XHTML and CSS;

Dynamic display and interaction using the Document Object Model (DOM);

Data interchange and manipulation using XML and XSLT;

Asynchronous data retrieval using XMLHttpRequest;

JavaScript -binding everything together.

Ajax uses a programming model with display and events. These events are user actions, they call functions associated to elements of the web page. Interactivity is achieved with forms and buttons. DOM allows to link elements of the page with actions and also to extract data from XML files provided by the server.

7. LIBRARY AND AJAX

Library users are more Web savvy than ever and have high expectations for information providers. In order to satisfy the increasing number of web savvy library users libraries must adapt the new trends and technologies.

Libraries and information agencies have been slower to embrace Ajax, but it's not for a lack of library-use cases. In a library setting, Ajax could be used for speeding up digital library search applications using a link to activate a process that matches multiple ISSNs to compile a list of electronic journals, or even making quick requests to validate a user's personal information as they log into a "My accounts" section of the catalog.

There are many AJAX based web sites and Web based library automation software available in the market which can really increase the speed and user friendliness of the sites. Online Public Access Catalogues can be created with the help of the AJAX technology which is going to benefit the users very much. Initially, Ajax might provide the means to improve the interfaces to library catalogs or other library-managed applications with a Web-based interface. Ajax can help overcome many of the limitations otherwise present in Web interfaces relative to graphical desktop interfaces. It will be interesting to see if Ajax can really improve library catalog interfaces.

Phoenix Live OPAC - OCLC Research

http://phoenix.orhost.org

8. CONCLUSION

Applications will move from the traditional desktop into the cloud and become available for free with added benefits of the dynamics of the Internet, like collaboration and social networking. Future is of Internet self-service applications.

REFERENCES

1. Robert A. Guth "Is It Time to Dump Your Desktop ? "The Wall Street Journal Online. www.wsj.com
2. Wikipedia.com
3. www.oclc.org

Index